THE NEW NAVVIES

A History of the Modern Waterways Restoration Movement

THE
NEW NAVVIES

A HISTORY OF THE MODERN WATERWAYS RESTORATION MOVEMENT

ROGER W. SQUIRES

Phillimore

1983

Published by
PHILLIMORE & CO. LTD.
Shopwyke Hall, Chichester, Sussex

ISBN 0 85033 364 4

Printed and bound in Great Britain by
BILLING & SONS LTD.
Worcester, England

CONTENTS

LIST OF PLATES
(between pages 148 and 149)

The following people are thanked for supplying photographs for the plate section:
R. Squires: 1, 5, 16, 20, 22, 24, 25, 28, 32, 33, 35, 36, 37, 38, 43, 45, 47, 49, 52, 53, 56, 57, 59, 60, 65, 69, 76, 77, 78, 81, 82, 85; British Waterways Museum: 2, 3, 4; C. D. Millington: 6; Chris Griffiths: 7, 8, 9, 11, 17, 18, 19, 44, 61, 62, 71; L. A. Edwards: 10, 46, 48; Forth & Clyde Canal Society: 12; Lancs. Canal Trust: 13, 14; J. S. Gavan: 15; David L. Finnis: 21; Aickman Collection: 23, 34, 83, 84; Shell U.K. Ltd.: 26, 31, 73, 75, 86; British Waterways Board: 27, 29, 39, 40, 41, 42, 54, 66, 68; Sleaford Navigation Society: 30; J. E. Marriage: 50; Ian Van Der Ende: 51; R. Murchison: 55; Droitwich Canals Trust: 58; M. J. Wood: 63, 64; Neath & Tennant Canal Society: 67; Gareth Lovett-Jones: 70, 79; M. A. Fryer: 72; John Wood: 74; Hoseasons Holidays: 80; Derek Pratt: 87.

LIST OF MAPS

LIST OF GRAPHS

FOREWORD

THE NEW NAVVIES

Between 150 and 200 years ago, bands of men travelled around the country building the canals. These men were called Navigators, or 'Navvies' for short. By their efforts they not only brought about a Transport Revolution, but also provided Britain, for the first time, with a network of reliable routes for the transport of bulk goods at economic rates. A factor that subsequently facilitated the Industrial Revolution which enabled Britain to become the world's leading industrial nation in the century that followed.

Over the last two or three decades new bands of workers have been going around the countryside rebuilding some of those early canals that had fallen derelict with the passage of time. These groups of 'New Navvies' are enthusiasts who believe that the derelict 'Water Byeways' not only can have a new lease of life, but can also serve a useful purpose in the years ahead.

Two features are significant in the development of this 'social adventure'. One is the rapid growth of the demand for more leisure space. The second is the renewed awareness of, and interest in, the whole environment in which we live. These factors, coupled with the willingness of individuals to devote their spare time to improve the amenities of the countryside have meant that the 'old' canals can now offer the prospect of a new value to the community and achieve a multifunctional use.

This book recounts how these 'old' canals came to be built, and records how new sets of local promoters are projecting the vision of their revival; showing by their physical efforts how such benefits can be achieved. In this way part of the national heritage is being redeveloped for the longer term benefit of the communities through which the waterways pass. Offering new leisure space, as well as the opportunity for the local economy to again benefit from the facility that originally provided the means for local industrial growth and wealth to be generated.

ACKNOWLEDGEMENTS

This book has been based on some 10 years of personal research into the way in which small groups of people around the country have set out to defeat bureaucracy and apathy and show by their own personal commitment, effort and sustained hard work, that new life can be brought to their local sections of canal.

During this period I have corresponded with, visited and discussed waterway restoration with hundreds of enthusiasts throughout the British Isles. To list them all would be a daunting task, yet they all must have my sincere thanks for the help and hospitality they have given me. Without their help, access to their records, and more so their memories, such a book about the development of the restoration movement over the last 30 years would not have been possible. I owe to them a personal debt of gratitude.

Of the many people I have met, some have offered particular inspiration to many others in the restoration movement. Of these I list but a few of the recognised leaders, who have equally given me so much of their valuable time and provided access and permission to use items from their records: the late R. Aickman, C. D. Barwell, the late Mrs. B. Bunker, L. A. Edwards, C. Hadfield, D. Hutchings, L. Munk, G. Palmer, and the late L. T. C. Rolt. To them all I offer my sincere thanks.

The most consistent and valuable sources of published information, apart from the journals *Waterways News, Waterways World,* and *Canal and Riverboat,* have been the past issues of the Inland Waterways Association *Bulletin* (now I.W.A. *Waterways*) and *Navvies* (formerly *Navvies Notebook*), and I am particularly grateful to the I.W.A. Secretary, J. Taunton, and the former Waterway Recovery Group leader, G. Palmer, respectively for making complete sets of each available to me. Equally my thanks to the editors of the numerous society journals and newsletters who made their archives available for research. Thanks also to Mrs. K. King who so efficiently converted my rough maps into a presentable form, and to Mrs. A. Hunter and Mrs. D. Wilson who typed the final manuscripts. Thanks, too, go to the various authors and publishers named in the text, for permission to reproduce copyright material, and to the late R. Aickman, H. Arnold, L. A. Edwards, C. Griffiths, Gareth Lovatt-Jones, H. Potter, D. Pratt, and R. Shopland, as well as various Society Press Officers, the British Waterways Board, and Hoseasons for providing a selection of photographs and charts to illustrate the book.

Finally, my sincere thanks are due to my wife, Amanda, for suffering so many hours of waterway restoration over the past decade; but for her assistance this book would never have seen the light of day.

To everybody, named and un-named, who has helped to make this book possible, I offer my sincere thanks. It is a tribute to their efforts, and I hope it will be seen as such.

Beckenham, Kent April 1983   R. SQUIRES

This book is dedicated to that ever-growing band of volunteer workers, the 'new navvies', who have individually worked so hard to revive the derelict waterways. The restored waterways are a lasting tribute to their efforts.

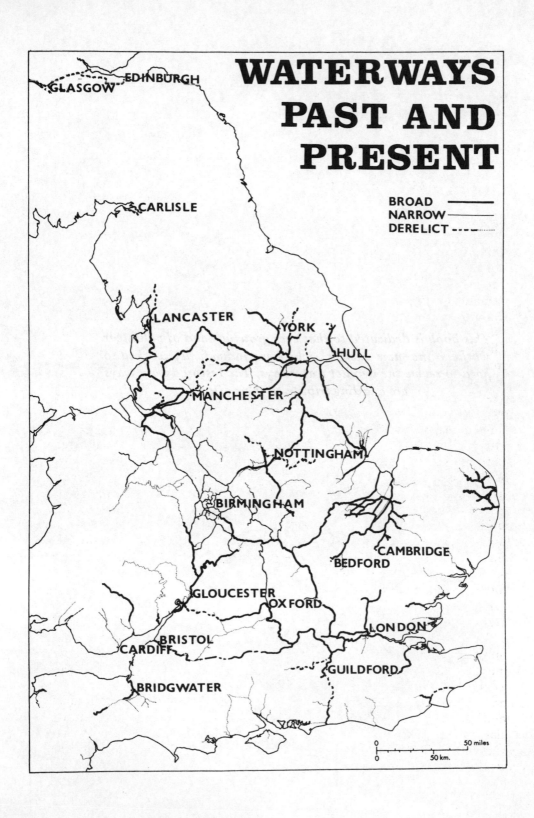

WATERWAYS PAST AND PRESENT

BROAD ————
NARROW ————
DERELICT ----

GLASGOW
EDINBURGH

CARLISLE

LANCASTER
YORK
HULL

MANCHESTER

NOTTINGHAM

BIRMINGHAM

CAMBRIDGE
BEDFORD

GLOUCESTER
OXFORD

LONDON

BRISTOL
CARDIFF

GUILDFORD

BRIDGWATER

0   50 miles
0   50 km.

Chapter One

THE WATERWAY NETWORK

RIVERS HAVE BEEN USED as transport routes from earliest times. Few improvements were needed to keep the channels free, as tidal scours originally swept far inland and offered a reasonable means of access for the small shallow-draft craft of the times. As time passed, so the gradual deposition of mud together with the natural debris of winter floods made river routes more difficult to use. Later, man-made obstacles, such as fish weirs and mill dams, further obstructed the main channels and did much to hinder such river traffic as existed at the time.

The earliest recorded artificial navigations in Britain were the Fossdyke and Caerdyke, built by the Romans between A.D. 61 and 70 to improve access to their regional staging post at Lincoln. The Caerdyke was over forty miles long and linked the River Nene, near Peterborough, with its access to the Fens and the Great Ouse valley, to the river Witham about three miles below Lincoln. The Fossdyke was some 11 miles long and linked the Witham at Lincoln with the river Trent, providing access to the variety of rivers that converge on the Humber estuary. The Fossdyke remains in use today, although it has been much improved throughout the ages. The Caerdyke, however, fell into decay following the demise of Roman rule, and is now only traceable in parts of its length. Excavations have shown that it was originally up to eight feet deep and 50 feet wide at the top, which compares well with the dimensions of the Narrow canals that were built some 1,700 years later.

It appears that many early navigations were allowed to decline in Saxon and Norman times. Even so, contemporary records show that Danish invaders sailed up the river Lea in 894 as far as Ware, and also up the river Severn to raid the city of Worcester at much the same time, indicating the sort of access then offered by river routes.

The era of major river development dawned as the need to transport larger loads grew. In the Middle Ages rivers and coastal routes were almost the only means of moving heavy goods, such as coal. The importance of river transport was confirmed in 1215 when the Magna Carta stated that the great rivers of the kingdom were to be open to all men. This authority was quickly enforced on the Thames and Medway with the prompt removal of the fish and mill weirs that had substantially restricted navigation before that time. The improvement of Britain's inland waterways was thereafter a continuous process.

The navigability of the principal rivers was first improved by dredging, the reinforcement of banks, the elimination of meanders, and the construction of

1

sluices and staunches to control the water level. The initiative for such improvement lay with town merchants, who hoped to benefit from the more reliable communications. Money was collected by those who promoted schemes to finance the work, and, over the years, tolls charged for the use of navigations repaid both the original capital invested and supported the continuing maintenance work required to keep the routes open.

One of the first rivers to be improved was the Severn. By the 14th century it was navigable by large craft to Bewdley, and for smaller craft as far upstream as Shrewsbury. By the 17th century the upper limit of navigation had been extended as far as Welshpool, though transit was difficult, especially during times of summer drought. Apart from the Severn, the most comprehensive network of inland navigations was that comprising the Fossdyke, the rivers Witham, Trent, and Yorkshire Ouse, and sections of their tributaries, the Swale, Ure, Wharfe, and Derwent. In 1462 Edward IV appointed the mayor and aldermen of York to be Conservators of the Yorkshire Ouse and its tributaries. Subsequent Acts were passed by Cromwell and William III for improving the navigation of the Ouse to York, confirming the value of the river as a trading link.

Before any improvement could be made Letters Patent or Acts of Parliament had to be obtained or passed, both to permit the work to take place and to provide the promoters with the legal authority to levy tolls. Thus, when in the Middle Ages the Fossdyke had become silted and difficult to navigate, an Act of Parliament was passed in 1671 which empowered the mayor and corporation of Lincoln to improve the navigation and also subsequently to levy tolls to pay for this work.

In much the same way an Act of 1571 had granted powers to the Corporation of the City of London to act as Conservators and spend money on the improvement of the river Lea. Similarly, under powers granted by a private Act of Parliament in 1698, the 'undertakers of the navigation of the Rivers Aire and Calder' proceeded to deepen and straighten these two important waterways. In the 17th century efforts were made to improve many other existing river routes. During this time rivers such as the Weaver were made navigable, and the Mersey and Irwell provided Manchester with its first reliable access to the sea.

Efforts to improve navigations were very much related to the technology available at that time. Perhaps the most significant advance came with the introduction of the 'Pound' lock to British waterways. Pound locks are thought to have originated in China, but their introduction in England can be traced through the Duke of Milan, whose artificial canals in Italy used pound locks with double mitre gates in the 15th century. Pound locks were first introduced into Britain in 1566 as part of an improvement scheme on the river Exe, which was promoted by the Exeter Corporation. A canal was built just south of the town in order to avoid the shoals and weirs of the Exe, and to enable craft of up to 16 tons to bring cargoes to the new town wharfs. The canal, or 'cut', included three pound locks with vertically rising guillotine gates. These three locks were followed some ten years later by another, not far north of London, on the river Lea at Waltham. This lock, however, used the mitre-type double gates.

By the 17th century certain associated factors were beginning to combine to provoke a profound social upheaval. Tudor enclosures and capitalisation of the land had the effect of widening the gap between wages and prices, whilst agricultural innovations both improved the productivity of the land and reduced the need for agricultural labour. The combination of these two events compelled the English peasantry to turn increasingly from agriculture to industry to augment their slender resources. As industry developed so the financial systems improved and the 'roots' were planted for an even more rapid conversion from an agricultural to an industrial society. One major component that at first retarded such a radical change was the inadequacy of transport facilities. The lack of good land transport thus delayed the growth of industrial concentration, which involved the change from domestic workshop to factory location, as both the supply of fuel and raw materials and the ability to distribute the finished products were governed by the limited efficiency of pack-horse trains, which wound through the muddy trackways constructed for less heavy use.

This obvious need for a more effective transport infrastructure prompted the new industrialists to consider ways to improve the efficiency of the nation's transport systems. Land transport was relatively costly. A horse could carry only two or three hundredweight in panniers, and, if it were harnessed to a wagon, this load might even be increased to two tons per horse, but this assumed a firm, level surface. Along a soft road, full of potholes or churned into mud, a team of up to eight horses might be needed to haul a wagon-load of four tons. The carriage of heavy goods of low value for many miles could not bear such high transport costs, and for longer journeys water transport was essential. Thus the need for the expansion of the waterway route system became increasingly important. Lack of civil engineering experience and the inability to raise the finance needed to complete the work at first retarded progress. In some instances, forward-looking individuals invested their own fortunes to complete river improvements and open waterways that had never been fully navigable. One such person was William Sandys of Fladbury who, under powers of Letters Patent, improved some 40 miles of the Warwickshire Avon between 1636 and 1640 at a personal cost of between £20,000 and £40,000.

Following in Sandys' footsteps, Andrew Yarranton developed a scheme to link the town of Stourbridge to Kidderminster, and thence to the river Severn, by the construction of a series of locks and weirs along the local brook. He completed this work by 1665, and the first boat-load of coal was conveyed from Stourbridge to Kidderminster on 9 March that year. In a similar way the improvement of the river Tone from Bridgwater to within two miles of Taunton brought another area of the country into the waterway network.

After 1665 many other places gained water access for the first time, and earlier navigations were improved and enlarged to accommodate the greater size of craft in use. The Exeter Canal, for instance, was extended in the 1670s and then enlarged again in the 1700s to take sea-going vessels of up to 150 tons.

The early 1700s saw the rapid spread of schemes for nagivational development. These encompassed such rivers as the Cam, between Clayhithe and Cambridge, in 1702; the Nene, from Peterborough to Northampton, in 1714; the Idle from East Retford to Bawtry, in 1720; and the rivers Bure, Yare and Waveney under an Act of 1722. Meanwhile, in the north of England the rivers Aire and Calder were made navigable from Leeds and Wakefield to Weeland under the authority of an Act granted by William III in 1699. This development was to become the first of a chain of works which resulted in a network of broad waterways, part canal and part river, that linked all the centres of the West Riding and so enhanced their industrial growth. Similarly, in the north west, navigations were being extended and improved. The River Douglas Navigation to Wigan was authorised by an Act of 1720, and the same year saw Acts authorising the improvement of the navigations of the Mersey and Irwell to Manchester and the extension of the Weaver Navigation to Winsford Bridge.

In the south west, an Act of 1700 authorised the improvement of the Bristol Avon to Hanham Mills, and an extension through to Bath was authorised in 1712. At the same time, in the south, works were proceeding in improving the river Thames. Its tributary, the Kennet, was opened to Newbury in 1723, and was capable of carrying craft loading 100 tons. This latter scheme was notable in two respects; firstly, it was the most advanced undertaking for the period in its construction, since it included extensive artificial cuts and many locks; secondly, it aroused most violent and active opposition from the people of Reading, who feared that it would take away their trade. The scheme, however, proved that the technique of canal construction, though crude, was already established, and that the true implication of the benefits that water transport could offer was rapidly being realised. The best estimate of the increase in the total length of river navigations in England suggests that it rose from at least 685 miles in 1650 to at least 960 miles by 1700, and to about 1,160 miles by 1725, by which time the pressure for substantial enlargement of the navigable waterway network was evident.

By the early 18th century South Lancashire, the West Riding and the Midlands were already established as industrial areas, but the river navigations were inadequate to serve their growing transport demands. Apart from the normal limitations to river traffic, caused by drought or floods, the barriers of the watersheds provided an apparently insurmountable problem, particularly in the Midlands where the industrial area was perched on the central watershed of England, over 400 feet above sea level. However, as trains of pack horses transported increasing traffic overland, between the Severn at Bewdley, the Weaver at Winsford, and the Trent at Burton, the need to connect the eastward and westward flowing rivers and thus to link the Midlands with Mersey, Severn, Thames and Trent became more apparent.

The potential solution to the problem first emerged in 1755, when an Act authorised the construction of the Sankey Navigation, or St Helens Canal as it was later called. This was the first wholly artificial waterway to be constructed that used a river only as a water feeder. Even before the Sankey Navigation was authorised, an Act had been granted in 1737 to enable the Duke of Bridgewater to transport his coal along an improved Worsley Brook. These powers were never used, but the concept of moving coal from Worsley to Manchester was later developed. The 3rd Duke of Bridgewater instructed James Brindley, a Leek millwright, to make a survey of a possible line for a canal in 1759. The survey was accepted by the Duke of Bridgewater who obtained an Act in 1760 to provide the necessary powers to construct the canal. The 10½—mile canal, level throughout, was modest in scale and the only engineering work of note were the two embankments over Stretford Meadows and Trafford Moss, and the stone aqueduct over the river Irwell at Barton. The canal was fed by water from the Worsley Mines and the various weirs, culverts, stop gates, and other contrivances, including the use of clay puddle to retain the water along the embankment section, provided the primitive technology that was subsequently to pave the way for the construction of other canals.

The financial success of the Bridgewater Canal provided the much needed impetus for the development of plans to link the rivers Trent and Mersey by canal. The project was finally promoted by the North Staffordshire pottery owners, Earl Gower and Josiah Wedgwood, and in 1766 James Brindley re-surveyed the line of a canal to link these two major rivers. At the same time Brindley began to envisage a bolder scheme, with a Grand Cross of some 260 miles of canals, linking the Mersey, Severn, Thames, and Trent.

The Grand Trunk Canal, as Brindley urged his promoters to call it, climbed from the Cheshire Plain in a south-easterly direction and pierced through the watershed at Harecastle to join the upper valley of the river Trent. The line of the Grand Trunk thence took the form of a broad 'V', drawn across the north Midlands. The northern arm extended to join the Trent at Shardlow, whilst the southern arm had two functions; firstly, a line using the Staffordshire and Worcestershire Canal to link with the Severn at Stourport, and, secondly, a longer line, by means of the Coventry and Oxford canals, to reach the Thames at Oxford. Due to his untimely death in 1772, Brindley did not survive to see his dream reach fruition, for it was not until January 1790 that the final link in the Grand Cross was completed, when the southern section of Oxford Canal was constructed and the Grand Trunk route at last became a reality. Although the completion of the Grand Cross was long delayed, the example set by Brindley and the Duke of Bridgewater was rapidly copied by others who saw similar benefits and profits from their local projects.

From 1770 onwards the number of new canal schemes rapidly increased, and in 1792 culminated in a riot of speculation, when a wide range of fanciful schemes was being dangled before gullible speculators. Some schemes, such as the Kington and Leominster, were started, never to be completed; others, such as the Oakham Canal and the Melton Mowbray Navigation, had a relatively short working life and were never able to repay the considerable investments made in them. Even so, the great number of schemes substantially advanced the knowledge of civil engineering techniques and the variety of skills learnt were valuable assets for the years ahead.

By 1830, the 'bubble' of the canal era had burst. At that time there were over 4,250 miles of navigable waterways, two-thirds of which were canals and the remainder navigable rivers, the majority of which had been completed in the previous 100 years. A measure of the impact of the period 1760 to 1830 can be gained when it is remembered that some £32 million was invested in navigation construction during these years. In that same period some of the most heavily-worked navigations had already been substantially rebuilt; the development of Telford's new Harecastle Tunnel and the long, wide and direct routes within the Birmingham Canal Navigations offered, perhaps, the best examples of the extent to which engineering skills had improved. In other instances, the original canals constructed by Brindley still provided the major transport arteries servicing the rapidly developing industries on which Britain's continued growth depended.

The downfall of the canals, as a major transport system, was almost as swift as their meteoric climb to prosperity. The decline was caused primarily because the waterway system was composed of a number of individual projects, each promoted to satisfy particular local needs at different times, and often without regard to the fact that they might eventually form part of an interlinking network of trunk routes. Secondly, the canals were still linked to archaic and often little improved river navigations. The Trent shoals and the Thames flash locks were not removed from their respective upper river reaches until the early 20th century. Thus the value of the Thames and Severn, and Trent and Mersey canals was drastically reduced, and they were unable to provide viable links to the major ports at the mouths of the two major rivers. A third factor was the extortionate tolls charged for short sections of the waterways forming parts of through routes, and the 'bar' tolls for all traffic entering certain canals. Although such tolls were reduced when competition came, the exploitation of the monopoly had often created an earlier loss in public sympathy and in consequence their subsequent support.

There was also a further constraint on canal companies in that the proprietors were not carriers, but merely toll takers. This was not changed until an Act of 1845 enabled canal companies to act also as carriers by amending the regulations that previously constrained them. Even so, as the great majority of the original canal carriers were small traders operating over particular waterways, the possibility for regular long-distance traffic working over the canal network and the quotation of through carriage rates was virtually impossible, and this further restricted trade.

During the first years of the railway era the new companies tended in the 1830s to concentrate on passenger and parcel traffic, and for a while the canals benefited both from carrying materials required for railway construction and held their existing levels of trade in the carriage of bulky goods. But as the railway network grew, so the competition between one railway company and another developed. The new railway companies found they could no longer afford to select their traffic and soon an all-out war of freight fares ensued between rail and canal interests.

There was no redress for the canal companies and many quickly sold their undertakings to the railway promoters, either by agreeing to withdraw opposition to the railway schemes or by threatening to promote rival railway schemes. The best example of the latter being the combined Ellesmere, Montgomeryshire, Shrewsbury, Chester, and Birmingham and Liverpool Junction Canal Companies which formed the Shropshire Union Railway and Canal Company in 1846. Because of the interplay of economic forces much of the canal system rapidly came into railway ownership. In three years alone, 1845 to 1847, some 948 miles of canal fell into railway hands.

Some canal routes were subsequently used to provide the paths for railway lines. The earliest and best known is the Croydon Canal, which was closed in 1831 to provide the route for the London and Croydon Railway. The resultant loss of these links in the canal network, combined with the active discouragement of traffic from some canals promoted by the railway owners in a variety of ways (by neglecting maintenance; by diverting water supplies; by raising tolls; and by closing waterways for lengthy periods on the pretext of carrying out repairs), soon took its toll, and one by one the canals were forced into decay through lack of use.

The advent of the railways meant that the continued development and modernisation of the canal system was virtually frozen. The Railway Companies were unwilling to extend or improve the canal systems that they controlled, while the canal companies that remained independent were too impoverished to contemplate further modernisation schemes. The net result was that, apart from the extension of various sections of the Birmingham Canal Navigations during the second half of the 19th century to meet particular colliery or works needs, the only other canals promoted, apart from the Manchester Ship Canal in 1886, were the Droitwich Junction Canal in 1852 and the Slough Branch of the Grand Junction, which was completed in 1883. This latter was the last link in an era that had its origin in the work of James Brindley some 120 years earlier.

During the 20th century the demise of the inland waterways became more and more apparent. Some small independent canals struggled on, either to be taken over by County Councils, like the Thames and Severn Canal in 1901, or to die, like the North Wilts and the Wilts and Berks canals in 1914. Others lost all traffic, but slumbered on, waiting for a new era to dawn, when perhaps they might again be needed as part of a waterway network in which they had a new rôle to play.

These various closures resulted in piecemeal disintegration of the canals as a transport system, which further diminished the ability to seek trade. Some waterways, however, spent a great deal of money on modernisation, notably the Aire and Calder, the Weaver, the Birmingham system, the Grand Junction, and the Leeds and Liverpool Canal, and retained some trade. It even seemed that there might be a new future for the inland waterways when a Royal Commission was created in 1906. Its report was presented in 1909, recommending the widening and deepening of the trunk waterway routes that form a 'Cross' to link the Thames, Severn, Trent and Mersey with the centre of Birmingham. It suggested that all these routes should be improved to take barges of at least 100 tons capacity, with the use of 300-ton barges on the river sections. Unfortunately the political problems of the time, together with the outbreak of the First World War, prevented action being taken.

In the 1920s further losses of traffic from the canals continued, forcing additional canal closures from lack of toll revenue. Thus, although in 1913 some 31,585,909 tons was carried on the British canals, this had dropped to 21,599,850 tons in 1918, and to an all-time low level of 13,000,000 tons in 1938. The dislocation of transport and the lack of maintenance during the subsequent war years created a further substantial decline in canal traffic, and by 1946 only 10,000,000 tons was being carried on the remaining canals.

The passing of the Transport Act in 1947 ended the era of private ownership for the majority of the existing 2,000-miles canal network, and on 1 January 1948 the British Transport Commission took control of most of the network. At that time there were still about 6,000 working boats, and the industry employed some 11,000 persons.

The final death knell for the narrow boat 'carrying' industry came with the long, harsh winter of 1962/3, when ice effectively blocked most of the canals for nearly three months. The fragile finances of the industry could not withstand the impact of such a long stoppage, and the nationally-owned narrow boat fleet was withdrawn and some of the craft sold. Thereafter only a few small and independent carriers tried to continue their trade, but with less and less success.

Fortunately, by this time, the vision of a new multi-functional rôle for the canals was being promoted by a small band of enthusiasts led by Robert Aickman, who had founded the Inland Waterways Association in 1946. At first they only achieved a few successes, but, as their aims became more widely known, so more and more like-minded people became sufficiently interested in the future of the canals to carry forward their own local campaigns. It is the growth of this revival that the subsequent chapters seek to plot and review.

Just as the original development of the navigation network was on a piecemeal basis, the same is equally true of the way in which the various revival campaigns have evolved. Often they have been promoted from the vision of one enthusiast, or a few local people, who believed that the derelict old canal could still become an asset to the local community.

The way in which the canal revival has taken place has differed from place to place, but often common factors are apparent and these are mentioned in the review that follows. To provide a complete picture of each group of waterways, Chapter Three includes a brief summary of the historical background to local canals, summarising their rise, decline and fall. Where restoration work is still in progress, an indication of the possible way ahead is also offered; for those projects that have failed, the problems that were encountered are similarly reviewed. In this way some of the components of the modern Waterway Restoration Movement are described in the period which has, perhaps, been most aptly named the 'Second Canal Mania'.

Chapter Two

THE 'NEW NAVVIES'

BETWEEN 150 and 200 years ago vast gangs of travelling labourers gave Britain a new transport system, when the country gained most of its canals. The work of the 'navigators' is well documented, as, indeed, is the rise and decline of the use of the waterways they created.

Now Britain has new squads of 'navvies'—men and women eager to undertake the back-breaking, often damp and chilling work of restoring some of the disused canals for leisure use. The growth of these new bands of workers is described here.

Voluntary work on the inland waterways started in earnest in 1950 with the commencement of the restoration work on the Lower Avon Navigation. Well before that date, intrepid boating enthusiasts always had to undertake a certain amount of canal clearance work simply to navigate some of the waterways. Early work of this nature involved weed and rubbish clearance from canals such as the Northern Section of the Stratford Canal.

Under the leadership of Douglas Barwell early groups of volunteers undertook work on the locks, including such tasks as pointing brickwork, cutting back undergrowth, weed clearance, and gate painting. Barwell often gave a lead by donning his own diving suit and undertaking underwater clearance work.

Initially, the work of the volunteers was concentrated in small local pockets, such as the work undertaken by the voluntary Water Bailiffs on the Basingstoke Canal in the early 1950s, or that on Linton Lock by members of the I.W.A., North Eastern Branch, at much the same time. Subsequently groups such as the Linton Lock Supporters' Club and the Stratford Canal Club were formed, primarily to continue the maintenance of re-opened waterways.

Perhaps the most significant advance for the 'navvies' came in 1957 with the foundation of the Coventry Canal Society, whose first task was the clearance of rubbish from the Town Arm of the Coventry Canal. This work, and a general renewal of interest in the canal, created a demand for new moorings for club members' boats. This led D. Hutchings to suggest the complete restoration of the derelict Wyken Arm of the Oxford Canal, which was owned by Coventry Corporation, in early 1958. The scheme was notable in that it was the first completely derelict section of canal to be restored and re-opened for boating purposes. The work, which was completed in 1959, provided Hutchings with extensive experience of the problems of dredging a mud-filled canal. It also provided a clear example of just how much could be achieved by using inexperienced volunteer labour. (Hutchings later led a rubbish clearance operation on the

9

Stourbridge Canal in 1959. On this occasion it was solely aimed at getting his boat past a severe obstruction.)

By 1960 Hutchings had been given the job of General Manager responsible for the restoration of the derelict 13-mile Southern Section of the Stratford Canal. In this instance the work was co-ordinated through the Stratford-upon-Avon Canal Society, which acted as agents for the National Trust.

The first record of authorised volunteer work on the nationalised waterway system came in 1958 when members of the Kennet and Avon Canal Association linked with members of the British Sub-aqua Club to repair Burghfield Lock on the Kennet and Avon Canal. This was ahead of its time, for it was not until 1964 that another similar joint effort was undertaken. On the latter occasion it was linked with the full-scale restoration of the Stourbridge Canal, Wordsley '16' Locks, by volunteer members of the Staffordshire and Worcestershire Canal Society, who were able to work alongside the paid B.W.B. staff. In all such early cases the members of the Associations or Societies were directly committed to the revival of the particular waterway on which they were working.

In late 1961 and early 1962 a new and more mobile force of volunteers was formed. This was the London Working Party Group, formed from the membership of the I.W.A., London and Home Counties Branch, led by Tim Dodwell. The group was started with the purpose of improving the Basingstoke Canal, partly to avoid further deterioration, and partly to prepare the way for the first London and Home Counties Branch Rally of Boats at Woking at Easter 1962. After the rally, further work parties were held on the canal, but operations soon faded when the problems of the overall restoration of the canal became too great for the minimal resources available to the group.

In October 1965 the group was revived, again by Tim Dodwell, and one of the first excursions made was to the Stourbridge '16' Locks restoration site. One of the six London volunteers who joined the group was Graham Palmer. In November the group, by then increased to 14 workers, went to join the Kennet and Avon Trust at Limpley Stoke, near Bath. Their next excursion was to the river Wey in December 1965. From that time regular working parties were held: January 1966, Sulhampstead on the Kennet and Avon; February, the river Wey; March, the Southern Stratford Canal; April, back to Sulhampstead; and June, back to the Stourbridge '16' Locks, where attendance was up to 10!

At this stage, Palmer reviewed the progress of the group. The average turnout for each of the previous six working parties was only 15, yet the London I.W.A. Branch membership was over a thousand. Even taking account of the enthusiasts' well-known preference for 'hot air' rather than hard work, it appeared that the working parties were not achieving the support they should. It occurred to Graham Palmer that perhaps communications were at fault. To test this, he decided to prepare an advance notice of all future working parties that could be circulated to branch members. The outcome was a small duplicated booklet, *Navvies Notebook*, the first edition of which was circulated in October 1966. It was distributed free to all members of the I.W.A. London and Home Counties Branch, which agreed to underwrite its production costs for the first year.

Members were offered the opportunity to subscribe to future issues, and over 70 took up the offer.

Navvies Notebook No. 1 (October 1966) outlined the aims of the Group:

> It is hoped eventually to cover all the voluntary work going on over the entire system. But the success of N.N. depends on you . . . All waterways Societies are invited to submit details of future plans and reports of past efforts.

Graham Palmer's initial hypothesis proved correct, and after the initial issue some 43 volunteers reported for work on the river Wey in November 1966, and 30 at Sulhampstead the following month. The next working party organised on the Stourbridge '16' Locks, in February 1967, doubled the previous attendance, and in March 1967 some 70 volunteers arrived for work on two separate restoration sites.

In April 1967 a further experiment was tried when the work on restoring the Stourbridge Canal fell behind schedule with the planned re-opening date ominously close. This was a scheme to send small working parties from London to assist on the site on every weekend throughout April. It proved to be a great success, and 50 Londoners worked on the final stage of the restoration scheme so that the work was completed on schedule.

The availability of members of this mobile group to visit various waterway restoration sites around the country prompted an increase in the number of local working group organisers. As they became known to the London Working Party Group Secretary their names and addresses were published in *Navvies Notebook*. This list grew rapidly, particularly after 1971, and by 1975 over 50 organisers were listed as offering regular work.

During 1967 the range of the alternative working sites grew as did the enthusiasm and strength of the London Working Party Group. One weekend in August 1967, 28 Londoners travelled to Marple to work on the Peak Forest Canal. They were joined by 20 members of the local Peak Forest Canal Society to make up the largest volunteer working party ever held on that canal. This highlighted one of the early problems encountered by the group, the lack of suitable equipment to assist in restoration work. This was partially overcome in a novel way, through the organised collection of trading stamps which were held by the Working Party Group Bank. Members also sought to publicise their efforts to raise additional funds. Perhaps the most beneficial publicity they received was from a two-page article in the *Daily Mirror* for 22 August 1967, entitled 'The Wasted Heritage'.

One effect of the publicity was the steady increase in the size of the working party, which was best shown on an excursion to assist with the restoration of Southcote Lock, near Reading, on the Kennet and Avon Canal, when 94 volunteers arrived to undertake the work planned. By early 1968 the circulation list of *Navvies Notebook* had risen to over 400 names, and this rate of growth continued throughout the remainder of that year.

The growing strength of the group was tested in September 1968 when members joined the Peak Forest Canal Society to mount a major canal clearance exercise at Ashton, code-named 'Operation Ashton'. Some 600 volunteers from many parts of Britain were mustered to clear a section of the Ashton Canal. During a weekend of pouring rain over 2,000 tons of rubbish was removed from the canal. The weekend cost the organisers £1,300, of which £750 was spent on plant hire and all the funds required were met by voluntary donations. This weekend working party proved to Palmer and others that a large-scale voluntary operation to clean and restore derelict canals was a viable proposition and could also be used to attract local support for the revival of a waterway.

A few months passed before the next suitable scheme emerged, where such local public support was needed. This was the battle organised by the Welshpool By-Pass Action Committee to save the obliteration of the route of the Montgomery Canal. As the result of consultation between the Shropshire Union Canal Society and the I.W.A., the *Navvies Notebook* publicised its second major working party at Welshpool in October 1969. Some 180 volunteers responded to the request, and a large section of the canal in Welshpool was cleared of rubbish. The longer term object of the event was to demonstrate that the canal, instead of being a nuisance, should be retained as a valuable amenity to the town. This was achieved and by 1970 a passenger trip boat was operating successfully on a restored section of the canal.

In *Navvies Notebook* No. 22 of January 1970, Graham Palmer reviewed the way ahead for the 'Navvies' movement:

> We now have a great power at our command, a great and evergrowing enthusiasm and we are, in the main, far more expert and efficient in our work. This progress, which has taken about three years to achieve, must not be frittered away on useless and non-urgent tasks . . . we are ready and have the capability to take part in a major restoration project on one of the remainder waterways.

To set the direction for the way ahead *Navvies Notebook* No. 25 of July 1970 published a map showing some 22 sites at which regular working parties were held. It also announced that the central co-ordinating organisation was being re-named the Waterway Recovery Group (W.R.G.), so that it could be more readily identified with its ideals. Its principal function, by then, was to co-ordinate effort, ideas, plant and money for voluntary waterway work. By this time the W.R.G. was starting to supply personal clothing required to protect the navvies, with a sales section for waders, safety helmets, and work gloves.

Under its new title the group was called upon to assist Dudley Canal Trust members with a major lock clearance, named the 'Dudley Dig and Cruise', in September 1970. Over 600 people attended for the weekend, and a lock and a section of the Dudley Canal were cleared of mud and debris.

In mid-1971 the *Navvies Notebook* was renamed *Navvies*. By then its circulation had risen to some 1,500 copies, for each of the bi-monthly issues. During this time the group was both adding to its stock of equipment and promoting a wider interest in the growing number of local waterway protection and restoration societies.

The month of March 1972 heralded the inauguration of the Ashton and Lower Peak Forest Canal restoration scheme. To give the project a good start a major

'Dig' code-named 'Ashtac' was promoted. The event saw 1,000 volunteers descend on the Ashton Canal and clear some 3,000 tons of rubbish from it.

The summer of 1972 saw the first Waterways Restoration Summer Work Camp, which later became an annual event. The pilot camp was held to assist with the maintenance of the Southern Section of the Stratford Canal, as was the second annual camp in 1973. Thereafter the venues of the Summer Camps were regularly changed, and by 1974 two separate Summer Camps were being organised.

By 1973 the total work force of volunteer navvies available through the W.R.G. was about 1,500 and still growing, with typical week-end working parties at each site attracting about 30 participants.

In October 1973 another new restoration scheme was inaugurated by a major working party, named the 'Droitwich Dig'. On this occasion some 600 volunteers descended on the Droitwich Canal and created a remarkable transformation during the course of one weekend. A subsequent 'Dig' at Deep Cut on the Basingstoke Canal in October 1977 achieved similar success, and again proved the effectiveness of the resources of the waterway volunteers.

During 1974 and 1975 the number of local Working Party organisers continued to grow, and by the close of 1976 some 55 separate groups were operating under the W.R.G. network. Since then the number of groups has remained fairly constant, with new organisers taking over the place of the old. By this time the W.R.G. had a fleet of vehicles, excavators, dumper trucks, a workboat, and assorted pumps and other plant available for loan to local restoration schemes.

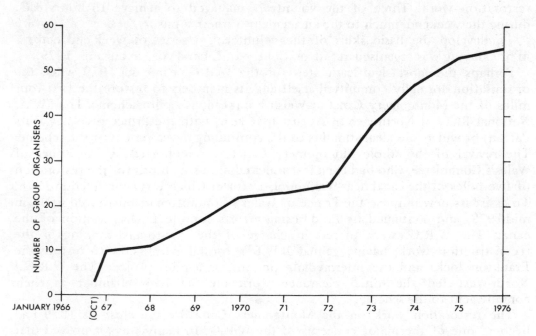

Growth of the number of voluntary working party organisers (1966–1976)

The W.R.G. was also running its own printing organisation to cope with the production and distribution of some 2,500 copies of each issue of *Navvies*—a level which has also remained fairly constant since that time.

The W.R.G. did not rest on its past successes, but continued to look for ways to improve efficiency. The period 1977 to 1978 thus saw a re-structuring of its own organisation. Various independent regional units were formed, with W.R.G./ North-West leading the way, to provide a nucleus of equipment and expertise which could be utilised for the benefit of each individual restoration scheme in their area. To supplement these area groups, a revitalised London-based mobile task force, aptly named W.R.G./C.O.S.M.O., was also formed. This group has since worked on developments throughout the country, undertaking both routine and specialised projects, and adding impetus to the local schemes.

The restoration efforts of the 'navvies' were partially retarded during the winter of 1978/79, when the Public Service unions, as part of their campaign of industrial action, refused to allow volunteers to work on any nationalised canals. Fortunately, the restrictions did not apply to the privately-operated waterways, and the volunteers were able to re-direct some of their efforts to reviving these, until the dispute was resolved.

It was on one of these non-nationalised canals that a weekend in April 1979 saw the start of a new scheme to raise funds for restoration work. Lock 19 on the Basingstoke Canal provided the venue for the country's first sponsored 'Dig'. Up to 40 'navvies' were in attendance at any one time, and over £400 was ultimately raised as a result of their labours to be devoted to financing further restoration work. Three of the volunteers managed to achieve 16 hours each during the weekend, much to the amazement of their sponsors.

To develop the basic skills of the volunteers, a series of week-end courses in bricklaying was organised at Sutton College of Liberal Arts in autumn 1979.

Perhaps the most significant step for the W.R.G. came in 1979 when the organisation formally committed itself and its members to restore the first four miles of the Montgomery Canal at Welsh Frankton, as a pilot scheme. The I.W.A. National Rally at Northwich in August that year, with the Prince of Wales as its Patron, provided the ideal stimulus to the continuing development of the scheme. The revival of the whole Montgomery Canal was supported by the Prince of Wales's Committee, who had been instrumental in raising funds for the restoration of five miles of the canal near Welshpool, a project which was completed in 1978. To assist its new purpose the Prince of Wales's Committee reconstituted itself, in mid-1979, and continued its fund-raising efforts for the English section of the canal. The W.R.G. were placed in charge of the day-to-day running of the reconstruction work, having gained B.W.B.'s formal permission to restore the Frankton locks and the intermediate pounds, as a pilot project. The W.R.G./ North-West led the initial clearance work on the lock chamber as their commitment to the scheme.

The restoration work on the Montgomery Canal by the close of 1979 had become one of the major concerns of the W.R.G. In many ways it proved that the volunteer 'navvies' had come of age, with official recognition of the rôle that they could play in developing additional recreational space. The potential success of the pilot project offered the volunteers the chance to show the high standard of professionalism that they could achieve. It also enabled the W.R.G. to exploit the full range of knowledge and skills accumulated during the previous decade. The W.R.G. was still entirely self-supporting, with no paid staff or official income. The group had no formal officers, except the editor of *Navvies* and a treasurer, but relied on a devoted group of volunteers, each of whom was responsible for some aspect of its work.

The success of the *Navvies* in England and Wales stimulated the Scottish Inland Waterways Association to launch a similar journal, *MacNavvies,* in December 1975, to co-ordinate the growing number of amenity development groups working on the Scottish canals. The combined aim of the two journals still remained the same as that of the original *Navvies Notebook*, when it was launched in October 1966: to co-ordinate all the voluntary work on the entire waterway network. It was unfortunate that *MacNavvies* ceased publication in 1978; even so, the original *Navvies* system continued to augment the progress of the regular workers of many local canal societies and did much to ensure the smooth flow of work, with maximum utilisation of available plant on a wide range of restoration schemes.

Surprisingly, it was about this time that the Waterway Recovery Group's own initial cohesion began to falter. Perhaps it was because the editor of *Navvies* was not so readily available to goad the group on to better things! The frequency of *Navvies'* publication also fell to an all-time low, with no issue between November 1979 and May 1980.

During 1980 the work of the volunteers on the nationalised waterways also nearly ground to a halt, with Union opposition rearing its ugly head again. Even so, work on the privately-sponsored waterways schemes, such as the Droitwich, Stroudwater, Buxworth Basin, Montgomery, and Basingstoke Canals still went ahead, and possibly gained more momentum because the efforts of the volunteers were concentrated on fewer sites.

The advantages gained from regularly publicised working party venues and co-ordinated operations suffered another severe blow when *Navvies* went through another crisis in 1981. No issue appeared between February 1981 and January 1982 because the editor, Graham Palmer, moved to a new job. Fortunately, local societies were not too affected by this, as their own newsletters directed members to old and new sites, whilst the W.R.G. centrally also were able to use local contacts to continue schemes at Welsh Frankton and elsewhere. No doubt there were losses to the 'navvying' system, in that new volunteers were not so readily attracted because of the lack of variety of choice. Also, the volume of work no doubt fell as the stalwarts continued, unassisted by new blood. In spite of this, major advances were made at new sites, such as Foxton on the Inclined Plane, and on existing projects, like Basingstoke and the Thames and Severn Canals, where local volunteers already had set targets to achieve.

The break in publication occurred, fortuitously, at a time when the Waterway Recovery Group itself was due for change. Until 1980 the Group had been run on

very informal lines. At that time the problems of V.A.T. and the need to give
more protection to the individuals involved became an ever-increasing concern.
It was concluded that the only possible course to cope with legal demands would
be to convert the former vast, loose and unaccountable organisation into a more
coherent whole, and for it to take the status of a wholly-owned subsidiary
company of the Inland Waterways Association (I.W.A.). As a result the Waterways
Recovery Group, Ltd., was formed in late 1981, with a new chairman, Alan
Jervis, at the helm. Because of his personal commitments, the original founder,
Graham Palmer, asked if he could stand down from taking the leading rôle,
but he remained a member of the 'Board of Directors', or Committee, that
thereafter took central policy decisions. A separate management committee,
consisting of regional representatives plus others with particular tasks such as
plant management, took over the lead in the 'day to day' operations. This new
arrangement meant that every individual 'navvy' could work through a local
designated Working Party Organiser who then had a regional contact who could
quickly lay on equipment or give advice.

In an effort to get the new organisation running smoothly a Working Party
Organisers' Conference was held in Wolverhampton in April 1982. This was
attended by over 60 representatives, and the new W.R.G. structure and aims were
outlined to them, together with the problems presented by such things as V.A.T.,
Building Regulations, the Health and Safety at Work Act, and Site Insurance. The
'simple' business of producing 2,500 copies of *Navvies* on a regular basis was
brought into perspective, and a list of plant for use on work-sites was circulated.
It was mentioned that Work Camps took up to a year to organise, and were
best undertaken by dedicated groups of 25 people; more being progressively
difficult to control! The additional amount of work capable of being completed
in this way, when compared to the usual monthly working party, especially
was stressed.

Specialist speakers on the subjects of Insurance and Working Party Safety
followed, and the important point was made that, to date, W.R.G. had an
enviable record in this direction; but that serious accidents could have
far-reaching repercussions, which could jeopardise future involvement on the
waterways, particularly at B.W.B. sites. The job of Work Party Organiser was
also explained.

At the end of the formal business, a somewhat subdued W.R.G. leader,
Graham Palmer, was presented with the Cyril Styring Trophy—a superb silver
replica narrowboat—in recognition of all the work he had done for W.R.G.

Perhaps the best news of all to emerge from the meeting was that the next
'Big Dig' (Spring 1983) was planned to clear the first three locks on the
Huddersfield Narrow Canal at Stalybridge—adding a further two miles to the
navigable network—precisely the job that the Waterways Recovery Group did
best. It was unfortunate that this 'Big Dig' subsequently had to be postponed
because of various difficulties encountered on the site.

Under the new organisation the *Navvies* journal began to appear regularly,
and began to gather momentum again by the close of 1982. A minor setback

came on 16 July 1982, when the Waterway Recovery Group were told that once they had completed their current works on the Montgomery Canal 'no further new works would be allowed to commence'. It took sometime for the politics behind this statement to be resolved, and it was clear that because of it the rest of the Montgomery Project had been set back by at least a year. This did not alter the target date for the completion of the pilot scheme. However, one effect of this was to make the North-West Branch of the W.R.G. take stock of 'where it was going'. The main debate concerned the relative importance of working parties, fund raising and publicity. The group decided that it was there mainly to get the job done. As a result, the local organisation was itself developed so that there could be four local working party organisers to cover each of the main areas of work, with a central organiser to ensure that they did not clash.

In January 1983, Alan Jervis, the new W.R.G. leader, set the movement one main aim for the year—'to increase volunteer involvement'. In particular he noted that, within the restoration field, there were many jobs to be undertaken, especially those relating to co-ordination. He therefore concluded his address with the rallying cry: 'So come on, some of you 2,500, volunteer for something in 1983'.

In recognition of his retirement from the W.R.G. leadership, Graham Palmer was asked to record for *Navvies* readers, what he thought the 'navvies' movement had achieved. He made some very valid comments. Firstly, he pointed to the spirit that the working party system engendered; with the satisfaction gained through achievement, which was only brought about by the unstinting support and the help of those that came along, and of those who helped from the sidelines. Secondly, he saw the working party movement as a way in which individuals could make a positive change and an impact upon the time in which they lived. Thirdly, by demonstrating a belief in such a practical way, he believed individuals were doing what they could to demand a share in the decisions with those that shape the country in which they lived. He concluded: 'a country gets the Government it deserves; perhaps by that same token we shall get the water-ways we deserve'.

During the period of Palmer's leadership, the Waterway Recovery Group deserved full marks for ideas. For instance, another way in which the national Navvies Movement tried to make more impact on those in power was by organising longer term and more comprehensive projects during the holiday periods. The idea of a summer holiday digging canals, knee-deep in mud, or balancing on a crumbling weir trying to repair it before the water level rises and washes it away, might seem a little bizarre. However, for those navvies who wanted to see more distant waterways, it also seemed a good idea. As a result, the concept of Summer Works Camps was conceived. Since the camps were inaugurated some ten years ago, students, clerks, factory workers, accountants and teachers, as well as many others, have come back year after year to join in such projects.

The idea of the Summer Work Camp was first promoted by the Waterways Recovery Group in early 1972. The concept was advertised in *Navvies* as 'a chance for all students, tramps and drunkards' to spend their summer holiday working to restore canals. Some 17 people turned up for the first camp, which took place between the 15 and 29 July 1972. The group were housed in Lowson-ford village hall and worked each day on the Southern Stratford Canal. Food was provided at 50p a day, to sustain the workers, as they rebuilt two culverts and removed a decaying cast-iron roving bridge, which was falling into the canal. Lengths of the towpath were also cleared to complete the transformation scene.

The first camp proved to be such a success, that a second camp was organised, centred on the Southern Stratford Canal, in August 1973. Some 27 volunteers arrived, and during their stay rebuilt two bywashes and renovated various of the locks on the canal. Perhaps the most notable achievement was the completion of some 250 feet of steel bank piling, just with the use of a sledgehammer, by unskilled volunteers!

In 1974, the holiday opportunities offered by the Summer camps were substantially expanded, with three separate sites on offer to the discerning volunteer. The Droitwich and Montgomery Canals figured in the prospectus, and, for the river enthusiast, a spell at Great Barford on the Great Ouse offered the ultimate in holiday dreams. Over 100 volunteers took up these special offers and cleared trees from the Droitwich Canal, as well as re-bricking Ladywood lock. On the Montgomery the work was centred at Llanymynech, where at first 30-plus volunteers had to share 4½ bedrooms, until the Llanymynech village hall was brought into service as the 'Navvies Rest', to serve as a base for the group whilst they worked on Pool Quay locks. At Great Barford the group slept in a small marquee, and by day filled gabbions from the remains of the old Barford lock. All these vital tasks were completed with success.

The year 1975 saw return visits to the Droitwich and Montgomery Canals, with 84 people putting in 141 weeks of work. Thirty-four of these volunteers were returning for their second and third successive camp, and four had come back for their fourth holiday to clear the locks and reconstruct the overflow weirs.

The year 1975 also saw the first of the 'Christmas Work Camps', where the active could fight the Christmas flab and get slim through healthy exercise in the cold winter air. This was on the Southern Stratford Canal and it became part of the annual winter blitz, which has since substantially improved the waterway for continuing pleasure use.

A new northerly site, at Howsham Weir on the Yorkshire Derwent, was offered to entice new recruits to the Summer Work Camps in 1976. Work here included the rebuilding of a damaged weir while the river still continued to flow down the main stream channel, as well as other site construction works. These offered thrills and possible spills for those who were willing to make the trek to North Yorkshire, and provided a new challenge for those used to dealing with drained canals. The ultimate achievements of the camp included rebuilding the 40-foot crest of the weir, rebuilding a sluice, and constructing three scaffold bridges, to offer access to the difficult island site where the main work proceeded.

Work continued on the River Derwent during the summer of 1977 and at two other work sites on the Droitwich and Montgomery Canals. The latter saw the first work on the 'Salop Riviera' at Frankton Junction, where the Mont-gomery joins the Welsh Canal. To enable volunteers to have a change of scene, the Camp season was extended to cover the whole of July and August, offering a full three weeks at each site.

In 1978 the Basingstoke Canal was the new venue on offer, together with the tried and tested Droitwich site, for those who preferred to work on the Midland canals. Vandals unfortunately damaged the Aldershot Hall just before the Navvies were due to move in. The Army came to the rescue with the loan of a hut at Mons Barracks, and volunteers gained a new vista of life. The Army Dental Corps, who had the next hut, were more than hospitable and provided access to hot baths and showers. A nice luxury for navvy life! They also offered access to their club facilities in the evenings for the waterway volunteers, and, in the end, they were persuaded to join the navvies on one of the lock sites, to show that they could do more than extract teeth! After three weeks at Basingstoke, the group moved in convoy to the second site at Droitwich, where the small marquee fell a little bit below the luxury that the Army had offered. Even so, the challenge of winching the Priestman Dragline from the Salwarpe mud more than made up for the less magnificent accommodation of the second site.

In 1979, the venues were again the Droitwich and the Basingstoke Canals, with the prospect of firmly carrying forward the achievement of the previous year. Each site gave more people the chance to learn, first-hand, the joys of 'navvying'. Both schemes were on non-B.W.B. waterways and had the prospect of complete revival in the early 1980s, provided that the necessary finance and flow of volunteers continued.

In 1980 one of the venues changed to embrace the Frankton Flight on the Montgomery Canal. At Droitwich, which provided the other part of the 'package deal', the newly-restored gas works manager's house, tastefully re-named the 'Droitwich Hilton' for the event, was the star attraction for the year. This 'package' was so successful that it was repeated again in 1981.

By 1982, the prospect of a wider range of venues had arisen, and the new scene for that year was two weeks at Uppermill on the Huddersfield Narrow Canal. This was carefully sandwiched between two four-week stretches at Droitwich, or an overlapping spell at Welsh Frankton, for those who could spare more time.

At Uppermill the task was a simple one—to clear one lock. The snag was that the lock was full of heavy quarry waste! The work would have taken the local canal society working parties about a year in odd weekends. At Droitwich the camp tackled the repair of a broken culvert. This was done section by section, by laying a reinforced concrete floor through the entire length of the tunnel, some 120 feet long, and could have only been undertaken by a team who were able to see the project through 'from end to end'.

The 1982 series of camps was the most ambitious that had ever been organised, with 12 weeks of actual work being undertaken by the teams. Their success proved that the concept was sound, but more particularly, the majority of the participants said they wanted to come back for more in 1983.

As mentioned earlier, the concept of the Winter Work Camp also emerged in the mid-1970s. That for 1978 was held on the 'Salop Riviera' and was advertised in *Navvies* No. 72, as 'otherwise known as the Frankton end of the Montgomery Canal—this area is noted for good working weather at this time of the year'. The camp extended from 27 December to the New Year.

The Winter Camp for 1979 covered a similar period of time, and was delightfully described in *Navvies* No. 76: 'the best moment of all is when you empty out your Christmas stockings, then put the stockings on your feet and head for the Montgomery Canal, where the annual Brass Monkey Meeting will occur'. The event lived up to all its promises, with the navvies being subjected to all kinds of weather—rain, show, sleet, mist, and even a 'flash' of brilliant sunshine. Fortunately, the accommodation was invigorating in itself, being on two floors of a building behind the *Queen's Head* hotel. The problem was that the floors were only linked by an outside stone staircase, and it was somewhat lacking in facilities! Even so, the 24 who took part enjoyed themselves clearing the locks and digging out tree stumps from the bed of the canal. By the end of the camp the group had cleared a fair stretch of the canal.

By 1980 the venue of the Winter Camp had changed to the Droitwich Canal, where '. . . the work will undoubtedly be very cold, very wet and utterly horrible, *but,* a splendid time is guaranteed for all'. This same package was offered again in 1981 and 1982.

Since the camps were first introduced in 1972, more and more people have been coming forward to join in the fun. When asked why they do it the majority reply, 'it gives you the opportunity to spend a cheap holiday giving practical help to restore one of Britain's derelict canals'. They often add that it gives them a chance to meet people, or old friends, working hard in the open air. Above all else, it lets them enjoy themselves, doing something very worthwhile.

Although the navvies who attend Camps and Working Parties pay for their own keep, they need materials and fuel if they are to make the best use of their time. In consequence one of the major tasks is that of raising the finance, which will enable the reconstruction work to proceed. Normally this task is undertaken by the local Canal Societies, on whose 'patch' the work is undertaken. However, sometimes there is a need to 'prime the pump'. In 1970 the I.W.A. inaugurated the National Waterways Restoration Fund, to provide capital finance to assist embryo and other restoration schemes. Between 1970 and 1975 over £50,000 was raised by the fund for distribution to those schemes with the greatest need. Between 1976 and 1978 a further £20,000 was donated to promote new projects. In 1978 a lottery was instituted to raise additional funds. The W.R.G. has done much to ensure that the best value was gained from this money, and has financed surveys to ensure official support where this was needed. It has equally financed its own progress and purchased much of the equipment used on the various work-sites around the country to supplement that owned by the local restoration societies.

Very little research work has been undertaken to evaluate the true strength or the origins of the volunteer workers. For the most part the end product of the re-navigable waterway, or the number of skips loaded with debris, are the main means of quantification of their rôle. As to their status, P. J. G. Ransom indicated in his book *Waterways Restored*:

> . . . the paid occupations of volunteer navvies ranged from doctors, lawyers and computer engineers to postmen, policemen, railwaymen and printers— almost every imaginable occupation except, unfortunately, craftsmen skilled in appropriate trades.

H. Hanson also undertook a review of just what makes modern navvies 'tick' in an article in *Canal and Riverboat* of June 1981. He asked some of the Surrey and Hampshire Canal Society members who operated the steam dredger each weekend why they devoted their spare time to digging out canals. A local college lecturer in physics indicated he got great satisfaction doing a job that improved the environment, with the facility to get in the open air and do something physical. He concluded by saying, 'it's unusual and fulfilling'. An administrator said that he came along to 'escape from routine'. Another said that he was there to forget the worries of his electrical repair business, whilst a bachelor admitted that it gave him something to do at the weekends! The others commented that they just felt that they could play a part in something that they believed worthwhile.

A useful review of the membership of the Grantham Canal Restoration Society was undertaken by M. G. Miller of Leicester University in January 1975. The results of this research were circulated to interested parties in May 1975 and indicated that the majority of volunteers were male (3 to 1) with an average age of 31.3 years. The majority of working party members being in the 20 to 39 age group. His survey found that the majority of working party members came either from the professional classes or from the skilled craftsmen group, the majority of whom lived within 20 miles of the working party site. He also found that the majority of working party members belonged to other Waterway Societies than the Grantham Canal Society on which the survey was based. The most popular attendance frequency at working parties was on a monthly or bi-monthly basis (32.4 per cent), but a sizeable group only attended working parties twice a year or less (36.6 per cent). Significantly 28.4 per cent of the working party attenders had had experience of working on other canals, giving a clear pointer to the value of the Navvies Movement in providing a variety of choice and a means of gaining wider experience of volunteer restoration work.

It would be wrong to draw firm conclusions from the results of just one survey. It is perhaps more appropriate just to accept that all of the volunteers live up to the motto 'I Dig Canals' which appears on the badges sold by the W.R.G. to raise funds, and to acknowledge the W.R.G. view that they are: 'dedicated to the restoration and maintenance of these unique water highways for all sorts of amenity uses'.

Chapter Three

REGIONAL PROJECTS REVIEW

CANAL RESTORATION, like the original canal construction, does not rest alone on the ability to 'dig'. Quite apart from the work of the new 'navvies', someone, initially, has to promote the project, gain public support for it, and seek legal powers to enable the work to proceed. Often these issues can take more time than the physical restoration itself!

An understanding of the potential problems for the modern restorationists can be gained by examining the past. The original navigation development schemes were promoted by local people on a piecemeal basis. Each group had the prime aim of improving access to their local community and, in doing so, promoting local industrial growth. Invariably the prospect of increased local wealth was the motive that stirred initial interest and ultimately the vista of rich profits was the incentive that persuaded others to support and invest in the local schemes. Because the various canal projects were promoted mainly to meet local needs, their designers paid little attention to the prospect of a larger-scale transport network, with a universal wide gauge, or to uniformity in canal equipment and structures. This initial lack of foresight was ultimately one of the major factors that led to the demise of many peripheral canal links. Incompatibility with neighbouring canals often created excessive handling costs and increased freight charges, and these also detracted from the development of an extensive provision for through traffic. This effectively stopped the canals from competing with the railways, with their standard gauge, for the long-distance bulk traffic contracts, and the regular and reliable income that these could offer. The multitude of small canal companies, each with their own problems and separate toll structures, similarly created difficulties for the canal carriers and further detracted from the development of a national carriage trade.

The decline in local traffic that followed as the railways spread their net, left the smaller canal companies with major problems and, because of their lack of financial backing and reserves, many soon were forced into a cycle of decline from which they could not recover; low toll revenue resulted in reduced maintenance, which in turn led to less traffic trying to negotiate the decaying canal. In this way, one by one the smaller canal companies were forced into liquidation and the rural canals that they owned allowed to close. As these branch canals were removed, so the main trunk canals lost valuable additional trade. This placed pressures on the major canal companies both to amalgamate and modernise in order to retain the minimal traffic available to them. Because of the severe financial pressures, these companies neither had the facility or the ability to rejuvenate the lost branch lines and had to allow them to decay.

The post-War revival of interest in the canals came much too late for many of the then defunct smaller canal companies, and they were unable to respond to the prospect of a brighter future. Nationalisation of most of the canal network took place on 1 January 1948, and this effectively stifled any immediate local initiative to rejuvenate the decaying canals for amenity purposes. It is perhaps for this reason that the first major restoration schemes for the revival of particular waterways were based on the river nagivations that had also fallen into decay.

The act of navigation reconstruction is, as indicated earlier, not just the simple matter of wielding a pick or shovel. It is almost as difficult as the promotion of the original navigation Bills; public and political support are the prime ingredients of each and every re-development scheme. The processes are much akin to those of the canal era, and the restoration schemes are developed by small bands of men who have a vision of just what can be achieved with derelict local canals, and who are willing to shoulder the brunt of the work in promoting the campaign, even though the end product offers no personal financial gain. By selling the prospect of the enhanced benefits that could accrue to the local community, these small groups seek to gain the necessary wider public and political support for their aims. Digging is thus very much the final stage in their campaign, to be considered only after all the political and legal battles have been won.

In much the same way as the early navigation proprietors had to form companies to promote their schemes, so the potential restorers have had to form recognised Societies or Trusts. As in the past, different projects have been promoted throughout the country at different times, depending much on local needs; one local scheme often provokes interest in another, and success breeds success. Likewise, as in the original canal era, there was at first little connection between the variety of local schemes, but, as the value of shared knowledge became recognised, so collaboration developed. The same has been true with modern restoration schemes. For it was only with the formation of the national Waterways Recovery Group in 1970 that true co-ordination became a practical possibility. For the most part, however, projects have been promoted by local enthusiasts and have since remained firmly in their control, with outside help and advice only being sought when required.

In much the same way as the original network of waterways grew from the river navigations, so did the first of the revival schemes. These were promoted to revive the decaying river navigations of the Lower Avon, Great Ouse, and Linton Lock on the Yorkshire Ouse, by groups of local supporters in 1950 and 1951. The first individual canal association was also formed in 1951, when enthusiasts in Newbury founded the Kennet and Avon Canal Association to fight for the complete re-opening of their local canal as a through route. The subsequent foundation of the Stratford-upon-Avon Canal Society in 1956 and the Coventry Canal Society in 1957 continued in much the same trend.

The factors relating to the formation of each of these and the many other local groups were much related to underlying public attitudes in each of the local communities at that time, but invariably the action was stimulated by the seriousness of the threat to their local canal. Because of the variety of circumstances involved, a review of each local development is needed to relate the achievements to their regional context. To assist readers in tracing these developments, the country has been divided into 20 sectors. These are defined on the master map opposite for ease of reference. It is in that order that the following regional reviews are made:

1. Scotland-Central Valley.
2. North West England.
3. North Lancashire and Cumbria.
4. North-Eastern England.
5. The Lower Trent and Don.
6. Lincolnshire.
7. East Midlands.
8. The Potteries.
9. North Wales and Border Counties.
10. The Great Ouse Valley.
11. Norfolk and Suffolk.
12. Coventry, Leicestershire, and Northamptonshire.
13. West Midlands.
14. Avon and Severn Valley.
15. Grand Union Canal.
16. South Wales.
17. Thames and Severn Links.
18. Southern England.
19. South-Eastern England.
20. South-Western England.

Preamble

The early history of 21 major schemes, developed and in part completed in the 1960s and early 1970s, has already been well recorded in P. J. G. Ransom's book *Waterways Restored* (1974); whilst the inter-relationship of these and many other local restoration projects to the development of the history of the national waterways restoration movement, through to 1976, was detailed in my own earlier book, *Canals Revived* (1979). However, as both these books are now out of print, and for completeness, the following regional accounts include an abbreviated sketch of the developments which took place before the mid–1970s. The remarkable achievements of the past seven years—especially where government funds, mainly through the Manpower Services Commission's various employment and work experience development schemes, have been used to revive those very waterways which early administrations sought to abandon—are given more detailed attention. Similarly pointers are offered to the likely way ahead.

In all these accounts, it must be appreciated that much planning and preparation has to go on behind the scenes to enable even the smallest event to take place. This often goes unnoticed and by its very nature, unrecorded. Often it is the 'backroom' boys who have enabled restoration to proceed. The accounts that follow make little mention of this. One can only hope that it is not overlooked by readers when they consider exactly what the efforts of the various local groups of 'new navvies' have managed to achieve during the past three decades.

*   *   *   *   *

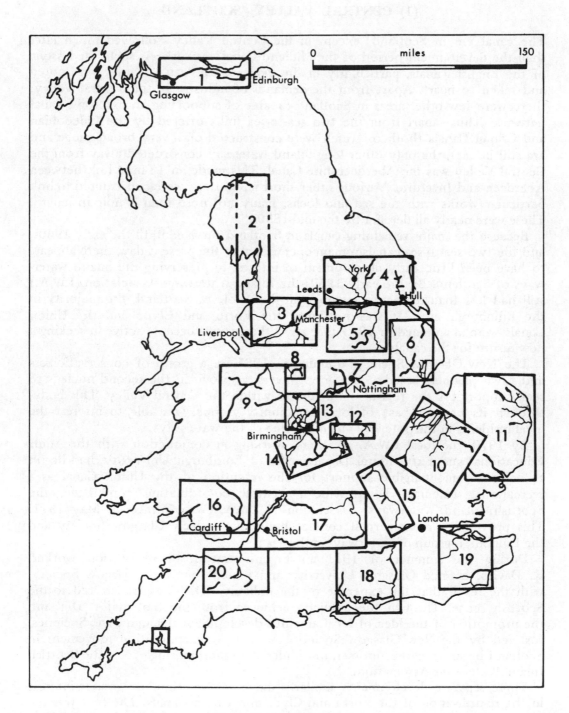

Key to Regional Locations

(1) CENTRAL VALLEY: SCOTLAND

The canal era in Scotland, except in the Central Valley, followed much later than the development period of the Midland Canal network. As such, the lessons of the English canals, particularly in the years of the 'canal mania' were noted and taken to heart. Apart from the demands of industry in the Central Valley, there were few other areas in Scotland capable of supporting an extensive canal network. Thus, apart from the two sea-to-sea links offered by the Caledonian and Crinan Canals (both of which were constructed on a very broad gauge and are still in use), the only other long inland waterway constructed away from the Central Valley was the Aberdeenshire Canal. This made an 18-mile link between Aberdeen and Inverurie. Various other short navigations were constructed to link particular works with the sea and lochs, many no more than a mile in length. These were nearly all derelict by the mid-1850s.

Because the major remaining canals in Scotland survived until the early 1960s, and the two sea-to-sea canals remain operational to the present day, there appears to have been little early development of interest in preserving the inland waterways of Scotland. By the early 1950s the Inland Waterways Association (I.W.A.) still had less than ten active members in the whole of Scotland, the majority in the Edinburgh area. It was not until the Forth and Clyde and the Union Canals were abandoned in 1963 that any other groups became active in seeking a new future for the canals.

The New Glasgow Society, founded in 1965 by a group of conservationists and town planners based at Glasgow University, provided the second nucleus to seek support for the revival of the canals within the Central Valley. This body, through its broader base of local community groups, was able to interest the local residents in the potential amenity value of the waterways.

By 1970, the local I.W.A. members, working in conjunction with the Adult Educational and Extra Mural Departments of Edinburgh University, had begun to achieve some tangible support for the retention of the Union Canal as a recreational amenity. To provide a central co-ordinating committee, the Scottish Inland Waterways Association (S.I.W.A.) was formed in May 1971. This provided a more formal contact between the New Glasgow Society and the Edinburgh group of waterways enthusiasts.

During the summer of 1971 an English waterways restoration worker, R. Davies, entered Glasgow University and joined the New Glasgow Society, with the result that the expertise of the publicity 'Dig' was transferred to the Scottish scene. Through the publicity achieved from the first major 'Dig' and the promotion of the idea of local amenity development through Civic Societies, fostered by the New Glasgow Society, the waterway restoration movement in Scotland began to gather momentum under the co-ordinating eye of the Scottish Inland Waterways Association.

Three separate developments similarly did much to stimulate greater interest in the re-utilisation of the Forth and Clyde and Union Canals. The first was the foundation of the Strathkelvin Canal Park Group based in Cumbernauld New

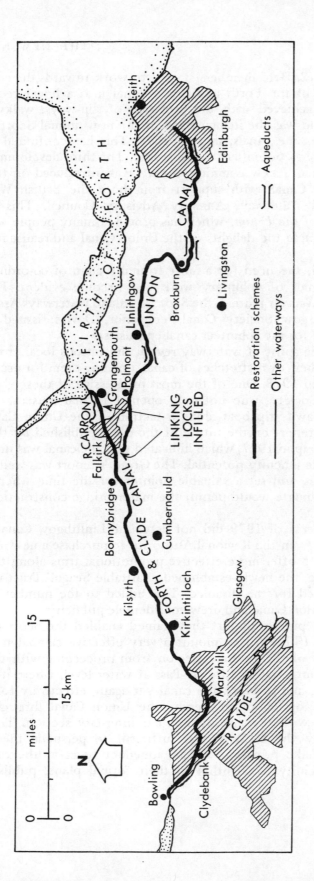

Map. 1.—Central Valley: Scotland
(1) Forth and Clyde Canal; (2) Union Canal

Town in December 1972. Here members started to work towards the conversion
of the central section of the Forth and Clyde Canal into a linear recreational
park. This they have achieved with the provision of slip-ways, walkways and
picnic areas. The second was the inauguration of the now annual Scottish Cross
Country Boat Race, via the canals, in July 1973. This has continued to show
that the canals still offer a potential through route. The third development came
in November 1974 when a new commercial craft was introduced on the Ratho
Section of the Union Canal, with support from both the British Waterways
Board and the Inland Waterways Amenity Advisory Council. This was the
restaurant boat, *Pride of the Union,* which has provided many people with their
first opportunity to sample the delights of the Union Canal and realise its longer-
term potential.

By the end of 1975, the need for a more formal system of co-ordination of
the various local schemes of voluntary work had become evident. Following
the idea of the English *Navvies* journal, the Scottish Inland Waterways Association,
through the New Glasgow Society Canals convenor, Davies, issued its own
newsletter, *MacNavvies,* for the volunteer canal enthusiast.

Aided by the growing spirit of waterway revival the various local groups each
continued to develop their own stretches of canal, opening them for use by small
craft between 1976 and 1978. One of the most progressive of these groups was
the Linlithgow Canal Society, who not only opened a canal museum, but also
inaugurated a horse-drawn trip boat along a section of the Union Canal. This
work complemented a report on the future of the canal published by the Union
Canal Development Group in 1977, which indicated that the canal was under-used
but offered considerable amenity potential. The Group's report was well received
by the local authorities and set a valuable pointer for the time when a more
favourable economic climate would permit the major bridge construction works
to be undertaken.

The economic problems of 1979 did not deter the Linlithgow Canal Society
from seeking grant aid from the Regional Authority to purchase a new motorised
trip boat to enable it to offer more effective promotional trips along the canal.
At about the same time, the newly-established charitable Seagull Trust was given
a boat specially designed for the disabled. This added to the number of boats
using sections of the Union Canal and drew considerable publicity.

These boats and the public support they gained enabled the Scottish Inland
Waterways Association (S.I.W.A.) to mount a very effective campaign to deter
the Highway Engineers of the Lothian Region from proceeding with their plan
to build the new Edinburgh Outer City By-Pass at water level, where it was due
to cross the canal line, and so block the canal yet again, effectively forestalling
the major restoration option of re-opening the Union Canal through Wester
Hailes and connecting with the already popular inter-city section. The public
outcry co-ordinated by the S.I.W.A. was sufficient to persuade the Lothian
Regional Council to make provision for an aqueduct to carry the canal over
the by-pass in the vicinity of Sighthill in their formal plans, published late
in 1979.

In June 1979 a Rally of small boats was held at Lochrin Basin in Edinburgh to campaign for the restoration of the Leamington Lifting Bridge. The Rally seemed to be a turning point for the revival hopes of the Union Canal, for in the same month came the appointment of a Project Officer, jointly financed by the Countryside Commission for Scotland and the Lothian and Central Regional Councils, whose remit was to co-ordinate activity among the various groups and organisations interested in the canal, and to investigate how the canal could be developed. One of the immediate effects was the creation of new societies at Broxburn, Winchburgh, and Wester Hailes, followed in 1980 by groups at Ratho and Falkirk.

At much the same time as these developments on the Union Canal, all the local authorities along the Forth and Clyde Canal agreed to prepare jointly a local (subject) plan, for which the Strathclyde Regional Council acted as co-ordinators. This initiative highlighted the need for the various interest groups along the Forth and Clyde Canal to get together. A preliminary public meeting was called by the S.I.W.A. in December with the result that a Steering Committee, representing S.I.W.A., yacht clubs, canoeing, local amenity and Community Council interests, promoted the foundation of the Forth and Clyde Canal Society, in April 1980 to co-ordinate the revival campaign. This proved opportune as the Forth and Clyde Canal Working party—composed of Local Authorities Regional Bodies and the B.W.B.—produced at about the same time a survey report which detailed the current state of the canal and reviewed its potential amenity rôle. Their report concluded that through navigation could be restored by removing some 60 major obstacles, at a cost of some £30 million. It pointed the way forward by a phased improvement of sections of the canal.

This theme of phased improvement was also developed on the Union Canal in 1980. One of the most promising plans to emerge was a Linlithgow Canal Society report, with detailed designs, which showed that a navigable culvert could be constructed at Preston Road to enable almost half the Union Canal to be navigable again.

The Report, which was supported by over 1,800 signatures, was presented to the Union Canal Working Group—a consortium of local authority and amenity groups—who agreed to give it their active consideration. Similarly, as the Union Canal was scheduled as an Ancient Monument (thus qualifying for protection to the structures and the route) it also enabled B.W.B. to justify the expenditure of £200,000 to restore the Avon Aqueduct near Linlithgow, when a scheme was proposed. This work included re-pointing, waterproofing and re-laying the towpath and the unique structure was restored to all its former glory.

The Avon Aqueduct was among many features of the Union Canal which were recorded in a set of eight leaflets produced by the Union Canal Project Officer in June 1980 as part of the campaign to interest people in the range of facilities the canal could offer. She also produced an audio-visual presentation about the canal and a transportable exhibition. All these substantially raised the level of local support for the revival campaign.

This theme of awakening public interest was similarly used by the S.I.W.A. in their effort to re-open truncated 18-mile summit level of the Forth and Clyde Canal, which was cut in half at Kirkintilloch by a culvert inserted to facilitate a road-widening scheme. For this a two-fold approach was adopted—one was the physical clearance of rubbish and the restoration of canal-side amenities; the other was to heighten public support for the replacement of the culvert to such an extent that the community and district councils would recommend the Strathclyde Region to make it a matter of priority.

By 1981 it seemed that this campaign was having some effect, when the local authorities' working party produced a draft plan which approved in principle that the canal should be revived by the phased removal of the obstacles to navigation, and envisaged a £4 million expenditure over 10 years. The first stage, costing £1.7 million, covered the 20 miles from Bowling to Dalmuir, and from Maryhill to Castlecary, and included the restoration of listed buildings, installing new slip-ways and replacing lock gates. The Local Authorities were asked by Strathclyde Regional Council to approve and fund the proposals and, as a sign of its intent, Strathclyde Regional Council agreed to spend some £13,000 on environmental improvements at Stockingfield Junction.

The Forth and Clyde Canal Society saw an opportunity to use these planned improvements to good effect and purchased two ex-Govan ferries for use as trip boats between Bowling and Kirkintilloch as a way or creating even greater public interest in the unique canal.

The year 1982 saw this same air of optimism generated on the Union Canal, especially when the Union Canal Project Officer's final report was presented in January. The study recorded the significant increase in the membership of clubs and societies associated with the canal in the period 1975–1980 and pointed to the variety of job creation schemes which could be developed to rejuvenate the canal. It pointed to the substantial fund-raising efforts of the Kennet and Avon Canal Trust and suggested the concept of a Union Canal Trust which could be used as a means of co-ordinating the fund-raising efforts needed for the removal of the various major obstacles along the canal. The report also suggested how the canal towpaths could be developed and how local authorities could optimise the recreational potential offered by the waterway.

The west was not to be neglected in this new air of optimism, and by the middle of 1982 major environmental improvements on the Forth and Clyde Canal, costing over £100,000, were already underway in Glasgow.

At about this time, the Forth and Clyde Canal Society completed the renovation of one of its two ex-ferry boats, and, in May 1982, this was transported overland to Hungryside Bridge, Torrance, where it was re-launched for use, giving trips along the canal near Kirkintilloch. By the close of the year a second ferry had also been installed on the canal, at Glasgow Bridge, for use as a cruising restaurant, and a canal-side stable had been renovated, at the bridge, to provide a second restaurant and land base for the operation.

Perhaps the most heartening feature of all this has been the way in which, over the last decade, there has been a marked growth in accord between the many local authorities concerned with the canals, and a change in attitude to one of positive action in restoration and development. It is unfortunate that voluntary work on the Scottish Waterways has suffered from the lack of firm agreements for volunteers to carry out major structural restoration works. Even so, the prospect of major advances over the next few years are good.

For this, one must not lose sight of the vision of a through route which has been kept alive through the Annual Two Days Canals Marathon, the 11th of which was held in 1983. This has gained publicity momentum of its own, as fleets of portable craft have travelled, mainly by water, between Glasgow and Edinburgh, being carried over the obstacles en-route. In the earlier years the rubbish and weed caused many competitors to drop out—but this is now a thing of the past. Certainly, since the first marathon was organised in 1973, the route has become much easier to complete, but none of the major barriers has yet been removed. Perhaps the next decade will provide the means for this to be rectified?

From the past nucleus of interest in Edinburgh, the waterway restoration movement has now encompassed the whole of the central valley. Many local groups are actively re-developing their own small sections of canal, looking over the Border at the way major English projects are reaping their rewards and learning from the mistakes that have been made. Hopefully the 'fill-'em in' lobby has now been stopped and the reverse in attitudes of the public and local authorities will surely mean that the Forth and Clyde, and Union, Canals will both ultimately be saved and re-created as through routes.

*   *   *   *   *

(2) NORTH LANCASHIRE AND CUMBRIA

The inland waterways of North Lancashire and Cumbria have always been segregated from the remainder of the canal network. The only means of access by boat is limited to the tortuous passage through coastal tidal waters. This isolation similarly has shown itself, until recently, in the re-development ideas for the waterways of the area. The first objections to the closure of parts of the Lancaster Canal came from the local users, prompted by the few Inland Waterways Association members in the area. However, they were unable to stop the Kendal section being closed and infilled.

The Lancaster Canal Boat Club members were the first organisation to become the guardians of the future of the Lancaster Canal, as early as 1955. However, as the boat club members were more interested in safeguarding the canal between Lancaster and Preston, and the local I.W.A. members were thin on the ground, some other local waterways enthusiasts, mainly from the Lancaster County Council Architects' Department, led by T. S. H. Wordsworth, formed a Restoration Group to fight for the renovation of the whole canal, particularly the decaying upper reaches, in late 1963. The group, with its amenity development outlook, was able gradually to gather broad support both from local Civic Societies as well as the users of the amenity that the canal offered; the ramblers, the naturalists and the fishermen. Unfortunately, their active support for the concept of the re-development of the canal, as a linear country park, came too late to prevent plans for a new motorway route from cutting the line of the Lancaster Canal, even though they were able to reduce the potential bill for making navigable culverts from £250,000 to only £20,000, by the use of their planning and civil engineering skills. When the upper section of the canal was closed in 1965, to enable the motorway construction to proceed, the battle appeared lost. To continue the Restoration Group's campaign, the Lancaster Canal Trust was formed in 1967 and has since fought a spirited rearguard action to protect the canal from further decay. This included the organisation of various protest cruises in 1967, 1968 and 1969. One of the first successes was the implementation of plans for scheduling some of the canal structures as Ancient Monuments, which proceeded in 1969. In 1970 the idea of using young offenders to restore the canal in the Kendal area was also actively promoted, and by 1973 enthusiasm in Kendal was sufficiently developed for the concept of a Kendal Canal Society to be launched and gain support. It was not until 1975 that Cumbria County Council became actively involved with the potential of protecting the line of the canal in the Kendal area. Its predecessor, Cumberland County Council, had considered the prospect of re-developing the Carlisle Canal as early as 1972. This scheme, which gained little support, was promoted by a local councillor who had seen publicity relating to waterway restoration elsewhere in the country.

The industrial archaeology of the Carlisle Canal and its potential as a centre-piece for a proposed re-development scheme did not go unnoticed. The concept of an Open Air Museum, based on a development at Blists Hill, near Ironbridge, using part of the canal to provide a feature of the past era being re-created, was mooted by the local museum curator in the mid 1970s. Both these schemes failed due to lack of public support in an area which did not readily associate itself with the era of the Industrial Revolution.

A small revival in the fortunes of the Lancaster Canal came in early 1974 when the Lancaster Canal Trust joined forces with the local boat clubs and the Kendal Canal Society, to organise a Rally of Boats on the Upper Reaches over Easter 1974. This Rally has since become an annual event and has attracted consider-able public support. It is also one of the main money-raising events for the Northern Reaches Restoration Fund, which was established by the Canal Trust. Soon after the Rally it was learned that the Central Lancashire New Town Corporation had announced its proposal to drop its plans to use the route of the Preston end of the canal as the path for a new road. As a result, the Trust were able to advocate the development of a new marina on the canal, as part of the recreational plans for the New Town.

The revival of interest in the canal was fostered by two other developments in 1975. The first was the active involvement of the chairman of I.W.A.A.C. in supporting the longer term re-opening of the Upper Reaches of the canal for pleasure craft, in the publication of a report, *Priorities for Action*. The second

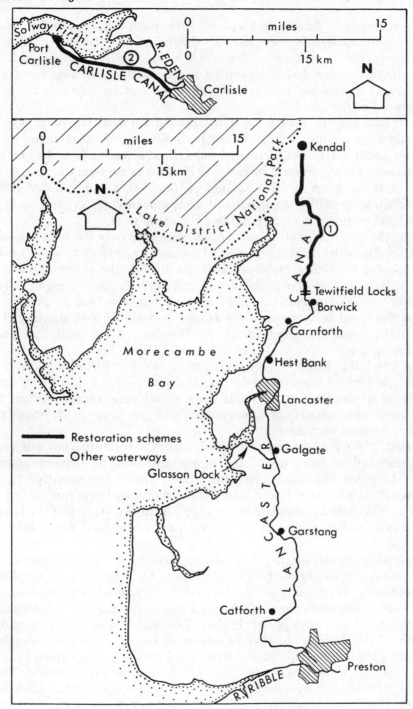

Map 2.—North Lancashire and Cumbria
(1) Lancaster Canal; (2) Carlisle Canal

was the opening of a Canal Museum and Information Centre at *Th' Owd Tithe Barn* restaurant, alongside the canal at Garstang, near Lancaster. Both events aroused hopes for the future of the whole canal. Unfortunately, lack of local authority finance in the 1970s prevented any immediate backing for the various revival plans and thus the Lancaster Canal Trust had to continue to fight alone for the survival of the canal.

One practical way in which the Trust moved forward was with a scheme to develop slipways on the truncated Northern Reaches so that these would still be used by small craft. The first of these slipways was built at Holme in 1977, and the second was completed in early 1978. This persuaded the B.W.B. to allow powered craft back on to the isolated sections at a reduced fee. They also undertook some dredging, hedging and towpath tidying, as well as building a few more light craft slipways, to stimulate the canal's use.

In 1979, the Sixth Annual Dinghy Rally was held over the Easter weekend on the short length between Stainton and Millness, in an effort to attract even more craft to use the isolated section of canal. Soon after the Rally, the Canal Trust heard that the portal of Hincaster Tunnel had been listed as being of outstanding historic interest. This persuaded them to consider how best to protect the dry section of the canal between the stop planks at Stainton and the tunnel mouth. One alternative was the purchase of the length of canal, and they started to explore this option.

During 1980 the Royal Engineers spent a week refurbishing the mouth of the tunnel, as part of a training exercise, and were given helpful support by the South Westmorland District Council. As a result, the tunnel portals and the adjacent areas were cleared of undergrowth and the horse-path, boundary walls and overbridge were all repaired.

In August 1980 the Central and North Lancs. Structure Plan was published. After representations from the Trust, it was amended to include commitments to both safeguard the canal structures and, more importantly, to prevent developments which were likely to impair either canal restoration, navigation, or drainage. This was a considerable advance for the Trust, as was the landscaping of the Preston end of the canal by Central Lancashire New Town Development Corporation.

Reports of progress on the Lancaster Canal must have stimulated further thoughts about the future of the Carlisle Canal. An article on the canal appeared in the December 1979 issue of the University of Lancaster's *Regional Bulletin,* and this was subsequently developed into a discussion paper by John Hartley of the Northumberland College of Higher Education. His paper proposed the restoration of the Carlisle Canal as a nucleus for a tourist and linear development, with revival planned in two stages: first, the lockless section from Port Carlisle to Dykesford; then, subsequently, the 6-lock section into Carlisle. The paper also envisaged secondary developments such as a towpath walk, cycleway, and a bridle path, together with an environmental study centre and a transport museum. Unfortunately, the calls for a more detailed feasibility study fell on deaf ears, and little more transpired.

The thoughts for the future of the Lancaster Canal developed, fortunately, at a faster pace. Perhaps one of the most exciting of these was a scheme undertaken jointly between the Trust and the Lancaster Boat Club to evaluate possible routes for linking the canal to the river Ribble, and thence to the remainder of the canal system. Surveys were put in hand by a civil engineer, and he was subsequently asked to cost the detailed plans.

During 1981 and 1982 the Trust continued its battles to protect the line of the canal from any permanent development, which would be prejudicial to eventual restoration, above the Tewitfield Locks. One of their aims was to have the whole canal designated a Conservation Area. They were strengthened in their resolve when B.W.B. were able to find the finance for the re-alignment of the canal bed at Holme, with reinforced concrete to navigable dimensions, to prevent further leakage, and were heartened when they heard other sections were to be similarly protected.

In summer 1982 the long-awaited costings of the Ribble Link were produced. These indicated that the project was certainly feasible and the most expensive option would cost £809,500 for the construction works. A cheaper project, at £574,000 did not offer the same overall advantages. Dr. A. K. Hughes, who made the survey which suggested the link could be made via Savick Brook using some four new locks, estimated that with land purchase costs the scheme could be completed for some £1½ million overall. The Trust and the boat club immediately agreed to create a sub-committee to follow up the plans.

On 5 August 1982 the North West Region of the Association of Waterway Cruising Clubs organised a cruise for some 20 boats from the Rufford Branch of the Leeds and Liverpool Canal to Preston Docks to publicise the need for the new link, especially with the demise of the docks and the promising new Preston marina plans. This cruise did much to strengthen local interest in the waterways— but much more support has still to be achieved if tangible advances are to be made.

It is unfortunate that the isolation of the area has continued to be reflected in the waterways revival plans. Various small successes are now becoming evident as more local people take an interest in their canals. The cause for reviving the Carlisle canal is lost, but the future for the upper sections of the Lancaster Canal seems slowly to grow brighter, thanks to the work of the Trust. However, there is one major difficulty to be overcome before the Lancaster Canal is completely re-opened or linked to the national network, and that is the problem of finance.

*   *   *   *   *

(3) NORTH-WEST ENGLAND

It is often claimed that the canal system in Britain as we know it today has its origins in the North-West of England. Some historians argue that St Helens Canal, or Sankey Brook Navigation, was the forerunner of the canal network, whilst the majority cite the Bridgewater Canal, constructed to James Brindley's design

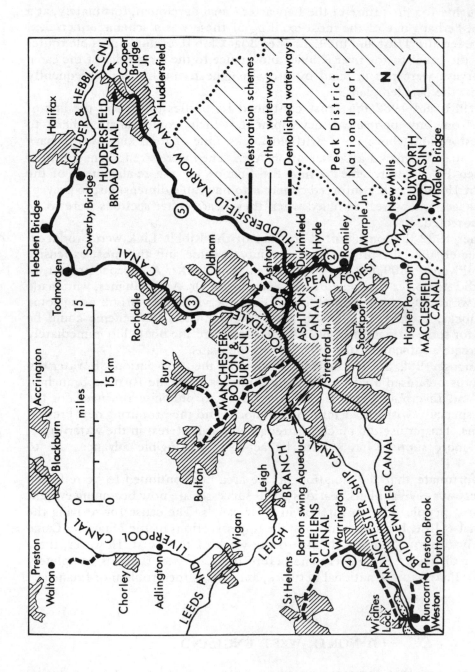

Map 3.—North-West England

(1) Buxworth Basin; (2) Ashton and Peak Forest Canals; (3) Rochdale Canal;
(4) St Helen's Canal; (5) Huddersfield Narrow Canal.

and opened in 1761, as the start of the canal era. The regular commercial use of the majority of the region's canals, until recent times, ensured that the birth of the restoration movement did not occur in the same area.

Early support for the continued use and the rejuvenation of the waterways in the North-West was generated by the Inland Waterways Association, and more particularly by the members of the I.W.A. North-Western Branch, founded in 1951.

The first activity came in the late summer of 1948 when the I.W.A. founder, R. Aickman, and secretary, L. T. C. Rolt, made a voyage through the northern waterways to try to gain public support for their use and retention. From this early publicity local interest gradually developed and grew. Thus when the I.W.A. held its Annual Rally at Macclesfield in 1953 the interest in the waterways of the area was already comparatively strong. When a British Transport Commission Board of Survey report was unveiled in 1954, suggesting the need to close some of the principal canals of the area, local enthusiasts were available to fight actively for their retention. Even at that time pleasure craft were beginning to make substantial use of the more scenic canals, and proposals were mooted for the restoration of Buxworth Basin as a marina.

Restoration plans were slow in coming to fruition, and it was not until the Bowes Committee made their report on the future of the canals in July 1958 that the local pace of events quickened. The Committee's report offered interested organisations the opportunity to make suggestions for the re-development of individual canals. This led to the formation of the Inland Waterways Protection Society, based in Sheffield, who started to take a particular interest in the future of the canals on both sides of the southern Pennines. I.W.P.S. members grasped the opportunity and started a local campaign to prepare restoration and re-development proposals for the Ashton and Peak Forest Canals, as well as Buxworth Basin.

Local support for the restoration was forthcoming, and, with the formation of the new amenity-orientated British Waterways Board in 1963, the political climate for the advancement of the various restoration proposals also became more favourable.

The I.W.P.S. ultimately devoted their efforts to the phased restoration of Buxworth Basin, but were instrumental, in 1964, with the local I.W.A. members in promoting the formation of the Peak Forest Canal Society. This local group were able to capitalise quickly on growing local authority support to carry forward their campaign for the restoration of the Ashton and Peak Forest Canals. They were authorised to carry out 'agricultural' work, but they soon extended their remit to replacing rotten lock-gate balance beams. Later, with B.W.B. permission, the Society members were also able to repair paddles and start the clearance of lock chambers in the Marple flight.

The provision offered by the 1968 Transport Act for local authorities to assist financially the British Waterways Board in the restoration of local canals provided the turning point for the local campaign. By this time the local press were becoming supportive, and an analysis of local press references to canals, conducted by J. Lett of Keele University, indicated that antagonism towards the canals had virtually ceased by the late 1960s.

Perhaps the greatest stimulus to this local support for waterway restoration came from 'Operation Ashton', held in September 1968, whilst the infilling of a section of the Rochdale Canal in Manchester, at a cost of £¼ million against a restoration estimate of £200,000, did much to focus local authority attention on the alternative costs involved.

A conference entitled 'Waterways in the Urban Scene', organised by the I.W.A. at the University of Manchester in April 1970, provided a further boost to local authority interest in the recreational and leisure potential of the waterways in the region. Plans for both the Sankey Valley Linear Park and the Tame Valley Park, through which the Huddersfield Narrow Canal passed, were similarly gaining momentum from growing local authority support.

By 1972 the amenity potential of the waterways of the region was more fully appreciated, and the local authorities were willing to subsidise B.W.B. work in recovering local canals. As such the agreement to proceed with the restoration of the Ashton and Peak Forest Canals, inaugurated by 'Ashtac' in March 1972, paved the way for the development of ideas for other restoration schemes. The I.W.A. and the newly-formed Littleborough Civic Society both promoted the idea of restoring the whole of the Rochdale Canal, whilst, in 1974, the Peak Forest Canal Society, after completing their work on the restoration and re-opening of the Ashton and Peak Forest Canals, joined forces with the I.W.A., West Riding Branch, and the Calder Navigation Society to restore the Huddersfield Narrow Canal.

By the end of 1975, the Greater Manchester Council was giving the lead to other local authorities in the region by developing a non-encroachment policy towards the canals within its boundaries. This enlightened attitude developed still further during 1976, 1977 and 1978, when, under the Job Creation Scheme, the Manpower Services Commission provided government finance to assist with the restoration of parts of the Rochdale Canal. This action greatly enhanced the longer-term prospect of re-opening a Northern Canals Ring.

The vision of a substantial increase in the local leisure resources did not, however, convince local industrialists in Huddersfield of the amenity value of their local canal. The Huddersfield Canal Society therefore had to fight a continuous battle to prevent various sections of the canal line being used as building sites. Even so, the constructive proposals outlined in their report, *A New Canal for Huddersfield,* and *Through Stalybridge by Boat,* showing just how the various obstacles could be overcome, together with their plans for a possible trip boat through the Standedge Tunnel, gained the Huddersfield Canal Society considerable public support.

The extent of the growth of public interest in the revival of the waterways was put to the test by the Rochdale Canal Society in mid-1978, when the Department of Transport published its plans for an extension to the M66 motorway. The road scheme envisaged the effective obliteration of a section of the Rochdale Canal. It seemed likely to put an abrupt end to any ideas for re-opening the complete canal as a through route. Fortunately, the Rochdale Canal Society put forward feasible alternative proposals to preserve a line for the canal at minimal cost, and the Department of Transport agreed to consider their ideas.

Road problems also loomed large for the I.W.P.S. in 1978 when they heard that long-mooted plans for the Chapel-en-le-Frith and Whaley Bridge By-Pass, for the A6, had emerged again. The Society had to rally local support to oppose the Department of Transport's preferred by-pass route, which seemed likely to ruin all that they had striven through the previous decade to protect and revive. To do this they enlisted the support of other amenity groups and jointly prepared a case to put to the public enquiry.

By the close of 1978 it seemed to local enthusiasts in the North-West that the tide of public opinion might be turning more strongly in their favour. A survey by Kirklees Metropolitan Council highlighted the recreational potential of the Huddersfield Canal along the Colne Valley, between Huddersfield and the Standedge Tunnel, and indicated that derelict land reclamation schemes, using Grant Aid, could considerably reduce vandalism. The B.W.B. responded to this statement by suggesting a list of projects, some of which could be undertaken on a job creation basis, while others benefited from grants from the West York-shire County Council and the Countryside Commission. Among these plans were ideas from local societies to signpost walks and undertake tree planting. It was also suggested that the local council should adopt the towpath as a public right of way. Elsewhere, the Tameside M.B.C. also accepted the principle of renovating and maintaining the canal through to Stalybridge. Even Bolton Council's Recreational Committee considered plans to restore some sections of the long-derelict Manchester Bolton and Bury Canal, around Little Lever and Kearsley, as local amenity sites, as part of a derelict land reclamation scheme for the valley alongside which the canal runs.

The Rochdale Canal Society's fight to protect their canal from the threatened M66 extension came to a peak in 1979 when the Department of Transport undertook a Public Consultation exercise. The Department refused to allow the Society to distribute the official questionnaires among its membership—a move which was cited as a 'negation of democracy' by the local press. As a result of this action the Society and the I.W.A. became even more determined to make their views known, and combined to organise a petition against the low-level road crossing plans, and rapidly raised 10,000 signatures in support of their aims. The Society also collected some 1,500 letters from their supporters, addressed to the Department of Transport, each making an individual plea for a more realistic approach. It was as a direct result of this weight of public concern that the Department of Transport ultimately conceded that adequate headroom could be provided to allow for a canal link. This news gave the Rochdale Canal Society Working Parties on the Ancoats, Brownsfield section of the canal an added stimulus to clear the enormous amounts of rubbish which had been dumped in this neglected section of the waterway in central Manchester.

The new, official enthusiasm for waterways revival was similarly marked in November 1979, when the local authorities along the St Helen's Canal announced the start of a phased scheme for revitalising parts of their canal. The first section tackled was between Bewsey Bridge and Sankey Bridge, where the council's plans involved clearing the canal and re-vamping the towpath as part of a linear park; which was ultimately envisaged to link the Widnes Docks area, through Warrington to St Helen's, using derelict land grants to finance the work.

The Huddersfield Narrow Canal was not neglected in this wave of enthusiasm, as the Huddersfield Canal Society carefully cultivated local support and reviewed the various options for the restoration of the section of canal adjacent to Standedge Tunnel, with the idea of running a trip boat as a short-term aim. Their plans received a welcome boost when they heard that the Saddleworth Historical Society had managed to negotiate a lease to restore the Woolroad Transhipment Warehouse at Dobcross. This strengthened the case for reviving the Uppermill section of the canal, from Wade Lock and the Woolroad Warehouse, as a pilot scheme and proposals were put to the B.W.B. with this in mind.

The breakthrough for the Huddersfield Canal Society came in early 1980 when they learned that the West Yorkshire County Council was reconsidering its policy statements in the County Structure Plan, especially where these concerned the canal. This was followed by news, later in the year, that the Society's Uppermill plans had been studied by the B.W.B. engineering staff, who had given them favourable support. By the close of 1980 the Society had gained a lease on the Marsden Tunnel End Cottages and planning consent for their renovation, a move which enabled them to enter 1981 with the facility to start work on the canal.

During 1980 the Rochdale Canal Society were similarly making great strides in their battle to rejuvenate their canal. A rally of boats in the Dale Street Basin provided a focus for public attention on the amenity value of the canal. One of the main attractions was a horse-drawn boat along the first section of the re-opened Ashton Canal. The rally provided an ideal platform from which to persuade the Greater Manchester Council to adopt a co-ordinated policy for the future development of canals in their area.

The Society's aims received a boost in July 1980 when Rochdale Council announced that they had received agreement for a further two-year extension of their M.S.C. Job Creation Scheme, with major lock renovation as part of the plans. This news prompted the Rochdale Canal Society to launch a major fund-raising campaign at the Sowerby Bridge end of the canal, where they promoted a 'Boats to Hebden Bridge Campaign' in an effort to restore that attractive section of the canal. The Society believed that £¼ million would be needed to re-open the 5-mile eastern section, and re-link it to the Calder and Hebble Navigation by a 'cut and cover' tunnel at Sowerby Bridge, where the line had been blocked by a car park. Their firm commitment to this scheme bore fruit, and a year later, in September 1981, a major breakthrough was achieved. That month was really the 'Month of the Rochdale Canal'. Firstly, a 'Big Dig' was mounted at Chadderton to clean up and improve the canal in the area, where the M66 extension was due to be routed. The aim was firstly, to encourage

Oldham M.B.C. to initiate a Job Creation Scheme in the area, and, secondly, to campaign for the re-opening of the canal all the way from Manchester to Sowerby Bridge. The event gained publicity and substantial local support, and many local councillors attended the event. However, even this was overshadowed when the news broke that Calderdale District Council, at the eastern end of the canal, had put a scheme to the Manpower Services Commission which envisaged the restoration, to full navigable standard, of the length of canal between the towns of Hebden Bridge and Todmorden—a distance of some 4½ miles. The plan involved the re-gating of 10 locks together with some dredging. Under the plan labour costs were to be covered by the M.S.C. whilst the £98,000 cost of materials was to be met jointly by the District Council, West Yorkshire County Council, and the M.S.C. The scheme also involved staffing a workshop at Halifax to design and manufacture the necessary lock-gates.

Such tremendous progress on the Rochdale Canal was similarly matched by substantial advances elsewhere. The Huddersfield Canal Society 'navvies', together with the W.R.G. using a 'Summer camp', started work on Loch 22 W at Uppermill, clearing the capping and concrete infill to see what the chamber walls were like, prior to full restoration. The aim of the project was two-fold. Firstly, to get some small piece of canal restoration underway, and, secondly, to provide, in the longer term, extended cruising ground for their newly-inaugurated electric-powered trip boat *Stan* which the Society had purchased and rebuilt for promotional trips along the canal. The Uppermill project was supported by funds raised at a highly successful Tameside Canals Festival, held in July 1981, which also involved a campaign cruise of 50 boats to the blocked entrance of the Huddersfield Narrow Canal. Some 15,000 visitors flocked to the rally site to lend their support, which was subsequently enhanced by the publication of an illustrated *Towpath Guide* by the Huddersfield Canal Society.

Elsewhere in the region, the I.W.P.S. were slowly progressing with their mammoth task at Buxworth, which received a welcome hand when contractors working for a local authority removed 4,500 tons of dried silt, already dredged from the basins, to cover refuse tips. During the whole clearance exercise it was calculated that approximately 70,000 ton-movement of silt had been undertaken by the I.W.P.S. co-ordinated volunteers. Even so, they still had several thousand tons of dried silt to move from the wharves. For this task, the morale of the new navvies was boosted by the arrival, late in 1981, of a rebuilt J.C.B. 6 D 'digger', which had been purchased by the I.W.A. for £3,000, and had been placed on long-term loan to assist with the Buxworth Scheme. This was doubly welcome because the I.W.P.S. had heard that part of the threat of the by-pass scheme had been lifted, with a confirmation in the Road Enquiry Report that the by-pass should not physically affect the area of the basin which had been scheduled as an Ancient Monument at their instigation. This was not the full cancellation that they had sought, but was sufficient to provide the stimulus for them to plan ahead, firstly for an I.W.A. Cruise of Boats in May 1982, and, secondly, to the projected date for the testfill of the Upper and Middle Basins in autumn 1983.

Towards the close of 1981, both the Rochdale and Huddersfield restoration schemes gained added impetus from the publication of a West Yorkshire County Council report, which evaluated the economic benefits of restoring navigable canals. This suggested that if both canals were re-developed to their full potential, the additial local income could exceed £4 million a year, apart from the welcome number of new jobs that would be created. As a small move towards achieving this, two large cheques from Council lotteries served to confirm the marked change in local public opinion towards these canals.

The year 1982 was Maritime England Year, and this provided another means to focus public attention on the inland waterways in the North-West. This happened in various ways. In the Mersey valley the local authority partnership erected Interpretation Boards at various sites. These included Fiddlers Ferry, Sankey Bridge, and Bewsey Lock on the St Helen's Canal. The aim was to allow residents and visitors alike to understand the importance of such features of the industrial past. The placing of these boards provided an overture to the re-opening of Widnes Lock in July 1982 as part of a £1.1 million scheme to provide facilities for water-based sports. Further along the St Helen's Canal another £567,000 scheme, under Derelict Land Grants, was also making great strides, through the renovation of the section between Bewsey and Liverpool Road, Great Sankey, together with a second phase, including the conversion of the Fiddlers Ferry section of the canal into a new marina, and the restoration of the lock into the Mersey due for completion during the late 1983. Further along the canal, in St Helen's itself, some re-excavation work on the old canal was planned under a scheme organised by the Groundwork Trust, who had been assigned grants of £9 million over the five years between 1982 and 1987 to reclaim derelict land around the town, including the canal, and for educating the public in its use.

This fervour for waterways revival was further enhanced in 1982 when it was learned that two of the region's earliest restoration schemes, the Ashton and Lower Peak Forest Canals, were included in the British Waterways Bill, promoted with the consent of the Secretary of State for Environment, for re-classification to Cruising Waterway status, with all additional legal security that this would bring.

Similar long-term commitments were being made in respect of both the Huddersfield and Rochdale Canals. On the former, the West Yorkshire County Council took out a lease on a Tunnel End Cottage at Marsden for use by a park warden, and Kirklees Metropolitan District Council signed an agreement to maintain the canal towpath between Marsden and Huddersfield as a public right of way. It also planned to develop picnic sites and place information boards at various points along the route. The Huddersfield Canal Society hoped that this was only the first step in gaining the Council's full commitment to re-opening the canal for through navigation between Marsden and Slaithwaite.

In the same way, prospects became brighter for the Uppermill section when the Greater Manchester Council signed a maintenance agreement to meet the additional costs, once the canal was restored. This provided the B.W.B. with the facility to issue its formal approval for the full restoration of the section to proceed.

Likewise, on the Rochdale Canal the year 1982 saw the various Job Creation Schemes, building on those originally started in 1976, rapidly making dramatic headway in reviving extensive sections of the canal. Perhaps the greatest achievements were in Rochdale Borough, where the local team finished work in the west of the Council's area and immediately moved on to Littleborough to complete a further section of the line. Similarly, in the east, the Calderdale District Council scheme doubled its workforce to complete its target of re-opening the Todmorden to Hebden Bridge section of the canal by the end of 1984. Even before then, a trip boat is planned to operate on part of this section in 1983, after access has been gained by the removal of a culverted bridge at the Hebden end, funded jointly by the Countryside Commission and the English Tourist Board.

In many ways the impact of this sudden wave of urgency, in the 1980s, to restore the region's canals, mirrors the way the restoration movement in the North-West was slow to get underway in the 1960s, yet once it started it seemed to achieve a momentum of its own. The major achievements of the mid-1970s, when the British Waterways Board assisted by the Peak Forest Canal Society were able to re-open the Cheshire Ring, provided the facility for the whole local restoration movement to carry themselves forward to even greater things. The fact that times have changed, with public support now orientated towards canal revival, is best identified by the large number of municipally-organised Job Creation and Community Enterprise canal improvement schemes.

Just as the Cheshire Ring was re-opened in the mid-1970s, so the Northern Canals Ring is the target for the 1990s. The positive attitudes promoted by the extremely hard-working and progressive local canal societies should do much to see that this will be achieved, with all the additional benefits which it can bring to the local communities along these trans-Pennine links.

*   *   *   *   *

(4) NORTH-EASTERN ENGLAND

The Yorkshire Ouse became a popular river for pleasure craft in the 1930s, and two major boat clubs, the Ripon Motor Boat Club, and the York Motor Boat Club, were formed at that time. By 1946 the use of the river by pleasure craft had again revived after the lull of the War Years. The year 1947 saw serious flooding in the Ouse Valley and many banks and the lock at Linton were seriously damaged. In 1948 the Linton Lock had become very dangerous—highlighted by the death of a member of the Ripon Motor Boat Club whilst using it. At about this time informal talks among local waterways enthusiasts concerned the prospective formation of a regional branch of the Inland Waterways Association to co-ordinate activity and re-development of the waterways of the area. The I.W.A. Branch, which was formed in York in April 1949, saw as its first rôle the dual task of getting Linton Lock repaired, and seeking the restoration of through navigation on the River Derwent to Malton. The former scheme

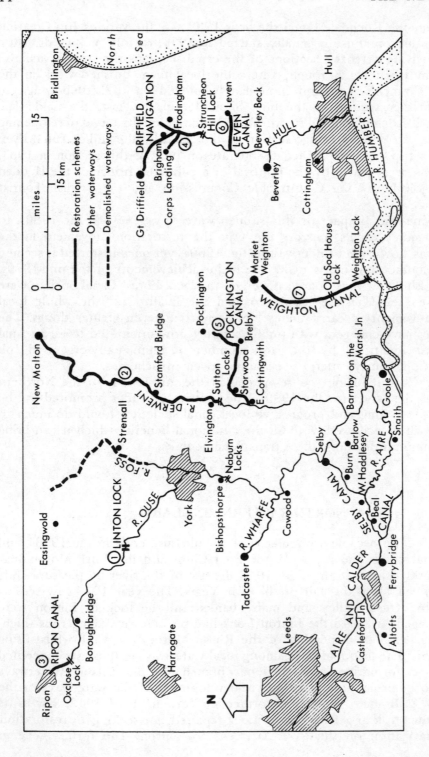

Map 4.—North-Eastern England

(1) Linton Lock; (2) River Derwent; (3) Ripon Canal; (4) Driffield Navigation;
(5) Pocklington Canal; (6) Leven Canal; (7) Market Weighton Canal.

offered the first success when Linton Lock was restored and re-opened by 1950 after the I.W.A. fund-raising campaign. This was followed in 1951 by the formation of the Linton Lock Supporters' Club to continue fund-raising and maintaining the lock in working order. In that same year the campaign to re-open the river Derwent took a downturn with the closure of Sutton Lock near Elvington. By the mid-1950s the strength of the waterways enthusiasts in the North-East was such that events started to develop on four fronts. The Derwent restoration campaign made some headway, whilst the Ripon Motor Boat Club and the Linton Lock Supporters' Club were both actively pursuing policies aimed at keeping the upper reaches of the Ouse, together with the rive Ure and the Ripon Canal, open to pleasure craft. Further east the Brigham Sailing Club had agreed to associate with the I.W.A. in safeguarding the Driffield Navigation. The year 1955 also saw the re-development of the Pocklington Canal as a longer-term restoration scheme.

The progress of the mid-1950s was somewhat dissipated in 1959 when an internal dispute in the Inland Waterways Association caused some members to resign and form the more boating-orientated Northern Waterways Association. Other members left to join the new Inland Waterways Protection Society. The effect of this split meant that the united efforts to preserve and restore the Derwent, the Pocklington Canal, and the Driffield Navigation, as well as to retain the upper reaches of the Ripon Canal, were not successful. Thus by the mid-1960s the newly-formed Derwent Navigation Trust had faltered, Linton Lock had been closed, the initial battles for the Driffield Navigation and Pocklington Canal lost, whilst the Ripon Canal had been blocked by a lowered bridge, and the opportunity to rejuvenate the Leven Canal had not been grasped when the canal had been offered for sale.

The lull was only a temporary setback in the waterways campaign, and by 1968 the North-East again saw progress. The Linton Lock Supporters' Club restored and re-opened the lock in 1966, and in the Derwent Valley the idea of a Pocklington Canal Amenity Society had been mooted, and the Derwent Restoration Scheme re-examined. In the same year the Driffield Navigation Amenity Society was formed to safeguard the Driffield Navigation.

The early 1970s saw progress on all fronts. In Ripon plans were promoted to restore the town basin. The river at Linton Lock was dredged; the Derwent Trust gained permission to restore the first lock on the Derwent; the Pocklington Canal Amenity Society started to restore the canal; a new Market Weighton Canal Society was formed to get the Weighton Canal re-opened; plans were made to restore the Leven Canal; and attempts were made to re-appoint the Driffield Navigation Commissioners and thus re-open the derelict upper reaches of the navigation.

In 1975 the I.W.A. helds its National Rally at York. The event was marked both by the extent of the campaign to stimulate more interest in the waterways of the North-East, as well as to review the progress by then achieved in the retention and rejuvenation of the waterways of the area. By this time, the majority of the local and county authorities in the Ouse Valley were showing their support of the waterway restoration movement. A distinct change of attitude, much of which was due to the persistent efforts of the inland waterways enthusiasts of the area in making their case publicly heard.

This commitment to the region's waterways paid dividends in various ways between 1976 and 1978, especially when a Job Creation project financed the clearance of part of the upper Market Weighton Canal and the Yorkshire Water Authority commenced work on restoring the 200-year-old Weighton Sea Lock. It was estimated that the lock would take over a year to repair, because of the extent of the work required on the drainage sluices and the sea-lock itself. The Market Weighton Canal Society therefore decided to postpone a planned publicity rally of boats until the work was complete in autumn 1979.

Perhaps the most significant advance for the region came with the creation of new Commissioners for the Driffield Navigation in 1978. This was an ideal 10th anniversary present to the Driffield Navigation Amenities Association (D.N.A.A.), who had been pressing the Charity Commission to re-activate the extinct controlling body and therefore provide new custodians for the waterway. They did this by arguing that the waterway was originally created as a non-profit-making amenity for the people of Driffield, and that it therefore should be classified as a charitable organisation and run by Trustees, administering it as a Public Charitable Trust. The legal wrangle to resolve the impasse of the 'lost' Commissioners extended over 10 years and ultimately cost the Association over £3,000. Fortunately, the I.W.A. Council agreed to match pound for pound the money raised by the D.N.A.A. with others, to a maximum of half the final account. The D.N.A.A. managed to raise half the legal fees, and the I.W.A. contributed the remainder.

The new group of Driffield Navigation Commissioners was appointed on 10 July 1978 and the re-activated body met for the first time in Driffield on 30 September 1978. Following the appointment of the Commissioners, the D.N.A.A. reconstituted itself to plan and promote the longer-term aim of the restoration of the navigation.

One of the first actions by the new Commissioners was to sanction the repair of Bethell's Bridge, which had failed to swing open in 1968 and had effectively prevented larger craft from reaching Brigham since that time. The preliminary bridge repairs were quickly put in hand by the D.N.A.A., with the backing of a local farmer, and the bridge was re-usable by the close of 1978. By then the new Commissioners were considering how the future of the waterway should be developed.

One of the first publicity events the D.N.A.A. committee organised in its new rôle was on 13 May 1979, when some of the new Commissioners were taken on a public cruise from Frodingham Bridge to Struncheon Hill Lock, returning by way of Brigham Landing on the main line of the waterway. This was followed by a second Rally of Boats at Frodingham Wharf in June 1979. Working parties also continued work on improving Bethell's Bridge with help from the local farmer who used the bridge as an access link.

Local farmers also helped the Pocklington Canal Amenity Society to revive their waterway, section by section. Offers were made of slurry pumps to clear the locks, but the main task was that of raising funds. The Society calculated that it needed to raise between £30,000 and £40,000 to restore three derelict swing bridges along the line, to extend the existing re-opened navigation section to Melbourne and the Village Arm. Their next task was to raise a further £5,000 for re-gating Thornton Lock, to restore water levels in the next section of the line.

During 1978 and 1979 work also progressed on the adjacent River Derwent Navigation. Volunteers from the Waterways Recovery Group assisted Derwent Trust members to complete the rebuilding of a weir at Howsham, where the lock was also repaired. Although the Yorkshire Derwent Trust owned a plot of land adjacent to the next weir at Kirkham Priory, which they had obtained as a site for a replacement lock, work did not proceed on the new lock construction as the Trust were unable to establish a formal Navigation Authority to operate and maintain the navigation works once they were revived. Even so, it surprised the Derwent Trust to find that the Yorkshire Naturalist's Trust had decided to publish a report, *The Yorkshire Derwent: A Case for Conservation,* which violently objected to the age-old navigation on the river being revived. The report argued that the high water levels required by boats could lead to flooding of farmland and so damage the eco-system of the lower-lying lands. The report, promoted by a local action group called Consyder, received quite a good local press and caused the Derwent Trust to wonder what might happen next.

Matters came to a head in spring 1980 when a Derwent Trust member donated his small cabin cruiser to take members of the public for trips on the Upper Derwent, between Malton and Kirkham. This was largely in response to numerous requests from local people. Another Trust member converted the boat for passenger use, and a photograph and a short article appeared in the local press, indicating that the boat was to be used in summer 1980 for public boat trips, with profits being donated to local charities. Immediately Consyder wrote to the landowners on the stretch of the river concerned, claiming there was no right of navigation and urged them to write to the Trust objecting to the 'trip-boat'. Four landowners heeded the Consyder circular and, in spite of the fact that many similar boats were already using this stretch of the river, threatened to obtain an injunction to prevent the Trust's boat from being used. Later their solicitor withdrew this and threatened to sue for trespass against anyone using the boat. This action postponed the operation of the trip-boat and called into question the right of the many other small boats currently using the upper reaches of the Derwent. The legal advisers to the Derwent Trust believed the action of the landowners was a threat to a Public Right and that the Attorney-General should be approached to begin a Relator Action to re-establish those rights. This the Trust decided to do, and they started to collect formal evidence of the long-standing usage of the river, particularly from the British Canoe Union and the Upper Derwent Boat Club.

The I.W.A. held its National Rally in August 1980 on the river Lea, which is one of the oldest legal river navigations. The Derwent Trust used this as a platform from which to launch a national appeal towards a Fighting Fund, setting a target of £20,000 to meet all potential legal costs. The I.W.A. Council responded with an offer of £6,000, and by the close of the year the Trust had raised a further £4,000 from other sources, including its own funds. This enabled the Trust to brief solicitors to prepare its case.

Just as the Derwent Trust were having to raise funds rapidly, so the Driffield Navigation Amenities Association and the Pocklington Canal Society were also seeking additional finance for their own restoration schemes. They were both fortunate in being recipients from the 1980/81 Shell Waterways Awards scheme. The Driffield Association received £450 towards the completion of their work on Bethell's Bridge, whilst the Pocklington Society received a major award of £750 towards new top gates for Thornton Lock, which would enable the next pound on the canal to hold water, and would effectively launch the second phase of the Society's plans to restore the navigation right through to the Canal Head at Pocklington.

The Pocklington Canal Amenity Society were also working hard elsewhere on the canal. By the middle of 1980 plans had been drawn up to make the fixed bridges up to Melbourne usable. Instead of rebuilding them as swing bridges, the Society hit upon the cheaper method of raising the fixed spans to offer navigational clearance underneath. These plans were put to local landowners, and the B.W.B., and were given active support. As a result, instead of costing some £14,000 to renovate, the rebuilding work on the first swing bridge (Baldwin's Bridge) cost only £600 on completion in 1981.

The restoration work on the Weighton Sea Lock was completed during 1980, and boats used it on special occasions. The local Canal Society and the Yorkshire Water Authority considered the best method of operation on a regular basis, for although a new lock-keeper had been appointed, his main function was to control the drainage of the area. The Society suggested trained licensed volunteer lock operators, so that the lock could be used at other times. The Water Authority agreed to consider this proposal, as the lock was not simple to use and any mistake could be disastrous for the whole area. Whilst the Sea Lock was under restoration, the lower 6-mile section of the Market Weighton Canal was dredged to improve drainage, especially in the area of the A63 road crossing, where the remains of two earlier bridges have caused considerable difficulties to through navigation. Above the first lock, at Sod Houses, about a quarter of a mile at each end of the two mile pound had also been cleared by the Canal Society through a Job Creation Scheme, and plans were also made to clear a section, from the top end to the Land of Nod, by spring 1981. However, further up the canal, work was limited to towpath clearance and caring for the lock chambers, which had been only partially cleared in the Job Creation exercise. This exercise had not had the expected success because of the reluctance of the local authority to help with the disposal of rubbish removed from the lock chambers. In an effort to stimulate more people to explore the upper reaches of the canal, the Society produced a *Towpath Guide* in summer 1981. They also tried to form a local boat club at Newport, on the navigable line, for more regular use of the Sea Lock.

Summer 1981 was used by Yorkshire Hire Cruisers to promote a campaign to get more people to use Yorkshire's waterways. They particularly highlighted the delights of the Upper Ouse, but noted the truncated top section of the Ripon Canal. They pointed also to the particular beauty of the section above Linton Lock, which itself had been restored by the Linton Lock Supporters' Club in 1966.

It was unfortunate that the Linton Lock area suffered badly from the serious flooding of the Ouse Valley in winter 1981. A large volume of silt was washed into the cut above the lock and the lock itself was damaged by the floods. This presented the Lock Commissioners and the Linton Lock Supporters' Club with the daunting task of raising the finance to carry out the repairs, without which the upper river would be closed. It was estimated that some 10,000 tons of silt would have to be cleared and this, together with the lock repairs, could cost some £6,000. Because of the importance of the project, the I.W.A. offered the group a loan of £1,000, which was later converted into a grant, and the Supporters' Club, together with local firms, raised a further £2,000 to get the work underway during summer 1982. A national appeal was launched in November 1982 to raise the balance required to meet the final contractor's bill.

In 1982 the *Ouse Recreation Subject Plan* was published by the North Yorkshire County Council. This outlined ideas for the development of the rivers Ure and Ouse to 1991. A new marina development for the Linton Lock area was part of the plan, but of more interest to local enthusiasts was a suggestion that the upper section of the Ripon Canal should be restored as one of the longer-term strategy objectives. The plan proposed that in the interim 'no development should be permitted that would prejudice restoration'. It also noted that 'the chances would be considerably enhanced by the formation of a restoration society'.

British Waterways Board local engineers responded to the suggestion of reviving the canal, and during summer 1982 undertook a preliminary survey of the derelict section of the canal in conjunction with a study of the associated Littlethorpe road bridge by the North Yorkshire County Surveyor. As a result they jointly produced a schedule of works and estimate of approximate costs. This considered two options for completing the works: (a) B.W.B. using its own labour; and (b) the least cost alternative, using volunteer labour and second-hand materials, etc. The work envisaged the rebuilding of two locks, dredging the channel, bank protection, tree felling, basin works, and replacing Littlethorpe road bridge, together with various other minor works. It was suggested that by using only B.W.B. staff the cost would be in the region of £600,000—but that volunteer labour, with careful supervision, could complete the work for some £250,000. The report suggested that if a decision was taken to proceed, the best way forward would be for a Restoration Society to submit its detailed proposals for approval by the B.W.B. and the North Yorkshire Council. Local enthusiasts seized the opportunity and called a public meeting in January

1983 to discuss the plans. Some 60 people attended, and added their support for
the idea, and subsequently the Ripon Canal Restoration Society was formed at
the first General Meeting on 8 February 1983. At that meeting it was suggested
that either Harrogate Council or North Yorkshire County Council might
promote a Manpower Services Commission scheme to get the works underway,
with active support from the B.W.B. The aim of the group was to get the canal
completely restored in time for the '1986 Festival' to celebrate the 1100th
anniversary of the granting of the city of Ripon's Charter.

Elsewhere in the region, by 1983, work was proceeding apace on the various
restoration plans. On the Market Weighton Canal working parties continued to
clear the Mill Lock and on the Driffield Navigation the bottom gates of
Hempholme Lock were replaced, and plans were made to start work further
up the line. On the Pocklington Canal fund raising towards the restoration of
Thornton Lock had reached some £3,000, and orders had been placed for the
installation of new top gates in spring 1983. Other schemes on the canal included
the raising of the remaining two fixed bridges near Melbourne, for which the
Society gained a further £1,000 Shell Waterways Award, and for the renovation
of the Canal Head area, which had become overgrown. To attract more support
for their work, the Society produced a *Visitor's Guide* which showed that five
out of the nine miles had already been restored, and that work on the second
phase of their scheme was well underway.

The only project in the region which had failed to make any further substantial
progress was that of the Derwent Navigation. Here the legal problems had not
been resolved satisfactorily, and, to make matters worse, the Yorkshire Water
Authority had even taken up an option of a contract clause to foreclose on the
99-year-lease on the locks, held by the Trust, and had offered them a renewal for
five years until the legal situation of the river could be resolved. However, by
early 1983, the Derwent Trust had raised the full £22,000 it needed to take legal
action, and their evidence was prepared. Depending on the local landowners'
stance, they planned to proceed with court action, to get the issue resolved,
during 1983.

The Derwent Trust seem confident that their case will succeed and hope to
get their restoration plans underway once the legalities have been resolved.
Elsewhere restoration plans are speeding up and it seems certain that the navigable
waterways of the region will be far more extensive in the 1990s than they were
in the decades before.

It is unfortunate that the waterways of the North-East have been beset with
more than their fair share of legal problems. However, the various individual
societies all now seem to be achieving real success. As the demand for recreational
water space grows, the safe waterways off the Humber estuary will offer the
facilities which people seek. It could well be that in the longer term, the future
of the region's formerly derelict waterways will be reassured.

*   *   *   *   *

5.—THE LOWER TRENT AND DON

The rivers Trent and Don, with their connection to the Humber estuary, were among the earliest commercial navigations and are still used today as arteries for waterborne trade. Because of their commercial nature they were not much used by pleasure craft during the inter-war years. In the post-war era much of the traffic on the waterways in the area remained in the hands of small family concerns who, facing the potential loss of their livelihood and way of life, became early members of the Inland Waterways Association.

The battle for the retention of the Barnsley Canal was waged while the I.W.A. was still young and inexperienced. Lack of local support combined with the blunt economic fact of inadequate return on investment capital made this a lost cause.

A similar situation was found by I.W.A. members of the North-Eastern Branch when they reviewed the Chesterfield Canal in 1952. Here again, lack of commercial traffic and a disinterested local population did not provide optimum conditions for a local campaign. However, the local anglers saw value in the amenity the canal could offer them, and added their support to the I.W.A. campaign.

By 1956 the campaigns for both the Dearne and Dove and Chesterfield Canals had reached a critical stage. Both canals were considered by the Bowes Committee, reviewing the future of inland waterways, but only the Chesterfield Canal was thought worthy of further attention. By this time the I.W.A. had already gained a consultant's view of the restoration costs, and its North-East Midlands Branch was developing an active local campaign to gain public support for their restoration ideas.

When the Bowes Committee published its report in July 1958, it recommended that the Dearne and Dove Canal should be closed, but that the Chesterfield Canal should be reviewed by a new body, the Inland Waterways Redevelopment Advisory Committee.

At this time some of the I.W.A., North-East Midlands Branch, formed a new group, the Inland Waterways Protection Society based in Sheffield, so that they could conduct the local campaign more actively by reviewing the potential of the canals and putting forward to the Redevelopment Advisory Committee cases for their retention and renewed use. The I.W.P.S. thus prepared reports on both canals and submitted them to the review body and the Ministry of Transport. To carry forward the local publicity campaign the I.W.P.S. also organised a Boat Rally on the Chesterfield Canal in May 1959.

Part of the I.W.P.S. strategy was that it should develop plans for the commercial revival of inland waterways. A committee led by A. Heaf devised a scheme for a new direct Leeds to London Inland Waterway route. The plan involved the use of the routes of the Barnsley and Dearne and Dove Canals as well as a section of the Chesterfield Canal west of Norwood Tunnel, and two new connecting links, of nine and 14 miles respectively, between Rotherham and Killamarsh and Chesterfield and Pinxton. The embryo scheme was presented

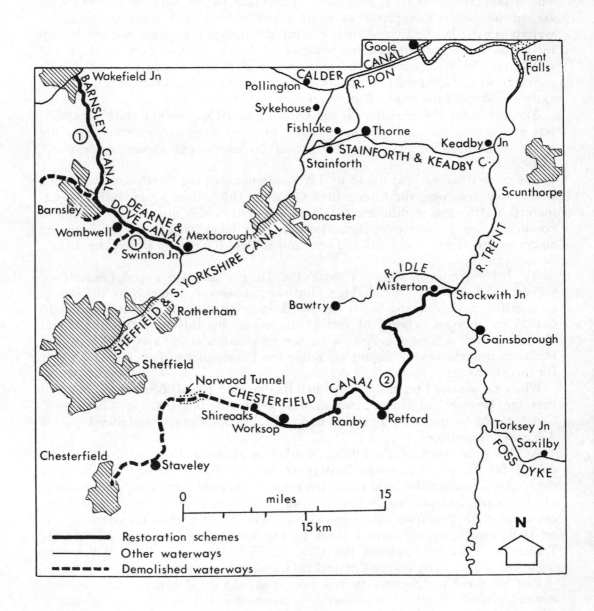

Map 5.—The Lower Trent and Don
(1) Dearne and Dove Canal; (2) Chesterfield Canal

at the Dearne and Dove enquiry in April 1960. However, when the closure of all but the first few yards of the Dearne and Dove Canals was announced in September 1960, even this scheme failed.

The future for the remainder of the Chesterfield Canal was not so bleak. As the waterways enthusiasts began to concentrate their attention on extolling its value as an amenity, so its prospects grew brighter, especially so when the local staff worked hard to upgrade various sections of the canal. The publicity gained from protest cruises slowly paid dividends, and the formation of the Retford and Worksop Boat Club in 1962 as guardians for this waterway gave its future greater security. The inclusion of the West Stockwith to Worksop section of the canal as a 'cruiseway' under the terms of the 1968 Transport Act provided the successful culmination to the first phase of a hard-fought campaign to preserve the canal.

The local I.W.A. Branch were not satisfied with this victory. They believed the 'remainder' section of the Chesterfield Canal, above Worksop, was one of the most interesting of the whole waterway system. Following negotiations with the South Yorkshire County Council Environment Department, they organised working parties to clear the towpath along the upper reaches of the canal, the greater part of which was a public footpath.

By 1976 it was realised that unless some more broadly-based yet local organisation was created, the battle to protect the remainder of the canal could be lost. The I.W.A. Sheffield Branch, and local organisations and individuals called a publc meeting in Worksop on 30 September 1976. It was at this meeting that the Chesterfield Canal Society was born. Its aims were 'to further the protection, conservation and restoration of the Chesterfield Canal, and to advocate the fullest appropriate use, by all interests, of the whole of the canal and its environs'.

By good fortune, the Bi-Centenary of the canal fell in 1977 and this provided the new Society and the Boat Club with an opportunity jointly to attract attention to its considerable value as a local amenity. A Rally of Boats was held in May 1977, and local councillors were among those who were able to enjoy the show. The rally was a great success, and particularly highlighted the derelict state of Morse Lock, the then current head of navigation above Worksop, where the rally was held. During the Bi-Centenary Year, the Chesterfield end was also given some attention by the Society members, who, with the Chesterfield Conservation corps, tidied the Tapton length of the canal in an effort to stimulate the council to review its future. The Society also cleared rubbish from the unique Norwood flight of locks and tried to deter the local council from infilling the Killamarsh section of the canal. The Society produced a booklet, *The Chesterfield Canal: Yesterday, Today and Tomorrow* in 1977, which identified all the items of historical importance along the canal route, in order to unite interest and support for its aims.

Local councils to the east of Norwood Tunnel responded to the Society's call to protect the canal, and in late 1977 two small Job Creation schemes were developed; one to clear the towpath in the Shireoaks area, and the other partially to rebuild the bulldozed walls of Morse Lock, which had been used to infill the lock chamber. These schemes gave impetus to the Society's campaign, and its aim for 1978 was to gain more local authority support for its long-term strategy to revive the whole six miles of canal from Worksop to the Norwood Tunnel. To achieve this, the Society organised a series of meetings, walks, exhibitions, and rallies, and liaised more closely with the four local councils along the line.

The canal got some unexpected national publicity in August 1967 when B.W.B. staff, dredging the 'cruiseway' section of the canal in Retford, inadvertently pulled out an old drain plug in the canal bed. Overnight, a mile and a half section of the canal was drained. This did not go unnoticed locally, and the Society were able to demonstrate the extent of national interest in the old canal.

By 1980 some results emerged from the Society's campaigns. At the western end of the canal, the Chesterfield District Council were considering the purchase of the first five miles of the line from B.W.B. to develop it as a linear park, whilst at the Norwood flight of locks, the Society had made a substantial improvement to the condition of the 13 locks, in four staircase sets. Similarly, east of Norwood Tunnel a £200 Shell Award made possible the inauguration of a trip boat along the summit level of the canal.

The trip boat, *The Norwood Packet,* was introduced on the canal at Kiveton Park and immediately created considerable public interest in this most scenic section of the canal. So much so that later in the year a new Youth Opportunities Scheme was announced aimed at clearing and re-making the towpath from the tunnel eastwards towards Worksop. The B.W.B. also dredged part of the summit level to improve the water supply on the canal, and improved the length of waterway used by the trip boat. This enabled the boat to make 28 public trips in 1982 and carry over 270 passengers along this scenic part of the canal.

By 1982 the Society had realised from discussions with B.W.B. and the local authorities that it would need to evaluate more critically its restoration plans. It was accepted that in the difficult economic climate it would be hard to complete the full restoration of the six miles from Worksop to Norwood tunnel, with 30 locks and two major blockages at Rhodesia and Shireoaks. So it produced a report in August 1982 under the intriguing title of *Route to Rhodesia*. This set out the benefits of, obstacles to, and costs of the restoration of the ¾-mile section between the present head of navigation at Morse Lock and Rhodesia, the location of the first major blockage, a culverted road bridge. The scheme involved rebuilding three locks, dredging and piling a short section of bank, and the construction of a new winding hole. The cost of the project was estimated at £66,000, of which £42,000 was allocated for new lock gates and paddle gear. The report was circulated to local authorities, councillors and the B.W.B., and quickly received a favourable response from the local District Council. A reply was received from B.W.B. which, though not giving unconditional support, did not rule out the development of the scheme, so long as funding could be guaranteed. To seek more public commitment towards the canal, the Society erected information panels at strategic points. The first was at Kiveton Park and a second at Retford, drawing attention to the features of the canal and stimulating interest in the Society's plans.

Although the Dearne and Dove and Barnsley Canals are now forgotten, and the 'Direct Leeds to London Route' is a thing of the past, the prospects for the upper section of the Chesterfield Canal continue to improve. Chesterfield District Council have indicated their keenness to restore their local section of the canal, to the west of the tunnel, on the truncated section of the line. Clearly the formation of the Chesterfield Canal Society in 1976 has provided the means of generating new support for the 'remainder' section of the canal.

*   *   *   *   *

6.–LINCOLNSHIRE

The majority of the waterways in Lincolnshire were developed to link with the main transport artery, the river Witham. The Romans realised the value of the east to west river and connected it to the lower Trent by what is now Britain's oldest surviving navigable man-made canal, the Fossdyke, which was constructed about A.D. 70. The Witham runs through low-lying fens and thus has always been an integral part of the drainage system of much of Lincolnshire. Although it was navigable in Roman times, there followed centuries of decline before it was much improved during the 18th and early 19th centuries. From this time commercial traffic rapidly developed, and Lincoln became, through Boston, one of the main centres of the country's trade. With the coming of the railways and the improvement in the road transport system, the Lincolnshire waterways, which acted as tributaries to the Witham, rapidly declined, and reverted to their drainage function. With the loss of trade so the wharfs and warehouses alongside the canals also fell into decay. Apart from the steady growth in the number of pleasure craft journeying from the Trent to Lincoln, and sometimes to Boston, interest in boating in the area was very slight, and only more intrepid enthusiasts explored what remained of the derelict waterways.

The first sign of interest in the waterway restoration, not surprisingly, came from Lincoln in 1965 where the state of Brayford Mere, after the demise of the commercial traffic, caused local concern. Before this, members of the Lincoln Boat Club had tried to get the Mere restored, but with little success. The local Chamber of Commerce eventually became the prime mover of the restoration scheme, with help and advice from the Inland Waterways Association, North-East Midlands region. After considerable debate it was agreed that an independent Trust should be formed to lead the restoration campaign. Work commenced on the project in 1968 and has continued subsequently as funds became available.

Because of the lack of waterway enthusiasts in the area no other restoration schemes were proposed until 1971 when both Louth Town Council and Sleaford Civic Trust separately reviewed the potential of the former canals that linked the two towns to the outside world. The scheme for the Louth Canal

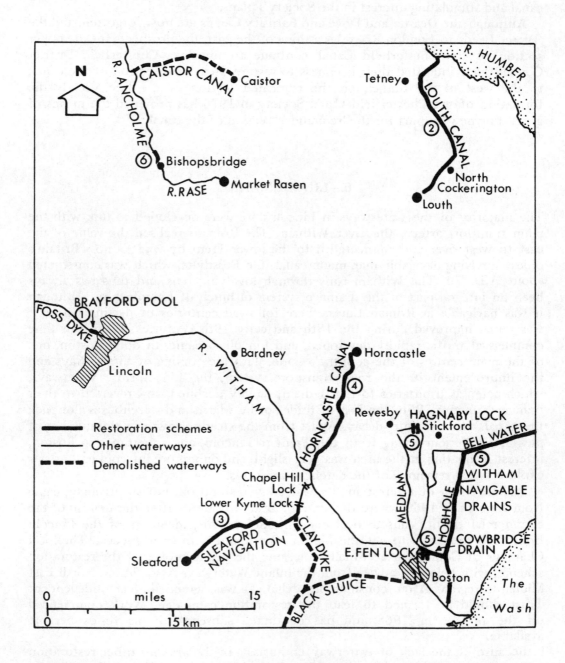

Map 6.—Lincolnshire

(1) Brayford Pool; (2) Louth Canal; (3) Sleaford Navigation; (4) Horncastle Canal;
(5) Witham Navigable Drains; (6) Rase and Ancholme

envisaged full restoration, whilst that in Sleaford only involved the town basin and wharf area. The far more elaborate Louth Canal restoration and re-development scheme was dropped through lack of finance, but that at Sleaford went forward with both county and local financial support. The local Civic Trust commitment proved sound as grants were also made available under the Architectural Heritage Awards scheme.

Perhaps the most significant advance for the promotion of waterway restoration schemes in the area was the Inland Waterways Association's reorganisation of their regional structure in October 1973. Under the boundary revision, a new Lincolnshire and South Humberside Branch was formed, based at Lincoln. This provided the few waterway enthusiasts in the area with the chance to pursue a common purpose.

Among the earliest events the new Branch committee and its members undertook was an involvement in the 1974 Lincoln Water Festival on Brayford Mere. This drew attention to Lincoln's unique waterways, and also contributed a useful amount to the meagre funds of the Brayford Trust for more improvements.

The Branch then considered whether they could assist in the extension of the existing network through the restoration of some of Lincolnshire's 'lost canals'. As a first step, they decided to press for the retention and fuller use of what they had. In May 1975 they organised a campaign cruise on the Witham Navigable Drains, which offered upwards of 25 miles of little-known but adventurous cruising off the river Witham, near Boston. The campaign cruise was a considerable success and provided the Branch with an up-to-date analysis of the potential cruising grounds and enabled them to produce a map, which subsequently appeared in *Waterways World* for December 1975. In the article associated with the map, it was suggested that if the derelict East Fen Lock was restored, it could offer a considerable extension to the unique cruising waterways. However, as a first stage it was accepted that the number of craft using the existing Navigable Drains would need to be substantially increased. The I.W.A. Branch issued plaques to all touring craft which could produce evidence that they had visited the Drains and had passed through Cowbridge Lock. Also, as part of their longer-term strategy, the I.W.A. Branch explored and developed local interest in the derelict Horncastle and Sleaford Canals, and investigated the state of the Thorpe Culvert.

Surprisingly, the first new impetus for waterway development came from the north of the region, with the foundation of the Rase–Ancholme Navigation Trust in June 1977. This group, based on the river Ancholme, realised that a campaigning body was needed if the stretch of the Ancholme between Harlem Hill Lock and Bishopsbridge was to be revived for regular use by craft. The Trust also set itself longer-term aims: to make the river Rase navigable as far as Market Rasen; to provide additional cruising waters away from the difficult Humber estuary; and to develop a link with the river Witham, on the lines of a scheme proposed in 1828, as a safe cruising route to the non-tidal section of the Trent. This latter plan was inspired particularly by the Trent–Witham–Ancholme water transfer scheme, developed by the Anglian Water Authority in the 1970s, by which water was pumped from Short Ferry Works, near Bardney, through an 11-mile pipeline to a reservoir at Toft Newton, thence feeding into the Upper Ancholme.

The new group organised a Rally of Boats to publicise their waterway, and then asked the Anglian Water Authority to take steps to improve Harlem Hill Lock, which was very difficult to operate and effectively blocked the route to Bishopsbridge.

A second advance in the Lincolnshire region came in November 1977 when the Sleaford Navigation Society was formed. This was prompted by a threat to destroy the unique Navigation Company House in Sleaford for a wharf area re-development scheme. However, it soon became clear that there was sufficient interest in the area to explore the possibility of restoring the complete navigation. The group therefore developed a plan for the Bottom Lock, and the one above, to re-open an additional 10 miles of river. It accepted that the last three miles, with five locks, presented a more difficult task, although the lock by the mill was already being renovated by the owner. Even so, it set itself the task of re-opening the whole navigation as soon as possible.

By December 1979, the Sleaford Navigation Society had completed the plans for the restoration of the Bottom Lock and discussed them with the Anglian Water Authority. At their meeting, the Society learned that the A.W.A. were in favour of restoring the navigation, but that there were problems of finance in the short term. However, in the longer term the Water Authority had plans to replace the sluice at the Bottom Lock and that when the work commenced in 1984 the new sluice could be designed with navigation in mind. The Society were heartened by this response, but pressed for much earlier consideration of their scheme. It set itself the task of raising funds, and its first major event, a sponsored walk in 1980, raised over £700. In May of that year the Boston Motor Yacht Club also tried to rally support for the navigation by holding a gathering of boats at Bottom Lock and a dinghy rally at South Kyme. These events were a great success and gained much publicity.

On 14 September 1979 the *Louth Standard* carried an article about the derelict Louth Navigation. The paper had discovered a scheme in the 'Five Year' Forward Capital programme of the Anglian Water Authority to restore the canal to navigation at an estimated cost of £2 million. According to the paper, 'public pressure has forced the A.W.A. to make some kind of commitment and the authority agrees that it is a sensible scheme'. The fact that the canal served as the main drainage channel for the area, as the river Lud linked into the top of the navigation channel and many other streams and drains were feeding into the line, undoubtedly accounted for the A.W.A.'s interest in the long-term re-development plan, which had earlier been suggested jointly by the local council and the I.W.A. However, two major problems had to be overcome. One was the numerous lowered road bridges, and the other the fact that at the sea end the former sea lock had completely disappeared. The scheme was not without its critics, and one Louth councillor, Roosevelt Wilkinson, went on record as saying he believed that £2 million was too much to spend on the scheme. Even so, this did not prevent East Lindsey District Council agreeing to meet the cost of a new slipway at the town basin in Louth in July 1980, part of the re-development of the basin area.

The cruising facilities of the Witham area received a boost in summer 1980, when Foxline Cruisers of Dogdyke, on the Witham, and Lincoln Hire Cruises of Lincoln, reached agreement for both companies' hire fleets to be operated from the Foxline, Dogdyke base. There would thus be some 15 craft available to cruise on the Fossdyke, Witham and Navigable Drains during the 1981 cruising season. The prospect of a larger fleet on the Witham interested the Anglian Water Authority, who were reviewing the recreational potential of their area as a result of I.W.A. Branch pressure to have water-based recreational potential identified in the long-term Structure Plan of the region. Because the river Witham was prone to floods, the A.W.A. were keen to see the Dogdyke base moved off the main river, and suggested to Foxline that they might develop a marina on the canalised, but derelict, river Bain. The A.W.A. would consider replacing the first lock on the derelict Horncastle Canal, which provided the entrance to the lower Bain. As there were extensive gravel workings at Tattershall, only 30 yards from the line of the old canal, and some of these were already converted into water-based sports facilities, the I.W.A. suggested that these also might be linked to the Horncastle Canal, as a move towards its longer-term re-development as a navigation, which by then was identified in the Structure Plan. Unfortunately, Foxline, after a poor season in 1982, decided to sell their Dogdyke fleet at the end of the year, and plans for the revival of the Horncastle Canal faltered just when the A.W.A. were planning to install a new sluice at the mouth of the river Bain. The local I.W.A. Branch, however, requested that it should still be designed with future navigational requirements in mind. Whether this can be arranged will depend on available finance.

By 1980, elsewhere in the region, the two main development projects were proceeding smoothly. The Rase-Ancholme Navigation Trust had commissioned Anglia Survey Consultants to examine the problems of upgrading the river Rase to navigable standards, and preliminary findings had not identified any snags. They had also raised funds for the construction of a winding hole at Bishopsbridge, so that larger craft could turn round at the present head of navigation. To enhance craft use, they conducted a full survey of the navigation, and through their Upper Ancholme Restoration Committee persuaded A.W.A. engineers to undertake remedial work on the worst sections identified in the Trust's *River Ancholme Survey 1980.* This included the construction of a silt trap at Harlem Hill, but did not achieve all that the Trust would have liked, as the A.W.A. were restricted in what could immediately be spent on the waterway, pending a decision on the *Binney Report,* which analysed the development of the area's drainage works.

More spectacular advances were, however, made by the Sleaford Navigation Society. Whilst the local Council were unable to repair the old Canal Company offices, it was still supporting the group in their aim to revive the whole navigation. By 1981, the Society had raised over £1,500 towards the restoration of the Bottom Lock, and a further Shell Waterways Award of £1,000 substantially contributed to the £10,000 needed for the complete Bottom Lock restoration.

The Society decided formally to promote a 'Bottom Lock Restoration Appeal', and prepared a very attractive brochure in May 1982. To launch their 'Appeal', the Society sent copies to every County and District councillor, a number of whom were invited to a reception in Sleaford in September 1982, when the Society fully outlined its prospectus, quoting examples of achievements elsewhere. At the meeting the Chairman of the I.W.A., J. Heap, presented the Society with a cheque for £1,000 and a personal cheque for £100. After the reception the Society wrote to the Councils for their support. The County Council offered £2,000, whilst the District Council indicated that the restoration scheme might qualify for a Manpower Service Commission Job Creation project. By the close of 1982, the Society had raised over £5,600 towards the restoration of the Bottom Lock. The full £10,000 was raised by February 1983, and orders for lock gates were placed soon after this.

Matters were not progressing as rapidly elsewhere. To stimulate further interest in the Louth Canal, the local I.W.A. Branch organised a walk along its route in September 1982, and the Rase-Ancholme Trust a cruise to Bishopsbridge in April 1982. Although all the boats completed the trip, the problems at Harlem Hill Lock had not been satisfactorily solved, which prompted the Trust to seek more remedial work.

Although only one of the waterways of the region is in sight of full restoration, the fact that the recreational potential of the remainder is under active review should ensure that future opportunities for restoration will not be lost. Meanwhile, the only project so far completed, at Brayford Mere, can attract more pleasure craft to the region, and thus pave the way for the development of other schemes.

*   *   *   *   *

7.–EAST MIDLANDS

The East Midlands region was at first serviced by the river Trent, the upper reaches of which were made fully navigable by 1719. In the canal era the first part of Brindley's Grand Cross, the Trent and Mersey Canal, linked the Bridgewater Canal to the Trent Navigation at Shardlow in 1770. The canal offered an immediate link with the Potteries, but the through route to the Mersey was not available until 1777, when the Harecastle Tunnel was opened. Two years later, in 1779, the Erewash Canal was opened, linking the Nottinghamshire and Derbyshire coalfields to the Trent and thence to the growing canal network.

As the value of water transport became evident so the Cromford, Derby, Nottingham and Grantham Canals were built, completing the water transport network of the region by 1800. From that time until the early 1920s these canals provided the routeways on which iron, coal, and heavy manufactured items were transported. From the latter date railways and roads rapidly absorbed the remaining traffic. Even so, in 1947, the potential loss of the Derby Canal as a commercial link with the coalfields was causing local concern. In the light of the publicity gained from their battle to re-open the Northern Stratford-on-Avon

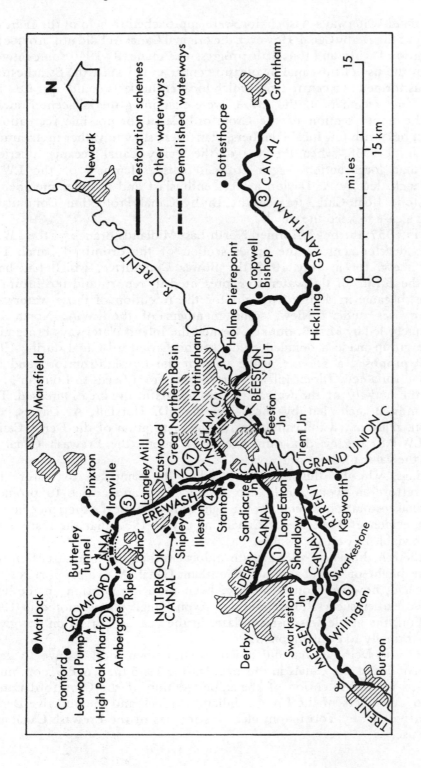

Map 7.—East Midlands

(1) Derby Canal; (2) Upper Cromford Canal; (3) Grantham Canal; (4) Erewash Canal;
(5) Lower Cromford Canal; (6) Upper Trent; (7) Nottingham Canal

Canal, the Inland Waterways Association were approached to help in the fight for the retention of the Derby Canal. However, the original Canal Act did not provide for Public Navigation Rights, and thus little progress was made. By 1949 some interest was shown in the use of the canal by pleasure craft, and in 1951 the Swarkestone Boat Club was formed as a centre from which local enthusiasts could operate.

By 1954 some members of the I.W.A. were examining the adjacent Erewash Canal and the upper section of the Cromford Canal for possible recreational development; but, with few local members, plans were slow to gather momentum. It was not until 1956, when the loss of the Derby Canal became a serious possibility, that local action began to materialise. Members of the I.W.A. Midlands Branch, led by A. Davies, a local enthusiast and founder member of the Swarkestone Boat Club, formed the Derby Canal Protection Committee, and prepared a case to keep the canal.

Similarly, in 1957, the newly-formed North-East Midlands Branch of the I.W.A. reviewed the development of the upper section of the Cromford Canal. This action was timely, for in July 1958 the Bowes Committee, which had been considering the future of the waterways, presented its report, and the future of the waterway became in doubt. To fight for the retention of those waterways whose future was under review, some members of the I.W.A. North-East Midlands Branch, led by Mrs. B. Bunker, formed the Inland Waterways Protection Society. The group made a detailed study of the Cromford Canal during 1959 and in 1960 proposed a scheme, using part of the Lower Cromford and the Erewash Canal, for a new 'Direct Inland Water Route from Leeds to London'.

By 1961 the activity of the waterways enthusiasts in the area increased. The I.W.A. Midlands Branch, led by local members D. Horsfall, A. Davies, and R. Torrington, rejuvenated the campaign for the restoration of the Derby Canal, whilst the I.W.P.S. organised a campaign cruise along the Erewash Canal to demonstrate the value of the waterways.

D. Hutchings, who by this time was leading the campaign to restore the Southern Stratford-on-Avon Canal, also offered help and advice to promote the Derby Canal restoration scheme. In the light of his practical experience he was able to offer evidence at the Derby Canal Enquiry in 1962 that the restoration plan was both viable as well as possible.

By 1963 there had been further growth in local enthusiasm, and attention was turned to the plight of the abandoned Grantham Canal. Active support for the Derby Canal had, however, come too late. Even though a petition on the lines of that of the earlier successful Kennet and Avon Canal was promoted in 1964 for its retention, the battle was lost and later in the year authorisation was given for the canal formally to be abandoned.

The loss of the Derby Canal did much to strengthen local resolve to keep open the remainder of the canals in the area. During 1965 the I.W.P.S. continued their campaign for the retention of the upper section of the Cromford Canal, whilst in 1967 members of the I.W.A. Midlands Branch and the abortive Derby Canal Committee, led by Torrington, cleared stretches of the Erewash Canal and promoted its use.

By 1968 the development of the waterways of the region as an amenity reached a turning point. Although the 1968 Transport Act included the Cromford, Erewash and Grantham Canals within the 'Remainder' waterways category, by this time local support for their re-development had grown sufficiently for people to take action to safeguard their future. In Grantham the Civic Trust took an interest in the canal, and at the other side of the region a group of enthusiasts examined the possible restoration of the Leawood Pump and the upper reaches of the Cromford Canal. Between the two, the fight for the Erewash Canal gave birth to the Erewash Canal Preservation and Development Association, formed by local people with the help of the I.W.A. and I.W.P.S.

In 1969 the Derbyshire County Council Countryside Committee considered a paper by Torrington, the I.W.A. representative, in which he suggested the restoration of Cromford Wharf and the Upper Cromford Canal to complement the amenity of the High Peak Trail, which was then being developed. This proposal was carried a stage further in 1970 when A. D. Stoker, for the Cromford Canal Group, proposed that the Derbyshire County Council should take over the canal from the British Waterways Board. In that year the Grantham Canal Society was formed by the Grantham Civic Trust to pursue the retention of the amenity the canal offered.

The year 1971 saw a gathering of support both for the Erewash and Grantham Canal restoration schemes. The local press gave substantial publicity to the former scheme whilst, for the latter, the I.W.A. Chairman, J. Humphries, provided the negotiating skill that gained the opportunity for such restoration.

The Arkwright Festival held at Cromford in summer 1971 boosted interest in industrial archaeology in the area, including the Cromford Canal, and led to the formation of the Arkwright Society to promote public interest. The Erewash Canal Preservation and Development Association (E.C.P. and D.A.) produced a guide to the Erewash Canal with much the same aim.

As local support for the waterways of the area grew so restoration proposals were evolved. During 1972, on the Grantham Canal there was a Rally at Hickling Basin, whilst at Great Northern Basin, the junction of the Erewash and Cromford Canals, work in re-opening the basin got underway. At the same time an idea was put forward to use the former canal reservoir at Codnor as a water-based recreation centre with a link to the canal system.

The Great Northern Basin was re-opened in 1973, and in that same year Grantham Canal Society also became a restoration-orientated body. The full value of the waterways was fully portrayed at the I.W.A. National Rally of Boats held at Nottingham during summer 1974, when plans for restoring navigation on the the Upper Trent, between Nottingham and Burton, were first promoted, as was a plan to revive the partly-infilled Lower Cromford Canal. The Upper Section of the Cromford Canal was taken over by the Derbyshire County Council for amenity development.

By 1975 an engineering survey had been completed for the restoration of the Grantham Canal, and similar surveys were underway for both the Lower Cromford Canal and the Upper Trent Navigation. Work also continued on the restoration of the upper section of the Cromford Canal.

The inauguration of a trip boat on the first restored section of the Upper Cromford Canal in 1977, and the re-opening of a short section of the Lower Cromford Canal together with the Jubilee Dry Dock at Great Northern Basin in the same year, indicated continuing progress. The foundation of the Nottingham Canal Society in 1976 was another sign that the region was taking a renewed interest in its canals.

Perhaps this interest is best exemplified in the work undertaken by the six partners of the Langley Mill Boat Co., Ltd., who were also members of the E.C.P. and D.A. They formed the boat company in June 1974 to meet the B.W.B. condition that, for an offer of a lease to extend the Langley Mill complex, a serious investment should be made. After protracted negotiations, plans for the dry dock, slipway and moorings were agreed, and the go-ahead given in September 1975. Provision was also made for the through passage of boats, should the Lower Cromford Canal be further restored at a later date. The operation involved some 10,000 man-hours, mainly in the evenings and at week-ends, and resulted in the doubling of the water area at Langley Mill by the time the works were completed in August 1977. This solved the major problem of water shortage in the Great Northern Basin by ensuring more reliable water levels.

However, even with this tremendous local support, all did not develop as the enthusiasts had planned. In 1978 the E.C.P. and D.A. were told that reservoir flood prevention requirements would not allow them to restore the Codnor Park Flight of locks at Ironville on the Lower Cromford Canal, as the first few locks on the line of the canal had to be adapted to offer an overspill route for the Butterley reservoir, in the event of its dam failing. Subsequently the Severn-Trent Water Authority published plans which envisaged a protective barrier across the Erewash Valley at Aldercar to act as a storage reservoir in the event of flood conditions. This plan meant that the line of the Lower Cromford Canal above Strutts Lock would be completely severed by a barrier, which could not easily be by-passed. Also the proposed Langley Mill by-pass road would cross the line of the canal to the north of Langley Mill, and a canal bridge could not be envisaged unless volunteers could find £30,000—more than the enthusiasts could afford. These blows effectively halted any immediate plans to re-open the navigation from the Great Northern Basin through to Butterley Tunnel by reviving the whole of the Lower Cromford Canal.

All was not lost, however. As a demonstration of their good faith in further waterways restoration, Derbyshire County Council funded the plant costs incurred by the E.C.P. and D.A. and the I.W.A. in the interim work of clearing the pounds on the Ironville lock flight, which had generated so much support from the local population; and the B.W.B. also cleaned out the summit pound, despite limited access, with a land-based dredger. Even so, open-cast mining continued above Langley Mill and the road by-pass embankment was built by the N.C.B. across the old infilled line of the canal as an access road. However, once this mining is completed, a Derelict Land Reclamation Grant could offer the possibility of building a completely new route to re-link the Ironville flight to Langley Mill. Therefore full revival might still be possible in the long term.

The E.C.P. and D.A. did not lose heart, but celebrated the bi-centenary of their canal in 1979 with a Rally of Boats at Ilkeston. The main theme at this event was the raising of funds for new gates for the entrance lock at the Great Northern Basin, as well as publicising the recreational value of the whole canal.

In much the same way as on the Lower Cromford, plans for the early restoration of the Grantham Canal suffered a series of setbacks in the late 1970s. Although the riparian County Councils and the British Waterways Board both accepted that the canal was of considerable recreational potential, they felt unable to allow volunteers from the Grantham Canal Restoration Society to start restoring the canal structures. Their work was thus restricted to clearing the towpath. Subsequently, plans were published by the National Coal Board for the development of a major new coalfield in the Vale of Belvoir, through which the canal passed. This scheme complicated still further the Canal Restoration Society's long-term aims; major land subsidence was likely to affect the canal line. However, the development of the new mines in the Trent Valley held out the prospect of the construction of a new water link with the river Trent, as an economical and environmentally acceptable means of removing coal from the new pits. After much heart-searching the I.W.A. Council agreed to support the British Waterways Board in their scheme for a new canal, so long as there was some provision for the inclusion of the original Grantham Canal in the plans.

Unfortunately, the B.W.B. decided not to proceed with the scheme for a new 11-mile canal across the Vale of Belvoir, as it duplicated a British Rail scheme to re-open some disused railway lines to handle the coal and colliery waste. The B.W.B. decision was announced at the Vale of Belvoir Mining Enquiry in October 1979, and was a disappointment to many objectors. They saw the canal scheme as the least environmentally objectionable method of removing the huge quantities of spoil, should the mining project receive official sanction.

The decision of the B.W.B. left both the I.W.A. and the Grantham Canal Restoration Society in a dilemma. In January 1980, the I.W.A. Council decided not to give evidence at the Vale of Belvoir Enquiry. It believed that it could not justify using its own funds to object, when the money could otherwise be used on restoration work. This was a shattering blow to the local restorationists, who felt that the I.W.A. had deserted the fundamental principle on which it had been founded: to fight for the revival of all canals. Fortunately, the Grantham Canal Restoration Society found a new ally in the Inland Waterways Amenity Advisory Council (I.W.A.A.C.), who decided to field a team of experts in the recreational use of waterways to support the case for the protection of the canal against the environmental effects of the proposed mining schemes. At the Inquiry, in March 1980, the I.W.A.A.C. Chairman, David Wain, argued that if the N.C.B. were given permission to open mines in the Vale of Belvoir, they should consider the sum necessary for retaining the Grantham Canal, in the face of subsidence, as a small price to pay for the winning of some 500 million tonnes of coal. This gave heart to the Restoration Society, who argued at the Inquiry that the £20 million, suggested by the B.W.B. for the retention of the canal, as opposed to the £5 million for its elimination, was unrealistic and that a sum of £12 million was nearer the likely overall long-term cost of retaining the canal, but that most of this should be underwritten by the N.C.B. as part of the cost of their mining programme.

The Grantham Canal Restoration Society believed that, even whilst the Inquiry was considering the long-term future of the area, there was, in the short term, a need to publicise the amenity value of the canal. To this end it brought out a popular booklet, *Walks in the Vale of Belvoir*, which emphasised the tremendous recreational value of the canal. Some 3,000 copies of the booklet were sold in the first five years. To build on this interest, the Society opened negotiations with the B.W.B. for permission to develop Denton Wharf as a picnic site. Plans were subsequently approved and the site was finally completed early in 1982. This was the first of several similar schemes envisaged for the canal route.

The Vale of Belvoir Public Inquiry closed on 23 April 1980, but whilst the Inspectors report was awaited, some of the members of the Grantham Society assisted colleagues in the young Nottingham Canal Society in two projects on their canal. One was the clearance of the arm leading into the former Fellows, Morton and Clayton warehouse, which the Nottingham City Council were considering restoring as a 'Canal and Commercial Museum'. The other was overcoming a breach, by laying a pipe across an embankment at Trowell, in a scheme funded by Broxtowe District Council, to retain adequate summer water levels in the Trowell to Cossall section of the Nottingham Canal. This latter scheme was quite significant, in that the Nottingham Canal figured quite prominently in the draft *Erewash Valley Environmental Improvement Plan*, published by Nottinghamshire County Council in mid-1980. Part of the plan also envisaged an 'Erewash Valley Trail', from the Pinxton Arm of the Cromford Canal southwards along the towpath of the Cromford Canal, through to Langley Mill, and then down the Erewash Valley. One snag in the proposal was that the Derbyshire County Council did not offer a similar plan for the west of the valley. However, they did negotiate to purchase the Pinxton Arm with a view to its subsequent environmental improvement and amenity use. It therefore came as no surprise when they joined with the Historic Buildings Trust, in 1980, to clear a length of the Lower Cromford Canal in Golden Valley— dredging it and refurbishing the banks, indicating that they had plans to designate the whole valley, from Ironville to Butterley, as a country park.

The Derbyshire County Council perhaps best demonstrated its new, positive attitude in its support for the Cromford Canal Society in its development of the Upper Cromford Canal. The Society, through its energetic manager, S. Stoker, developed the first section of the canal as a tourist attraction. By 1979 the Society's horse-drawn trip boat *John Gray* had carried over 6,000 passengers in the season through to High Peak Wharf. This public support prompted the Society to put forward a scheme to the County Council for a lease on the canal which would enable them to restore and maintain it. The lease was duly granted.

In August 1979 the Society succeeded in re-opening the 130-year-old Leawood Pump House, with the steam-operated Beam pumping engine in full working order. This development, which had taken eight years to complete, provided an added attraction. During 1979 and 1980 the Society also started on the second phase of its development scheme, dredging a further 1½ miles of canal to Gregory Tunnel, using a Job Creation scheme. This work was further enhanced in 1981 when the Pilgrim Trust made a donation of £1,200 to the Society to finance the conversion of a fixed bridge over the canal at Leawood into a swing bridge. Once this was completed, and a new turning basin constructed at Whatstandwell, the trip boats could use the extended canal cruising grounds. It was also planned that a museum and workshop should be developed at Cromford Wharf, as funds allowed.

Spring 1982 saw the publication of the Belvoir Enquiry Inspector's Report. This refused permission for the N.C.B. to proceed with the three mines in their original plan, but asked that the plans be revised and re-submitted taking more account of waste disposal and the environmental problems of mining. This left the future of the Grantham Canal uncertain. The Grantham Canal Restoration Society were specially heartened by the Inspector's comment: '. . . the canal is an object of great local interest'. This gave them new hope and prompted them to consider plans offering a balance between human recreation and the needs of wild life. The Grantham Canal Trust, an umbrella body looking after the broader interests of the canal, met subsequently.

Perhaps the most pleasing feature of 1982 was the announcement by the B.W.B. that the Secretary of State for the Environment had given his consent for a British Waterways Bill to be promoted to upgrade the status of certain 'remainder' canals. Among these was the Erewash Canal, between Long Eaton and Langley Mill. The Bill received Royal Assent in early 1983, as plans were agreed for the development of a new marina at Langley Mill; both offered additional long-term security to the canal which local enthusiasts had fought so hard to revive.

No doubt the sad spectacle of the derelict and partly infilled Derby Canal has had much to do with the considerable change in public attitude towards the waterways of the area over the last decade. Various restoration schemes offer tangible evidence of public, local authority, and County Council support for all that now has been achieved. Future progress now depends on matters mainly outside their direct control.

* * * * *

8.—THE POTTERIES

The Potteries, the Churnet valley and the town of Leek all have early associations with the canal era. James Brindley, a Leek millwright, is regarded by many as the engineer who paved the way for the construction of over four thousand miles of inland waterways which ensured that by 1840 every town of size in England was on, or near to, a canal. As such he probably deserves the title of 'Father of British Waterways'.

It was Brindley who conceived the idea of the 'Grand Cross', with canals linking the Mersey and the Thames, and the Trent and the Severn, providing easy access to the four great ports of London, Liverpool, Bristol, and Hull. The implication of such a network and its value to the Potteries was quickly grasped by Josiah Wedgwood, who realised that the Grand Cross scheme would ease the problems of the pottery industry, which hitherto had to rely on the packman, packhorse, and horse wagon.

The partnership between Wedgwood and Brindley promoted the canal from the Trent to the Mersey, which Brindley regarded as part of the Grand Trunk Canal.

The Trent and Mersey Canal offered direct access to the Wedgwood factory at Etruria, and provided the stimulus for the construction of the Caldon Canal to link the Etruria Works with the limestone and flint supplies of the Churnet Valley. The Caldon Canal also led to Brindley's premature death. While he was surveying the route he caught a chill and died on 27 September 1772, before the Caldon Canal was constructed.

The name of Brindley became well-known and many people developed an interest in his life and works. One follower was the headmaster of Bradnop Parochial School at Leek, Harold Bode, who studied the life and times of one of the few local men to achieve national acclaim. The potential loss of a working memorial to the works of Brindley, such as the Caldon Canal offered, inspired Bode to campaign locally for its retention. Fortunately, the merits of the canal were already known to the founders of the Inland Waterways Association, and many members of the association were also members of the Stoke-on-Trent Boat Club, based on the Newcastle Arm of the Trent and Mersey Canal.

The catalyst of the local restoration campaign was provided by the I.W.A. National Rally of Boats held in Stoke-on-Trent in August 1960. It drew together the various local interests, the Inland Waterways Protection Society, local youth organisations, boat club members, and waterways enthusiasts in the common aim of restoring the canal, and the Caldon Canal Committee was formed in 1963. Committee members soon started work in clearing sections of the canal. In 1968 the Canal Committee was reformed as the Caldon Canal Society and registered as a charity, a more acceptable negotiating body for developing restoration plans, sponsoring working parties, and organising fund raising. Local and county authorities supported the canal restoration programme which commenced in August, and the B.W.B. undertook the major engineering work. Two years later, on 28 September 1974, the restored Caldon Canal was formally re-opened as a lasting tribute to its originator and engineer, James Brindley.

In 1977 agreement was reached with B.W.B. for the Leek Arm of the Caldon Canal to be restored, and in 1978 plans were submitted by Stoke-on-Trent City Council for the development of the Etruria Museum project at the junction of the Caldon and Trent and Mersey Canals. At last it seemed that new life was flowing back into the waterway, especially when Johnson Brothers, the local pottery manufacturers, commissioned their third purpose-built narrow boat, the *Milton*

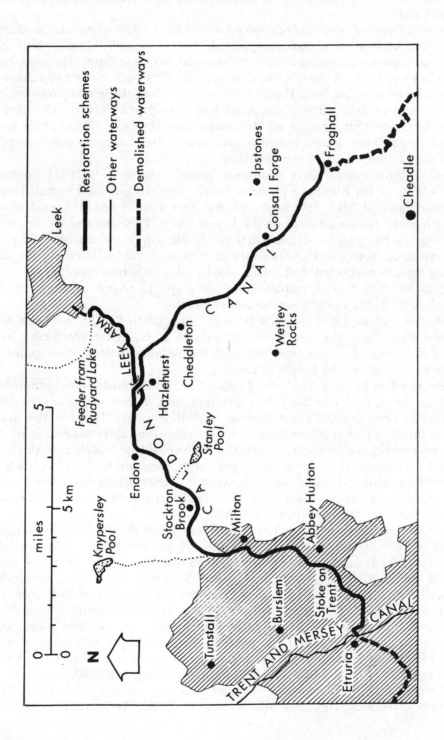

Map 8.—The Potteries
(1) Caldon Canal

Princess, late in 1978, to convey products between their various depots adjoining the Caldon Canal.

The theme of revival was also reinforced over Easter 1979 when a horse-drawn passenger trip boat service was inaugurated from Froghall Wharf, where the derelict canal warehouse was partially restored to act as a base. The trip boat now takes visitors through the Churnet valley, part of which is normally inaccessible except by canal or on foot. It also traverses a section of the waterway which, at one stage, was so decayed that the water had to be piped along it! The owners of the trip boat not only provide an 'insurance' that the canal would never again be allowed to fall into decay, but also gave many the chance to see the upper reaches of this unique canal for the first time.

Few realised how quickly that 'insurance' would need to be tested. It came all too soon when, to his horror, a pleasure boater moored on the Froghall length had the experience of being left 'high and dry' overnight. A serious breach in the canal bank drained the water away on 24 August 1979. This shut the section from Consall Forge to Froghall yet again. Fortunately the trip boats' season was nearly over, otherwise an even greater loss could have been incurred. Even so, the first engineering reports suggested that repairs could take over two months, once the contract was let. The B.W.B. responded quickly and managed to complete the repairs by 5 April 1980, in time for the Easter cruises.

Towards the end of 1979 the B.W.B. also managed to dredge the Leek Arm between the tunnel and the new terminus, outside Leek, where the feeder from Rudyard Lake joins the Arm, and enlarged the winding hole at that point to attract more boats to use the length of canal.

For a short while in early 1980 the Caldon Canal could boast two commercial carrying operations. One was the Johnsons' fleet, and the second stemmed from Stoke-on-Trent City Council's assumption of full responsibility for the maintenance of the canal towpath in their area. To raise the safety standards of the walkway, emergency works were undertaken between Planet Lock and Stockton Brook, and this involved a motor boat and butty bringing in 100-ton loads of limestone ballast and red ash shale each week to reconstitute the towpath and provide better access to it. Plans were also made to install mooring rings and seating, with future central government grants.

The B.W.B. continued their commitment to the canal during 1980 by re-lining Hazelhurst Aqueduct and waterproofing the whole structure. Unfortunately, this exhausted their meagre maintenance funds for the canal. When the Leek Tunnel was found to be unsafe in July, since the canal was still a 'remainder' waterway, the repair could not be given priority. By the end of the year, the tunnel remained closed, as it did throughout 1981. It was not until autumn 1982 that sufficient funds became available for structural surveys, and plans were made to de-water the tunnel over the winter period, aiming to re-open the length for the 1983 cruising season. Unfortunately, this was not to be. The cost of repair was estimated at £300,000, and that money was not available.

The closure of Leek Tunnel struck a sad note for the Stoke-on-Trent Boat Club, which celebrated its 25th anniversary in 1982. To commemorate the event they held a 'Gathering of Boats' on 24 July at their base at Endon, on a short arm off the Caldon Canal which they had taken over in 1976 to ensure that the re-opened canal was well used by boats. The founder members of the boat club were some of the most ardent campaigners for the restoration of the canal. It therefore proved a fitting reward when they heard that a B.W.B. Bill was being promoted in the 1981/82 parliamentary sesssion, to re-classify the whole of the Caldon Canal, and the Leek Branch between Denford and Wallgrange, as a 'Cruising Waterway'. Such a move offered the best guarantee possible that their hard-won canal would be maintained in future as a matter of priority. At last it seemed that the revival campaign had proved its worth in one of the major centres of the Industrial Revolution.

*   *   *   *   *

9.—NORTH WALES AND BORDER COUNTIES

The canals of North Wales and the Border Counties came under the same ownership in 1850, some five years after the merger between the Ellesmere and Chester Canal Company and the Birmingham and Liverpool Junction Canal Company to form the Shropshire Union Canal and Railway Company. The group of canals, with the involvement of the major shareholder, the London and North Western Railway Company, remained profitable, and thus did not suffer the same early decline, caused by the railways, as the other major canals, except in the Shropshire Coalfield area where canal subsidence forced the construction of a railway network for trade to continue at a high level.

The major decline of the canal network occurred after the Railway Act of 1921 which re-grouped the railway companies, including the Shropshire Union Canal and Railway Company, into one major operational unit. Thus the Shropshire Union Canal System came under the control of the London, Midland and Scottish Railway, and the tonnage carried on the canals quickly dropped. In 1929 the canals still carried 433,230 tons, but by 1940 this had fallen to 151,144 tons. A sharp decline in tonnage during the Second World War led to an L.M.S.R. Act of 1944 authorising the abandonment of the whole of the former Montgomeryshire Canal from Newtown to Carreghofa, together with the Guilsfield Branch; the Llanymynech branch to Frankton Junction and that to Weston; the line from Hurleston Junction, including the Prees, Whitchurch, Ellesmere and Llangollen branches; the old Shrewsbury Canal from Shrewsbury to Donnington, with the Newport branch and Humber Arm; and the remaining section of the Shropshire Canal. The loss of 175 miles of canal created little local dissent and only one line was saved, that from Llantisilio to Hurleston, which was needed as a water supply channel for the Autherley Junction to Ellesmere Port section of the Shropshire Union Main Line, which was to be retained.

The restoration movement in the area developed from the premise that pleasure craft were still allowed to use the water supply channel to Llangollen and Llantysilio. The beauty of the canal was well known to two of the Inland

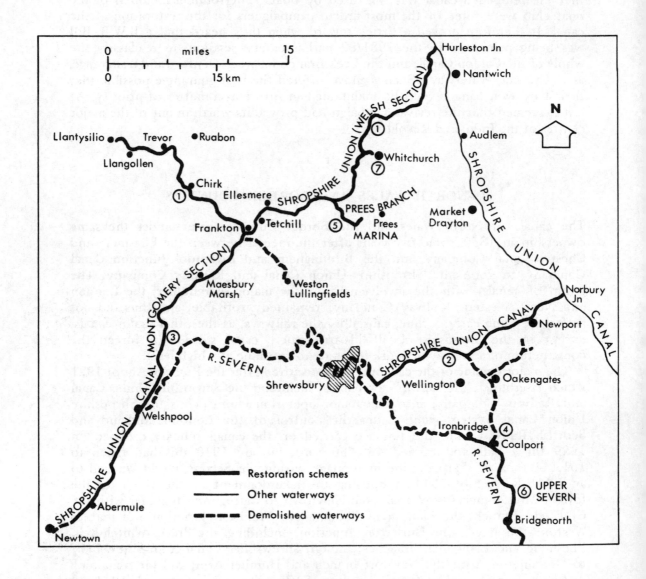

Map 9.—North Wales and Border Counties
(1) Llangollen Canal; (2) Shropshire Canal; (3) Montgomery Canal; (4) Coalport Canal and
Hay Inclined Plane; (5) Prees Branch; (6) Upper Severn Navigation; (7) Whitchurch Arm

Waterways Association founders, R. Aickman and L. T. C. Rolt. They, with fellow member and author, Eric de Maré, were thus quickly able to persuade other waterways enthusiasts that the Llangollen Canal must be retained. Fortunately, the I.W.A. gained considerable early support, especially from local canal engineers, and this, combined with the value of the canal as a water transfer line, had much to do with the success of the campaign to keep the canal from being blocked by lowered bridges. It is often said that success breeds success. This is true of the Llangollen Canal which, once it was agreed to use it for pleasure craft, became the centre of canal hire craft schemes promoted by R. Kerr, the Waterways Manager of the British Transport Commission, and local enthusiast, D. Wain.

The need to maintain the Llangollen Canal also proved to be the salvation of the first section of the Prees Branch, next to which the waterways' puddling clay pits were located. The extraction of this clay in the early 1960s, coupled with the growth of pleasure craft using the Llangollen Canal, enabled the scheme for restoring the Prees Branch and the development of a marina on it to be a viable proposition by the early 1970s.

The strength of the membership of the North Western Branch of the I.W.A. also led to the battle over the Shrewsbury and Newport Canals when the British Waterways Board proposed they should be de-watered in 1964. Although the campaign to restore the canals was ultimately unsuccessful, it later benefited the waterways restoration movement of the region in three ways. These were:

1. The development of substantial local support for the canals and their heritage;
2. The training of a large group of enthusiasts in the strategy of organising a restoration campaign;
3. The birth of the Shropshire Union Canal Society, which later provided the medium through which another major restoration scheme was able to develop.

Support for the retention of the remnants of the industrial heritage in the Shropshire Coalfield, considered to be the cradle of the Industrial Revolution, and the part played by the canal era in that revolution were naturally interlinked. Also, the growth of the new town of Telford and the enthusiasm of local industrial archaeologists, Barrie Trinder and Neil Cossons, led to the development of the Ironbridge Gorge Museum Trust in 1968, and the establishment of the 42-acre Open Air Museum at Blists Hill, with extensions at Coalbrook Dale and Coalport. The Hay Inclined Plane and the tub boat canal that serviced both the Blists Hill blast furnaces and the adjacent Brick and Tile Works, included within the museum site, were early targets for restoration. For, in their restored state, they offered the many visitors a clear example of the way in which the industrial revolution evolved in this inhospitable section of the Severn Gorge. The waterway restorationists thus participated with the industrial archaeologists in the restoration of this unique section of the former Shropshire Canal network between 1969 and 1975.

The Shropshire Union Canal Society (S.U.C.S.) originated from the failure of the Shrewsbury and Newport Canals restoration scheme. This group of enthusiasts, already over 300-strong when their first project failed, has since developed what must be the best-known of all current waterway restoration schemes, the Montgomeryshire Canal.

The S.U.C.S. turned their attention to the plight of the Montgomeryshire Canal following their first abortive campaign, which provided members with the necessary experience, abilities and skills. Their work has since been recognised by the Prince of Wales's Committee. Such recognition now provides the stimulus for the group to deal with the almost insurmountable problems created by lowered main road bridges and road development schemes.

In view of the considerable significance of the Montgomery campaign to the development of the waterway restoration movement as a whole, it is perhaps worth spelling out what has been involved and achieved so far. The problems stem back to 6 February 1939 when the canal banks burst about half a mile below Welsh Frankton flight of locks. Stop planks were put in, but these left a mile of drained canal and some boats were trapped on the navigable section to the south. Although there was a statutory obligation for the L.M.S. Railway Company, as the owners, to repair the breach, because traffic revenue was less than £40 per year they deliberately played a waiting game. There were local objections, but the boat owners were individually 'bought off' and the breach was never repaired. Between legal abandonment in 1944 and 1967 a short stretch of the canal at Newtown was sold, and a few minor road bridges were lowered as the structures became unfit for modern traffic.

Moves towards restoration developed first in 1967 when the Shropshire Union Canal Society (S.U.C.S.) pressed the British Waterways Board (B.W.B.) to repair a collapsed weir on the River Tanat, which supplied water to the canal's central section. This action was successful and led to the S.U.C.S.'s decision to launch a campaign to restore the whole canal.

Matters came to a head in 1969 when proposals were made to use the canal bed through Welshpool as a town by-pass. Local protestors and S.U.C.S. members united to resist this plan and won a victory at the Public Enquiry held to examine the road development scheme. During this campaign one of the major events of waterway restoration history occurred. The S.U.C.S., in conjunction with Graham Palmer and the I.W.A. working party group (which became the Waterway Recovery Group in 1970), organised the Welshpool 'Big Dig' on the weekend of 18/19 October 1969. This was a spectacular success. The whole canal in central Welshpool was cleaned up during the 'Dig' by nearly 200 volunteer 'navvies', and the publicity and support that their efforts gained was a turning point for the future of the canal.

It did not, however, safeguard the other sections of the line, and a minor bridge at Refail was lowered in 1971. That year two greater problems emerged, when it was learned that two main roads crossing the canal were likely to be improved. One scheme, on the A5, was later temporarily shelved, but the other around the village of Abermule went ahead. Fortunately, the S.U.C.S. were able to persuade the Department of Environment to provide a bridge offering navigable headroom.

The 'Big Dig' at Welshpool led to the complete restoration and re-gating of Welshpool Town lock, and under a scheme, 'Operation Eyesore', the Welshpool Town Council paid part of the costs for the town section to be dredged. This enabled a trip boat, *Powys Princess*, to run along the town section of the canal, and attract more interest in the waterway.

In October 1973 a marked change in attitude towards the future of the canal was apparent, with the announcement that the Prince of Wales's Committee, together with the Variety Club of Great Britain, intended to give full support to the complete restoration of a seven-mile section of the canal between Welshpool (Gallowstree Bank Bridge) and Ardleen. As a result, the Montgomery Waterway Restoration Steering Group was formed to administer the £350,000 environmental revival scheme. The restoration was to be a joint effort between the B.W.B. and S.U.C.S. The Prince of Wales showed his personal support by touring the works and then officially re-opened the Welshpool Town Lock on 23 May 1974. Later that year the I.W.A. and the Waterways Recovery Group (W.R.G.) announced plans to restore the first four miles of the canal from Welsh Frankton to Queen's Head, subject to satisfactory agreements.

Restoration work quickly proceeded on the first part of the seven miles, together with the work on the Pool Quay Locks. The S.U.C.S. separately worked on the restoration of the Carreghofa Locks, further along the line. A slipway was also planned for the canal at Welshpool to allow that section to be more readily used by trailable craft, and the Manpower Services Commission financed a Job Creation Project to clear the towpath and wharf in Maesbury Marsh.

By 1976 over three miles of the Prince of Wales's section had been restored, and in July that year the Prince inspected progress and inaugurated a trip boat, *Heulwen-Sunshine*, designed and built to accommodate the physically handicapped.

However, royal patronage and the backing of various official bodies did not mean that the future of the canal was safe. In 1975 plans were announced by Powys County Council to culvert the humpback Walls Bridge, south of Llanymynech, and in 1976 by the Welsh Office for a by-pass at Ardleen. The latter plans offered no navigable headroom even though it was on part of the canal that the Prince of Wales's Committee planned to re-open. Fortunately, solutions were found. At Walls Bridge a temporary culvert was built across the canal, on a five-year lease, to allow heavy traffic to reach a local quarry, yet not stopping the canal from ultimate restoration. For the Ardleen by-pass a scheme was devised whereby one of the two nearby Burgedin Locks would be removed and a new lock inserted beyond Maesbury; the intervening level could then be dredged to lower the canal by some three feet, thus offering navigable headroom under both the planned by-pass bridge and also a second dropped bridge at Maesbury. The difficulty with this option was the additional expense. It meant that when the first stage of the Prince of Wales's project was due to be completed in 1978, only just over five of the seven miles could be re-opened to through navigation, and work on the remainder was suspended until the funds could be raised to build the new lock and lower the bed of the canal. This did not deter craft from making good use of the restored five-mile section, especially when a winding hole below Burgedin Locks was made fully operational in summer 1978.

Although work had come to a halt on the first 'Seven Miles', restoration had not stopped elsewhere. For during 1978 and 1979 the B.W.B. repaired the Vyrnwy Aqueduct, and part of the adjacent section of the canal between it and Carreghofa locks was also dredged. The locks themselves were also being restored by the S.U.C.S., who had already invested some £7,000 in their works. It therefore came as a great shock when Powys County Council indicated that it wanted to lower Williams Bridge, midway between the locks and Vyrnwy Aqueduct, and could not afford to rebuild it at a higher level. The council also wanted to verify its legal rights over the canal bridges and decided to seek a High Court Writ of Mandamus to clarify its responsibilities.

The S.U.C.S. and I.W.A. did not let this battle go unfought. Their campaign to save the bridge included a visit from the Prince of Wales, a picture on the front page of *The Times,* and a telegram to the Prime Minister, but to no avail. At a Court Hearing on 15 March 1979 it was confirmed that the County Council had the legal right to lower the bridge. This they did in July 1980.

Even so, 1979 was not all bad news for the revival campaign. Powys Council Planning Information Service started to distribute leaflets describing the canal and its path to restoration. The Prince of Wales's Committee appointed a Montgomery Canal Interpretive Projects Officer to co-ordinate and develop public interest in the Welsh Section of the Canal, and especially stressed the value of the amenity. At the same time, the I.W.A. and W.R.G. were making considerable progress re-building the locks on the Welsh Frankton flight. It was this latter project which, in September 1980, provided the venue for an 'Open Day' on the canal to which some 400 councillors and government officials were invited, to see what the volunteers had achieved. The visitors were also shown the S.U.C.S. progress at Carreghofa Locks, where work on one of the pair of locks neared completion.

The 'Open Day' was aimed at building on the commitment expressed in the Shropshire County Structure Plan that 'nothing should be done or permitted to be done, or tolerated by default which would be contrary to ultimate restoration for navigation'. It was hoped that when the Powys Structure Plan was prepared later in the year it might offer the same commitment, especially when it was debated by the Council in autumn 1980.

To co-ordinate all this effort in both England and Wales a new umbrella organisation, the Montgomery Waterway Restoration Trust, was formed in mid-1980. This developed the rôle of the Prince of Wales's Committee over the whole canal. The Trust held its first meeting in June 1980 and on 11 July 1980 the Prince of Wales visited the canal, to talk to the Committee of the new Trust and to inspect progress.

The Montgomery Trust adopted a strategy of directing resources, as they became available, to areas of selected priority. The first priority was the opening of the four miles to Queens Head, including the Welsh Frankton Locks, repairing the 1936 breach and restoring the leaking Perry Aqueduct. Secondly, it planned to extend the Prince of Wales's section northwards by taking the canal past the road crossings at Ardleen and Maerdy, which involved the lowering of the bed of the canal for a mile and building a new lock at an estimated cost of £2 million. The remainder of the Trust's programme included the connection of the first two stages, the reclamation of the dry length at Pant, and six culverted road crossings, followed by the extension of the navigation southwards through Welshpool towards Newtown.

The first stage came a little nearer to completion when, on 10 October 1981, John Biffen, M.P., took part in the ceremony to install a new top gate at Welsh Frankton. While he was not able to promise any government finance, it was an opportunity for the I.W.A. Manchester Branch to hand over a cheque for £2,500, the first instalment from their 'Lock Gate Appeal' fund. By that time the I.W.A. and W.R.G., through the Trust, had spent some £40,000 on restoration of the locks. To commemorate the impressive work of the volunteers, the W.R.G. prepared a medal to be purchased by anyone who had worked on the canal restoration.

The re-gating ceremony enabled the W.R.G. to set a target for the completion of the re-building of the whole Welsh Frankton flight for May 1983. They were assisted in this aim by the receipt of a £1,000 Shell Waterways Award in early 1982. At last all seemed to be progressing fairly well, especially when it was learned that the Powys Structure Plan had been amended to read, 'there will be a presumption in favour of proposals to use the Montgomery Canal for recreational purposes. No permission should be granted for any development inconsistent with the restoration of the canal north of Whitehouse Bridge (Welshpool)'. This did not cover the whole of the canal line into Newtown, but it seemed to pave the way for most of the Trust's aims to be achieved. Subsequently the Secretary of State for Wales approved an amendment to the plan, protecting the whole of the line in Wales for ultimate restoration. This offered an added stimulus to the hard-fought campaign.

Suddenly, in 1982, the stormclouds gathered again, when the B.W.B. issued a surprise statement: 'Future restoration of the canal is not certain. No new Works to be commenced after work at Frankton and Carreghofa is completed. The situation will be reviewed in the Autumn'. The Montgomery Trust met with Sir Frank Price, Chairman of B.W.B. on 5 August 1982 to establish why the Board had issued such an ultimatum. It was agreed by all parties at this meeting that 'an economic study should be undertaken to assess the benefits arising from the restoration of the Montgomery Canal'.

W. S. Atkins and Partners were appointed in December 1982 to undertake this study, which was commissioned by all the groups involved in the Montgomery Waterway Restoration Trust, principally the Welsh Development Agency, the B.W.B., Shropshire County Council, the I.W.A., the Wales Tourist Board, and the Development Board of Mid-Wales. Work started on the £40,000 research project in January 1983 and its report was due to be completed by mid-April, after which the Trust hoped that they could proceed with new vigour.

The consultants undertook their work, and the W.R.G. continued on the Welsh Frankton flight. They also instructed professional engineers, working as volunteers, to undertake an extensive soil survey to establish what additional work needed to be undertaken before they could re-water the dry section through to Queens Head, where the new A5 improvement scheme was planned to give navigable clearance over the canal. Further down the line, work by the S.U.C.S. at Carreghofa Locks was nearly completed; the delivery of the final set of gates was due in spring 1983. Even the section of canal between Newtown and Welshpool was getting a new lease of life, thanks to a team from the Community Task Force, who were clearing the canal between Abermule and Garthmyl, financed by an M.S.C. Community Enterprise programme. However, progress after that very much depended on the Consultants' report. To maintain the momentum in the interim, the local I.W.A. Branch organised a Rally of Boats at Frankton Junction on 28/30 May 1983. This concentrated minds on the main task of raising sufficient finance for the restoration efforts to proceed.

Events elsewhere in the region have tended to be overshadowed by the importance of the Montgomery campaign. It was the thrust of that campaign which prompted a second attempt to revive interest in the Shrewsbury and Newport Canals. This was undertaken by a new Shrewsbury and Newport Canal Group, formed in 1976. They endeavoured to gain local council support to protect the line of the canals, and undertook substantial towpath clearance between Uffington and Rodington, as well as restoring Brick Kiln Bridge. Unfortunately, the group did not get the backing it had hoped for, and, in 1981, decided it could not achieve its long-term aims. Even so, in 1978 it did play a small part in the restoration of the former, 1835, Howard Street Canal Company warehouse in Shrewsbury, at the old terminus of the canal, which was converted into a theatre complex under a Job Creation scheme. Similarly, some members were also involved in the Hadley Park Locks Project, organised by the Wrekin College Canal Restoration Group, who gained a £100 Shell Waterways Award for their work in clearing the towpath and lock surrounds to preserve this part of the old Shropshire Canal as a nature reserve. Other than that, the only part of the line which has been saved is the short section in the Blists Hill site of the Ironbridge Gorge Museum.

In the light of this lack of local commitment to the waterways, it was surprising that, just as the second battle for the Shrewsbury Canal link was accepted as lost, so another scheme to link Shrewsbury to the navigable river and canal network was being proposed. In fact, the idea came from a member of Bridgnorth Council, who thought that it would be a good thing if boats could again navigate the Upper Severn.

A detailed survey of the river through to Ironbridge was made in summer 1982, and an outline review was conducted up river to Shrewsbury. The result was a plan in December 1982 to make the river navigable for pleasure craft, from the present head of navigation below Bewdley to Ironbridge. The first stage of the scheme envisaged the construction of 13 weirs and locks between Stourport and Ironbridge, using the techniques developed on the Upper Avon. The scheme received initial support from Bridgnorth Town Council, Bewdley Town Council, and the Ironbridge Gorge Museum Trust. Several other bodies also expressed interest, including the members of Stourport Town Council and the I.W.A.; however, Shropshire County Council rejected the plan on the grounds of cost. The aim of the proposers will be to create a Trust to carry the scheme forward. In the interim, it was accepted that a fully-detailed scheme should be prepared by Sir Alexander Gibb and Partners, or similar consultants, in the hope that the cost will be funded by the I.W.A. and local councils along the route. However, much depends on convincing the Severn Trent Water Authority and the local anglers that more boats on the river will be acceptable.

In contrast, one group who needed no convincing of the potential of visiting boats was the Whitchurch Town Council. They had been unable to benefit from the growing number of pleasure boats passing along the nearby Llangollen Canal, as the Whitchurch Arm was abandoned under the 1944 Act, and had since been partly infilled. Following local interest about the possibility of generating additional trade, the Town Clerk was asked to produce a preliminary report for the council, in early 1982, which examined the problems and advantages from restoration of the Arm. A meeting with B.W.B., I.W.A., and local canal society representatives persuaded the council to vote unanimously for a full feasibility study to evaluate how the one-mile Arm, which terminates in the centre of the town, could be restored. On 12 July 1982 the University of Aston's Faculty of Civil Engineering were commissioned to carry out the study as part of the following year's students' work experience project. It is hoped that their report will be completed by summer 1983.

When one looks and sees how successful the early revival of the Llangollen canal has been, it is easy to forget that, even after a canal is re-opened, it can soon be closed again! This has been the experience on the upper section of the Llangollen Canal over the past few years. First, there were the problems of the Pontcysyllte Aqueduct itself, which needed major repair in the early 1970s. Subsequently, in July 1978, seepage under some canal-side houses at Llangollen caused the canal to be closed and drained for another four months, at the height of the tourist season. Then again, in March 1982, a serious breach washed away part of the canal bank, west of Trevor. On this occasion the repair work took nearly a year to complete and cost over £250,000. Fortunately, this length of the canal is a major water transfer supply link, and the cost of the repairs can be justified on this basis alone. It does, however, raise the issue of the problem of keeping canals open once they have been revived, especially when they generate little direct income. There is no doubt that this was what concerned the B.W.B. when they called for a viability review of the restoration of the Montgomery Canal, before allowing the plan to proceed. In many ways the Montgomery Canal could become the major revival project for the 1980s—also hopefully, the one which is most likely to be achieved. The restored canal can bring new life and a new look to this little-known and unspoilt area of the Welsh border lands, without destroying the beauty and peace which visitors might seek on this most scenic rural waterway.

10.–THE GREAT OUSE VALLEY

The river Great Ouse and its associated tributaries that drain into the Wash have provided the region with both a transport and drainage network. The problems of the drainage of the low-lying fenland area have taxed men from earliest times. The history of the drainage of the Fens has been so well recorded by H. C. Darby, in his work *The Draining of the Fens,* that there is no need to dwell here on the extensive transformation of the lower reaches of the Great Ouse into a rich agricultural area readily serviced by water. As commerce moved away from the waterways to other speedier means of transport, so pleasure craft appeared on the waterways. The Cam has long been associated with skiff and punt. At the turn of the 19th century it was thus considered viable to restore part of the Ouse Navigation for pleasure craft. It was equally useful in the late 1930s for the River Board to seek to restore the navigation through to Bedford for both maintenance and pleasure craft.

The war years affected the river both through lack of dredging and the loss of pleasure craft. However, pleasure craft soon reappeared on the river, and local concern about restrictions to the cruising network grew. It was in this climate that the Inland Waterways Association, Fenlands Branch, was formed in October 1949, and the Bedford Boat Club by like-minded people in 1950. By then the idea of restoring the Ouse through to Bedford was a well-discussed subject, but it needed additional public support before the scheme could be launched. The Lower Avon restoration scheme provided an example, and with support from members of Bedford Rotary Club the restoration scheme was projected. A rousing speech by P. Scott, by then well-known for his support of the waterways, combined with reports of the recent re-opening of the Northern Section of the Stratford-on-Avon Canal, set the scheme in motion.

At first the Great Ouse restoration scheme made rapid progress, with the re-opening of Bedford Town Lock in 1955, but the loss of the leading members of the committee, combined with the severe economic climate of the mid-1950s, retarded progress in getting Cardington Lock restored and the initial impetus of the campaign was lost.

The local waterways campaign was rejuvenated by the formation of the East Anglian Waterways Association in 1958, led by the energetic former Honorary Secretary of the I.W.A., L. A. Edwards. This group, based on representatives from boat clubs of the waterways draining into the Wash, gained its strength from the tremendous upsurge of interest in boating on the Ouse and Nene, and on the drains termed the Middle Level that connected these two major rivers.

One of the first tasks of the E.A.W.A. was to clarify the legality of the Navigation Rights over the River Ouse from St Ives. The I.W.A. solicitor, R. S. W. Pollard, provided proof that the Public Right of Navigation still existed. The E.A.W.A, together with the I.W.A. Fenlands Branch, were thus able to take direct steps to support the revival of the G.O.R.S. campaign to re-open the river through to Bedford. In November 1961 the River Board started work in restoring Cardington Lock, and the Society offered to provide lower gates

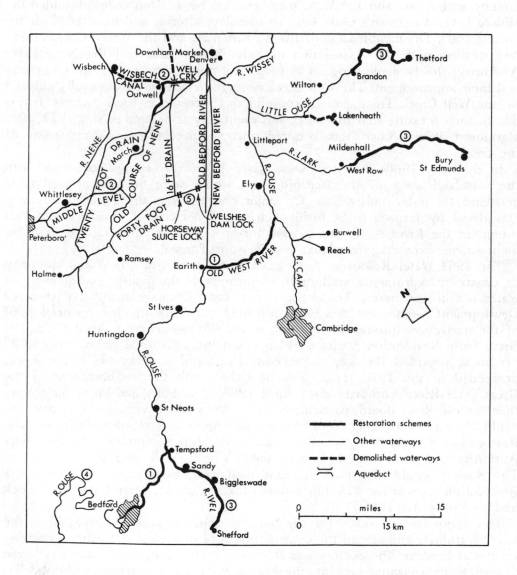

Map 10.—The Great Ouse Valley
(1) Great Ouse and Old West River; (2) Well Creek; (3) Ivel and Lark and Little Ouse;
(4) Upper Great Ouse; (5) Horseway Sluice Lock

to retain navigation access, at a cost of £1,000. The lock was re-opened in February 1963.

At this time the I.W.A. founder, R. Aickman, and chairman, L. Munk, led a campaign to revive the ailing Middle Level navigation, Well Creek. Some local boating enthusiasts and E.A.W.A. members, led by L. Doubleday, founded the Middle Level Waterman's Club, both to stimulate interest and to offer pilots for visiting craft. The combination of I.W.A., E.A.W.A. and the Waterman's Club, in co-operation with the Association of Nene River Clubs and the Nene River Authority, slowly made progress in increasing public interest in the waterways and their improvement. The Well Creek restoration scheme, successfully pursued by the Well Creek Trust, had its roots in this increase in local interest. It was due to their pressure that the Creek was eventually re-opened in May 1975, after Marmount Priory Lock was restored and volunteers had cleared parts of the Creek.

In the early 1960s the Great Ouse River Authority became concerned with the washland areas of the Bedford Ouse which were being converted from grassland to arable cultivation. Of major concern was the summer flooding, considered by farmers to be highly detrimental because of toxic residue. This prompted the River Authority to plan for an extensive land drainage improvement scheme extending from Roxton to Newport Pagnell.

The 1963 Water Resources Act placed an obligation on the Water Authority to construct hydrometric stations to monitor both the quality and quantity of water within river basins. The availability of Land Drainage and Water Resource Development Grants for this work provided the basis for the restoration of of the navigation through to Bedford, which was re-opened in April 1978. The Great Ouse Restoration Society, which raised the additional finance of £5,000 per lock, provided the key to success. The rapid pace at which the works proceeded in the 1970s must also be linked with the establishment of the Great Ouse River Authority on 1 April 1965. This body had far wider powers than the old River Board, particularly in its rôle as the navigation authority, and could license boats, and from the revenue provide navigation facilities. The Restoration Society was therefore able to develop a rapport with the River Authority and press them to re-open the link between Roxton and Cardington. The Society could also back its aims with cash, because it had launched a Restoration Appeal for £15,000 towards further works, after Cardington Lock had been revived in 1963.

The major breakthrough for the Society came in January 1968, when the River Authority announced the construction of a new weir and water measuring station at Roxton. The Society was able to offer the additional finance required to introduce a navigation lock into the scheme, and work commenced without delay. The new Roxton Lock was opened by the Duke of Bedford on 12 August 1972.

Even before the work at Roxton was completed, plans were being considered for a new lock upstream at Great Barford. There was little land drainage benefit, and it seemed likely that much of the estimated cost of £140,000 would fall on the limited navigation budget. Fortunately, in October 1972, Bedford Town

Council agreed to contribute £100,000 towards the cost, as a way of ensuring that the river was re-opened to Bedford.

The Great Ouse Restoration Society also offered £5,000 and offered to provide volunteer labour for some of the work, if this would reduce the overall cost. Subsequently an agreement was reached whereby volunteers, organised by the I.W.A., Cambridge Branch, and the Waterways Recovery Group, were responsible for the demolition of the old lock structures and for recovering the bricks to be used for gabions to protect the river bank. The scheme got underway in April 1974 and took nearly two years to complete because the site was flooded completely on two occasions.

In 1973, the River Authority announced its plans to construct a new lock at Willington. This was to avoid the need to replace the former intervening lock at Old Mills. Work commenced in June 1975, and the Society agreed to contribute a further £5,000 towards the navigation works. Such rapid progress was made that the Society and the Great Ouse River Division of the new Anglian Water Authority, which had superseded the River Authority on 1 April 1974, were able to celebrate a double re-opening on 8 May 1976. A flotilla of craft took a party of guests from Roxton to above Willington and back, and the Society handed over £10,000 at a small ceremony at Great Barford Lock.

Work started in August 1976 on the final barrier to navigation. This scheme, at Castle Mills, included a new lock, new automatic sluices and other works. It also involved the demolition of the old staunch below the former lock. The complete scheme was expected to cost over £370,000, and the Society agreed to find a further £5,000 for additional navigation equipment. The lock was completed in April 1978 and the Great Ouse Restoration Society celebrated the re-opening through to Bedford by a programme of events in Bedford over the week-end of 28/29 May 1978. For the Society, this was the culmination of a 27-year campaign. The task completed, the Society decided to wind itself up, and the residue of its funds was transferred in January 1979 to the Well Creek Trust.

Some of the members would have liked to see it promote further developments up the Great Ouse valley, where the Water Authority was continuing its scheme of water control works. In fact, in 1974, the Eastern Sports Council had produced *A Regional Strategy for Water Recreation* which suggested 'no further development of the river upstream from Bedford be allowed'. At that time the Society had tried to get the statement changed, but without success, even though it was known that the Water Authority planned to continue to develop their flood alleviation works upstream. Much the same apathy also befell the enthusiasts' ideas for restoring the navigation on the River Ivel through to Biggleswade, and for a longer-term scheme to link a restored Little Ouse Navigation from Thetford to a restored Waveney Navigation at Bungay, although the East Anglian Waterways Association try to keep both schemes alive.

1978 was a year of success for the Great Ouse. But further downstream concern was developing for some parts of the Middle Level Navigations, particularly for Horseway Lock which was falling into further disrepair. In 1979 it was heard that changes in the land levels could also mean that a section of the west Middle Level system might be lost to navigation. Negotiations were opened between the I.W.A. and E.A.W.A. and the Middle Level Commissioners to ensure the navigations were protected. Events unfortunately went from bad to worse—Horseway Lock was closed and padlocked, as it was deemed unsafe. The I.W.A. and E.A.W.A. both maintained that the permanent closure was not justified, as a right of navigation existed, and threatened a Relator action to prove their point. They also considered legal action, when they learned that Bevill's Level and the South West Section of the Old River Nene might also be blocked off by new sluice gates. After considerable wrangling and threatened injunctions, the Middle Level Commissioners, in 1982, agreed to restore Horseway Lock and also to build a new lock at Ramsey to keep open the South Western section of the Middle Levels, where the water levels were to be changed. Unfortunately, during the intervening period, the closure of Horseway Lock had led to the deterioration of Welshes Dam Lock, and the I.W.A. approached the Anglian Water Authority, under whose jurisdiction it fell, to seek its full restoration to coincide with the re-opening of Horseway Lock in 1984.

Elsewhere in the region events were on a slightly brighter note. In 1979 the Recreation Advisory Committee of the A.W.A. recommended that a further two-mile section of the Lark Navigation be re-opened to Mildenhall. The A.W.A. estimated the cost at between £40,000 and £60,000, and decided to seek local authority aid. The local Forest Heath District Council supported the plan, but because of the financial climate was not immediately able to make the 70 per cent contribution sought by the A.W.A. This did not deter the I.W.A. Cambridge Branch, who firmly advocated the revival scheme and investigated the creation of a restoration society to promote it, together with the long-term idea of re-opening the whole navigation through to Bury St Edmunds. These plans received a boost when a new 200-berth marina and chalet park was opened at Isleham Lock in 1982, thus bringing more traffic to the little-used lower reaches of this attractive fenland river.

The year 1980 similarly brought good news for those who feared that the navigable lodes off the river Cam might have to be closed due to deteriorating banks. The A.W.A. announced it would be spending some £400,000 over the following 20 years, to rebuild the Lode banks and to dredge the channels. The first of these works started in 1981.

In much the same way North Bedfordshire Borough Council's plan to develop the river in Bedford also got underway in 1980, and a new marina, canoe slalom course, moorings, and a riverside walk, were developed to enhance the amenities of the river within the town boundaries.

Looking back, it can be seen that the creation of the all-embracing Anglian Water Authority provided that vital link in the restoration chain, with the facility to combine its land drainage and amenity development rôles to revive and preserve navigations. However, it really depends on the ability of the local waterways enthusiasts to gain public support and commitment to their goals for anything to be achieved. This will be the key to any future restoration of the Ivel, Lark and Little Ouse Navigations. The success of the Well Creek Trust and the Great Ouse Restoration Society in bringing their respective restorations through to satisfactory conclusions, must encourage new targets to be set, so that the growing interest in, and demand for, further extensions to the waterways of the area can be satisfied.

The fortunes of the waterways of the Great Ouse Valley have changed drastically over the years. It now appears that the other derelict navigations in the valley may be restored, as local demand for recreational water space grows.

*   *   *   *   *

11.–NORFOLK AND SUFFOLK

East Anglia, with its many sheltered inlets and tidal rivers, has from earliest times offered ease of transport by water. The area known as the Broads perhaps offered the most comprehensive system of interconnected waterways, and thus it was the rivers Bure, Yare, and Waveney, together with Great Yarmouth Haven, that were subject to some of the earliest Navigations Acts in 1670, 1722, 1747, and 1772 respectively. The river Stour was made navigable as early as 1705 and substantially improved under an Act of 1781, and the adjacent Ipswich and Stowmarket Navigation, based on the river Gipping, was made navigable under an Act of 1790; the river Blythe Navigation was opened from Halesworth to Blythburgh in 1757. The Broadland rivers and the river Blythe were worked by Norfolk Wherries, whilst the Stour and Gipping were worked by Thames sailing barges and specially-built Stour lighters. After the coming of the railways, traffic declined quickly on the southern rivers, but Norfolk Wherries continued to work the Broadland waterways until well after 1900.

Constable drew early attention to the beauty of the Stour Valley, but pleasure traffic did not develop on the river, except for a few rowing skiffs. The Broads, on the other hand, had become a fashionable boating area by 1880, with a wide range of small craft, large sailing cutters, and adapted sailing wherries available for hire by the week. Since that time the hire craft industry has continued to grow, and the cruising season has gradually extended to attract many thousands of devotees each year. Thus many parts of the area have now almost reached saturation point at the height of the season.

With such interest in the pleasure use of these waterways it is thus rather surprising that any of them were allowed to go out of active use. The answer seems to lie in the demise of commercial craft, combined with the costs and problems of maintaining the navigational works, and in the attitude of the landowners of property adjacent to the waterways. The loss of commercial craft meant the loss of tolls to pay for lock maintenance, whilst the pursuits of the pleasure boaters were not always in harmony with the ideals of the landowners. Thus by the early 1900s the navigation locks were already poorly maintained, and, except on the Stour where the lower four locks were renewed in the 1930s, soon prevented craft from sailing upstream.

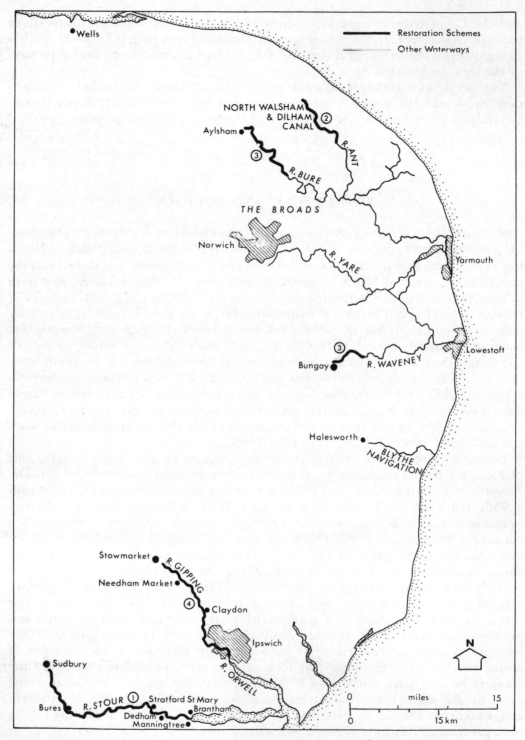

Map 11.—Norfolk and Suffolk
(1) River Stour; (2) North Walsham and Dilham Canal; (3) Bure and Waveney Navigations;
(4) Gipping Navigation

In the waterway restoration era one of the earliest navigations to receive attention was the river Stour. One of the early members of the Inland Waterways Association was L. A. Edwards, an enthusiast whose interest in the waterways of East Anglia had led him to attempt the majority of them in the late 1930s. One of the first pleas for a campaign to restore the navigation was made to the few enthusiasts of the area in November 1946. Surprisingly, because the estuary navigations were perhaps so good, the I.W.A. gained few supporters in the area and the appeal went by default.

Edwards continued his lone campaign to revive interest in the river and other derelict East Anglian waterways, but with little success. It was not until 1953 that any prospect of restoration emerged, following a surprise request from the secretary of the North Walsham Canal Company for advice. Soon afterwards the Chelmsford Boat Club, through their chairman, J. E. Marriage, took an interest in the restoration of the river Stour, and started the 'Save the Stour' campaign.

By 1955 an engineering survey of the Dilham Canal was made by the I.W.A. consulting engineer, C. Boucher, and a small committee formed to consider the revival of the derelict Upper Reaches of the rivers Bure and Waveney. Edwards led the campaign, which was promoted in an article in *Motor Boat and Yachting* of March 1956, when the case for restoring all three waterways was made. The Broadland Society, later the Broads Society, was formed in June 1956, but after a successful start, revealed the deep conflict between local landowners and those who promoted the Broadland Pleasure Craft industry. This stunted progress. Boucher conducted an engineering survey for the restoration of the derelict navigations of the Bure and Waveney at this time, but little positive action resulted.

Edwards and other local enthusiasts formed the East Anglian Waterways Association in March 1958. They set out both to prove legal rights to use navigations and to gain as much publicity as they could to promote the public support for their aims.

The 1960s saw slow progress on the river Stour as well as on the Broadland waterways. When the chance came in 1967 to restore the branch of the Dilham Canal, the Dilham Dyke through to Dilham Staithe, the E.A.W.A. became a limited liability company and undertook the restoration work to re-open the dyke. Similarly, in order to re-open the lower reaches of the river Stour, the Stour Action Committee became the River Stour Trust, Ltd., in 1968. It was immediately plunged into battle over the Brantham barrage scheme. With little money and no financial support from the parent I.W.A., it was forced to accept boat rollers around the barrage, rather than a lock—and an empty promise by the then River Authority of future navigation improvements upstream.

It was not until 1974 that progress could be made, when the Stour Trust sought and gained permission from the new Anglian Water Authority to restore Flatford Lock, and in the Broadland area the new North Norfolk District Council reviewed the amenity potential of the North Walsham and Dilham Canal.

In September that year the I.W.A. formed a new branch in Ipswich to cover Norfolk and Suffolk. Its Steering Committee immediately reviewed the restoration potential of its waterways, and highlighted the river Gipping, or the Ipswich and Stowmarket Navigation as it is locally known, as its first project.

Of prime importance in 1975 was the progress made by the restoration to full navigational use of Flatford Lock by the River Stour Trust. The formal re-opening ceremony on 29 March 1975 set the scene for progress on the other locks of the lower river, and working parties started to clear Stratford St Mary's Lock, towards subsequent restoration. Plans were also made by the I.W.A. Ipswich Branch, to start work on restoring some sections of the Gipping Navigation, and even the re-opening of the derelict Blythe Navigation was discussed.

In the Broadlands area, plans progressed for the re-opening of the North Walsham and Dilham Canal, a steering committee for a planned local Canal Society was formed. The Broads Committee of the Anglian Water Authority considered the restoration of the derelict Bure and Waveney Navigations, with the active support of the Water Space Amenity Advisory Commission. However, the financial climate at the close of 1975 meant that the prospect of early progress on either of these projects seemed bleak.

Unfortunately, a dispute in 1976 over the proposed terms of the Anglian Water Authority's Bill dampened hopes of an early resolution of the legal problems of the river Stour, and refusal of permission in 1977 for the River Stour Trust to restore Stratford St Mary Lock placed yet another barrier in the way of re-opening 'Constable's river' to craft. The Anglian Water Authority's Bill was debated in the House of Lords that year. They ruled in favour of the public Right of Navigation on the river, but this did not preclude the A.W.A., who became the navigation authority, from proposing by-laws which could substantially restrict navigation usage, especially their proposal to ban powered craft from 21 miles of the overall 24 miles of river navigation. When the Stour Trust heard these plans it mounted a campaign to alter the proposal. The A.W.A. refused to move, so the Trust decided to force the issue to a Public Enquiry, which was ultimately held in Colchester in June 1981. Even so, the dispute did not deter the Trust from pressing forward during 1978 with its plans. In fact, they organised two Job Creation schemes: one was to facilitate the restoration of an old Stour lighter, recovered from the mud; the other was the complete restoration of the main arm of Sudbury Basin, which had become filled with rubble. This complemented the work of the local dramatic society, who were converting the large derelict former waterside grain warehouse into a theatre. The basin restoration scheme was estimated at some £40,000. Fortunately, the Manpower Services Commission provided some £25,000 for the wages of the nine men employed by the Trust for a year, but the Trust had to find the balance for materials and hire of equipment. Trust members raised a substantial amount, and grants were also received from Babergh District Council, the Pilgrim Trust, and the I.W.A., who made a £2,500 contribution from their National Waterways Restoration and Development Fund. It was hoped that restoration would be completed by May 1979, but the wet winter and spring delayed the project until October that year, when it was completed.

In 1979 the enthusiasts focussed their attention on the future of the Broads, and the creation of the new Broads Authority. The journal, *Waterways World,* carried a review of the Broadland navigations, and especially highlighted the derelict sections of the rivers Bure and Waveney, noting that on the Bure light craft could still reach Aylesham, if they could be portaged around the locks (three of which were derelict, and two had disappeared), because the former navigation levels were still generally maintained. Similarly, on the Waveney, craft could still traverse the four miles to Bungay, if they could be carried past the three derelict locks. The article also mentioned the Dilham Canal, which could be used by canoes as navigation rights still existed, but noted that various earlier restoration schemes had not made any progress.

It was to the North Walsham and Dilham Canal that the newly-formed Norwich I.W.A. Branch turned its attention in March 1979, especially when it was learned that a bridge over the entrance section to the navigation was likely to collapse. The Branch alerted the new Broads Authority who arranged for the bridge to become a Listed Structure, and put forward plans for its restoration and for the clearance of the canal between Tonnage Bridge and Honing Lock. Various difficulties prevented the I.W.A. Branch from making immediate progress, but by 1982 the bridge had been re-built by its new owner, and much of the first section of the canal line had been cleared of undergrowth, which had almost blocked the canal route to Honing Lock, by the I.W.A. and other volunteers. What future work is undertaken on the Dilham Canal very much depends on the owners of the waterway, and on the difficulty of achieving an acceptable balance between wild life and enthusiasts exercising their navigation rights.

In 1979, the Ipswich and Stowmarket Navigation (Gipping Navigation) was reconsidered for revival. John Marriage wrote an article in *Waterways World* on the state of the line. This indicated that the navigation could easily be restored throughout its length, and that local anglers would also benefit from the raised water levels. The article also mentioned that Suffolk County Council were willing to encourage greater use of unpowered craft on the waterway, and that Anglian Water Authority had plans to improve the channel for drainage, thus offering scope for more extensive restoration. However, the local climate for major action was not right, and I.W.A. Branch members had to lower their sights and to cultivate interest in their longer-term aims by towpath clearance in the Ipswich area and by organising walks and talks.

The River Stour Trust, on the other hand, were keen to maintain the momentum of their substantial achievements in the Sudbury area. For 1981, they set themselves the task of restoring the infilled Gas Works Arm at Sudbury, and the renovation of a second granary, which might become a museum for the Navigation as well as the Trust's headquarters. Luck was on their side, and in July 1981 a team of highly skilled U.S.A.F. Civil Engineers, from 819 Squadron, came to Sudbury on a six-week training exercise, and undertook all the dredging and site clearance free of charge. The Trust were well pleased, since to have cleared the 100-yard basin by normal means would have cost well over £15,000.

Also in 1981 the Stour Trust announced its plans for building a new lock at Great Cornard, where the old lock had been replaced by a sluice, to extend the navigation down river to Great Henny. Their architects' scheme so impressed the local landowner that he agreed to allow a small piece of his land to be used. The local council also gave the scheme outline planning permission. This was the signal for the Trust to launch a national appeal for £50,000 to complete the project.

The year 1982 started well for the Stour Trust, when a Youth Opportunities Project replaced two of the four unique lock lintels on Flatford Lock. The cost of the beams was met by a £200 grant from Babergh District Council, and the Manpower Services Commission funded the labour. A Dedham Vale Landscape Conservation Project also reinstated the river bank, repaired towpaths and planted trees on the lower reaches at Brantham. The Trust also heard that the A.W.A. had plans for flood alleviation on the lower river which might require the restoration of the two lower locks. Simultaneously, fund raising towards the Great Cornard Lock appeal was surging ahead and, with a further Shell Waterways Award, nearly £2,600 had been raised in the first year.

It therefore came as a shock to the Trust when the decision resulting from the Public Enquiry into the Anglian Water Authority's by-laws was announced in October, upholding the A.W.A. by-law banning non-manually propelled craft between Henny Sluice and the sea. This setback immediately provoked the Trust into renewing its fight for the waterway's full restoration, and the amendment of the by-law.

The Trust planned a protest cruise for 27 March 1983 before the by-laws came into effect, and considered with the I.W.A. what legal action to take. It also called on all members to write in protest to the various authorities concerned.

Fortunately for the Trust the by-laws did not restrict the use of craft on the Sudbury-Henny reach, so their plans for Great Cornard Lock could proceed undeterred. Nor did it dissuade supporters of the Trust from assisting with working parties. Such were held in early 1983 at Stratford St Mary Lock to carry out tree and shrub clearance, ensuring that the growth did not threaten the fabric of the lock sides and make future lock restoration more expensive. However, the Trust has got to fight even harder for its longer-term aim of through navigation on the river Stour.

Over a span of 30 years the campaign of Edwards, Marriage, the Stour Trust, the I.W.A. and others to restore the derelict navigations of Norfolk and Suffolk has progressed slowly, in the face of local conflict, few inland waterways enthusiasts, and lack of substantial active local public demand for more recreational space. This is, perhaps, surprising in one of the centres of the English pleasure hire-craft industry.

*   *   *   *   *

12.—COVENTRY, LEICESTERSHIRE AND NORTHAMPTONSHIRE

The canals of Coventry, Leicestershire and Northamptonshire provide a contrast between early and later canal schemes. The Coventry Canal was part of the original Brindley 'Grand Cross' and, with the Oxford Canal, formed one of the inter-river links. In contrast the Old Union Canal, later to become part of the Grand Union Canal system, was built to supply a more direct link between the Trent Valley coalfields and the markets of London and the eastern area of England. The history of the Coventry coalfields and the part they played in the development of Coventry, within the West Midlands industrial area, is well known. That the Coventry Canal was able to maintain commercial traffic until 1970 is of historical significance. Surprisingly the Old Union Arm to Welford also retained regular coal traffic until as late as 1939, and boats still brought coal to Welford Wharf intermittently until 1946. This was largely due to the rural nature of the area and the lack of a local railway line.

The Midlands region, with its comprehensive canal network, was one of the earliest centres of the waterways restoration campaign, first with the Northern Section of the Stratford-on-Avon Canal, and later with the Avon Valley restoration schemes. The organisation behind these schemes was developed by enthusiasts who formed the Midland Branch of the Inland Waterways Association in 1947.

Because of existing commercial traffic on the Coventry Canal, the first attentions of the area enthusiasts were directed elsewhere. A direct threat to the future of the Coventry Arm prompted a local campaign to interest the local population in its amenity value. Support for this campaign came from two sources: the growing local body of canal pleasure craft owners, and, more particularly, a group of young architects in the City of Coventry Planning Department led by D. Hutchings and L. Davies. The former had a particular,

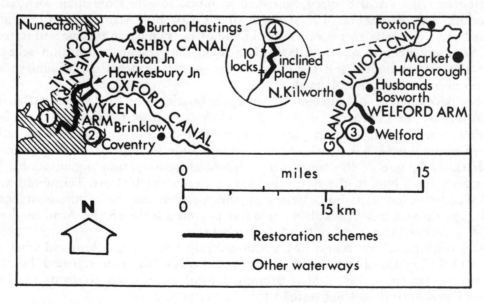

Map 12.—Coventry, Leicestershire and Northamptonshire
(1) Coventry Arm; (2) Wyken Arm; (3) Welford Arm; (4) Foxton Inclined Plane

vested interest insofar as he had recently married and had made his home in a converted narrow boat moored in the City Basin at Coventry.

The combination of the threat to the Coventry Arm, the prospect of oil rationing created by the Suez crisis, and a nucleus of I.W.A. members, led by H. R. Dunkley, willing to stage a Boat Rally at Coventry, persuaded the I.W.A. to change the venue of their proposed Stourport Rally to the Coventry Town Basin. The local debate about the Town Basin became polarised before the Rally was held. The I.W.A. members, on the one hand, called for its retention, and a local council group, led by A. J. Waugh, chairman of the influential General Works Committee, sought the canal's closure and its development as part of the town's new road network.

The I.W.A. Rally Committee, led by Hutchings, managed to gain the support of the then mayor of Coventry, Pearl Hyde, after a cruise for council members along the Coventry and Ashby Canals. This cruise attracted substantial publicity to the amenity of the Coventry waterway and led to the foundation of the Coventry Canal Society.

The boat-owning members of the Canal Society for some time had been seeking a base to moor their boats. A proposal to abandon a former colliery basin and canal arm on the outskirts of the town offered them an opportunity. The Society members, led by Hutchings, put forward proposals in early 1958 for re-developing the Arm as a Club Boat Base, and by the close of that year they had been given a lease on the Arm, and started work restoring it. This work on the Wyken Arm was significant, because it provided Hutchings with the chance to gain practical experience of canal restoration and clearance, and a strong local cohesion between members of the Canal Society, who had so much to gain from their own base, moorings, and clubhouse. The strength of the Coventry Canal Society, gained in this way, was later to prove the backbone of the campaign to save and restore the Southern Section of the Stratford-on-Avon Canal. This restoration scheme gave the restorationists the chance to show what volunteers could achieve by the economic restoration of canals.

The development of interest in pleasure boating on the Midland Canals, promoted by the Coventry I.W.A. Rally and by later boat trips on the canal, led to the growth of interest in pleasure hire craft on the waterways. One early entrepreneur was G. Baker, who later became a founder director of Anglo-Welsh Cruisers, Ltd., one of the leading boat hire and construction organisations. In his search for a base in the East Midlands he found the Welford Terminal Basin and Warehouse derelict, but offering all the requirements for a hire-boat base. Although he was unsuccessful in his quest to gain a lease on the Arm, he drew I.W.A. members' attention to it and its derelict state.

As a result, local awareness of the vulnerability both of the Arm and much of the Old Union Canal was highlighted by a British Waterways Board Interim Report of January 1964, which prompted local enthusiasts to form the Old Union Canal Society in 1964 to fight for its retention.

The Society gained support from the I.W.A. Midlands Branch, of which the Coventry Canal Society was also an associate member, and campaigned locally for public interest in the history and amenity that the canal offered. Baker, who by then had gained a lease on the Market Harborough Canal Basin and started a boat hire base, was also active in his support for the development of the area's waterways.

The provisions of the 1968 Transport Act enabled restoration of the Welford Arm to progress, and by 1969 it had been re-opened. Unlike the Wyken Arm, the Old Union Canal Society were unable to gain mooring rights for their members, but the opening in 1981 of a hire craft base at the terminus of the Arm has assured its future use. Since then the Arm has been improved, and now the restored warehouse buildings, neat yard and new turning basin show how a canal should be maintained.

The Coventry Canal Society has developed interest in the waterways to the west of the area. Speakers from the Society have regularly visited other groups and organisations to give talks and slide displays. The Society members publish in their booklet, *Coventry's Waterway: A City Amenity,* an example to others of the amenity value of a multifunctional use of the country's canals. One of the earliest of the Canal Societies, it sets a valuable example of how to retain and revitalise a local canal.

In the east of the area, the Old Union Canal Society supported the Leicestershire Branch of the Council for the Protection of Rural England, when it put forward in 1970 a plan to the Leicestershire County Council that agreement should be reached with the British Waterways Board to make the upper area of the derelict Foxton Inclined Plane more accessible to the public. As a result the upper area of the plane was cleared of scrub and undergrowth, which had grown over it since the last structures were removed by scrap metal merchants in 1928. The C.P.R.E. were unable to clear the lower area because it was private property. However, the Inclined Plane area was scheduled as an Ancient Monument in 1973. Subsequently, Leicestershire County Council developed a new car park and picnic area at Gumley Bridge, near the site, and with the C.P.R.E. published a guide by P. Gardner and F. Foden, *Foxton Locks and Barge Lift.*

More general interest in the Foxton Inclined Plane was generated in November 1978 when a detailed article about it appeared in *Waterways World.* This compared Foxton with its modern counterpart at Arzviller, on the Marne-Rhine Canal in France, which attracted thousands of tourists each year, as well as saving peniche operators the slow trek up 17 locks. As a result, various interested persons wrote to the editor asking if restoration of the Foxton Inclined Plane had been considered, indicating that an independent viability study was justified, and commenting that a rebuilt Foxton Inclined Plane would make a spectacular working museum, attracting thousands of visitors a year. This renewed interest prompted the Leicestershire Branch of the C.P.R.E. to create in 1979 a Steering Committee for a local restoration society. This was founded in 1980. Since then the project has not looked back. By December 1981 the Society had not only raised over £1,000 towards its aims, including a £150 Shell Award, but also had gained the support in principle of the local and district councils, as well as of the Department of the Environment, for their 10-year plan to restore the plane to full working order. The Society had become a charitable trust in November 1982 and by that time had already cleared the tops of both planes, laid out a guided walk around the site, and submitted detailed plans to rebuild the boilerhouse as a study centre and small museum. In no small measure was that success due to the publication of a small pamphlet on the *Foxton Inclined Plane* and a *Guided Walk* leaflet.

It seems unfortunate that the Hawkesbury Engine House Trust, at Sutton Stop on the Coventry Canal, have not achieved similar success in their quest to stop the old canal pumphouse from falling into further decay. Even the stalwart campaigner Dunkley has been unable to raise the £20,000 required to renovate the 1837 Engine House, for use as a trip boat and activity group base, even though detailed plans for the project were approved in May 1980. No doubt the hard economic climate has played its part. However, by early 1983 the group had raised just over £1,000 towards restoration of the the roof, which could halt the decay.

In 1982 the Coventry Canal Society commemorated its 25th anniversary. Its founder members can look back on their achievements. The restored Wyken Arm is now home for over 80 of their members' boats; the whole Coventry Arm has been dredged, and has fully recovered from the disastrous breach of 15 December 1978. The City Council have landscaped parts of the line, and the future of the City Basin seems secure. The whole area can be well satisfied with the restoration successes it has achieved—if only the Hawkesbury Engine House can be saved!

*   *   *   *   *

13.—WEST MIDLANDS

The Birmingham Canal Navigations lie at the centre of Britain's canal system. At one time they formed an interlacing network of waterways over 200 miles long and with over 200 locks. It began between 1768 and 1772, when James Brindley built, and local businessmen financed, the narrow, winding Birmingham Canal from Birmingham to Wednesbury coalfield and the Staffordshire and Worcestershire Canal. This connected south to the Severn and north to the Trent and Mersey Canal. The system grew slowly, benefiting hundreds of works and collieries, and linking with the other trunk waterways. Much of the central growth was promoted by the Birmingham Canal Company and two other independent concerns, the Wyrley and Essington and the Dudley Canal companies, which later joined with the Birmingham Canal Company to form the Birmingham Canal Navigations.

The introduction of canals to an area utterly devoid of rivers that could be made navigable hastened the industrial revolution, and, by linking coalmines with works, attracted a concentration of heavy industry to the canal banks. At its height the B.C.N. served more than 550 private side basins, linking factories with mines and railway interchange basins. It is thus not surprising that as late as 1888 the B.C.N. transported nearly eight million tons of goods annually, and even in the early 1950s about one million tons a year of short-haul traffic remained.

To the west of the region the Staffordshire and Worcestershire Canal, also designed by James Brindley as part of his 'Grand Cross' system, linked the Trent and Mersey Canal, at Great Heywood, to the River Severn at Stourport. Stourport, originally known as Lower Mitton, owes its existence entirely to the canal, and is an outstanding example today of a canal town. The canal was opened in 1772 and rapidly became a commercial success. Regular commercial traffic remained on it until the early 1950s, when the final consignments consisted of the regular carriage of Cannock Chase coal, from the Hatherton Branch, to Stourport power station.

From the Staffordshire and Worcestershire Canal at Stourton Junction a link with the Dudley Canal and the B.C.N. network was provided by the Stourbridge Canal, opened in 1779. This important link was a short route to the River Severn and carried heavy traffic until the late 1940s, after which it rapidly declined to near dereliction.

This latter canal was the vehicle for the growth of the restoration movement in the region, though one of the first successful canal restoration campaigns took place in 1947 in the Birmingham area at Lifford Lane, Kings Norton, on the Northern Section of the Stratford-on-Avon Canal, to the south-east of the city. This was led by members of the Inland Waterways Association who had formed a Midlands Branch based in Birmingham. In view of the large amount of commercial traffic on the Birmingham Canals at that time the group initially turned their attention to the river Avon to the south-east. However, with the demise of commercial traffic and the rapid decay of some of the peripheral canals in the Birmingham network, some of the boating enthusiasts organised their own clearance work on the less-used B.C.N. routes. One route, which was heavily locked and little used, was the Stourbridge Canal. Fears for the future of canals in the area grew after the publication in July 1958 of a committee report, chaired by L. Bowes, on the *Future of the Waterways*. This report, and an internal dispute in the I.W.A., led to the formation by a group of local canal enthusiasts in February 1959 of the Staffordshire and Worcestershire Canal Society. At first its members pursued interests in their own canal, but later turned their attention to the Stourbridge Canal, which offered them a through link to central Birmingham.

By mid-1959 the I.W.A. Midlands Branch had been revitalised by a new chairman, D. Hutchings. He was also a member of the Coventry Canal Society, and had been instrumental in the restoration by volunteer labour of the Wyken Arm. The I.W.A. made the first move in the battle to keep the Stourbridge Canal open. The I.W.A. were later joined by members of the Staffordshire and Worcestershire Canal Society in a campaign to re-open the Stourbridge Arm and to protect the Stourbridge Canal.

Two events, both led by Hutchings, did much to gain local public support. The first was the free dredging of the Stourbridge Arm by volunteers, and the second was the 1962 Stourbridge I.W.A. Rally.

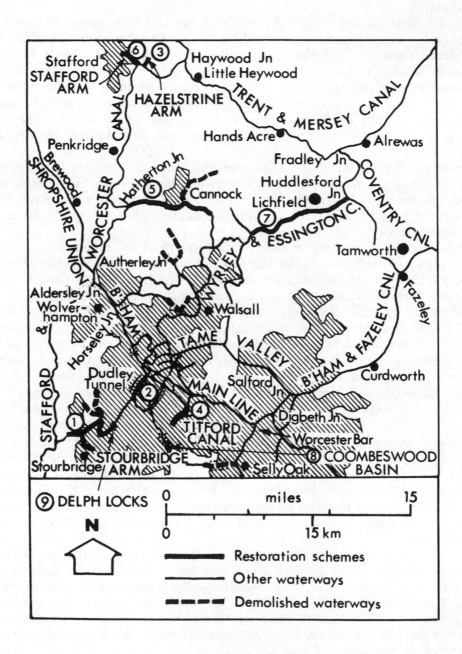

Map 13.—West Midlands
(1) Stourbridge 16 Locks; (2) Dudley Tunnel; (3) Hazelstrine Arm; (4) Titford
Canal; (5) Hatherton Branch; (6) Stafford Arm; (7) Wyrley and Essington
Canal; (8) Coombeswood Basin; (9) Delph Locks

The inauguration of the new British Waterways Board, on 1 January 1963, provided the change in canal management that local enthusiasts sought. Leaders of Staffordshire and Worcestershire Canal Society persuaded the local M.P., J. Talbot, to take up their case, and discussions took place between the Society and the Board. The Society chairman, J. Robbins, a civil engineer, and the vice-chairman, D. Tomlinson, made a balanced negotiating team, and with the co-operation of two B.W.B. members, F. Parham and C. Hadfield, managed to reach agreement for the canal to be restored by volunteers. The event was significant in two respects: firstly, it was a test project for the volunteers to prove their ability, and later it provided the new 'Navvies' group with the chance to flex their muscles and gain restoration experience.

As the Stourbridge restoration project developed so the future of the adjoining canal, the Dudley line through Dudley Tunnel, became more precarious. Again, the I.W.A. and Staffordshire and Worcestershire Society members joined forces, on this occasion with members of the Coventry Canal Society, to fight for its retention. A Dudley Canal Sub-Committee of the Staffordshire and Worcestershire Canal Society was formed to protect the canal line and try to clear it of rubbish. The archaeological and geological relevance of the Dudley Tunnel drew support from many quarters, and in January 1964 the various interested parties joined together to form the Dudley Tunnel Preservation Society. Dudley Town Council became interested in the plans and became one of the first councils in the region to support a waterway restoration project. The 1968 Transport Act later made it possible for the riparian local councils financially to support restoration works.

The interest of the Dudley Council in waterway restoration was followed by its neighbour, the Borough of Warley, who examined the amenity value of their local canals. Matters came to a 'head' when the 1968 Transport Act indicated that many of the Birmingham Canal Navigations were classified as 'remainder' waterways, whose future was in doubt. Again, the I.W.A. and the Staffordshire and Worcestershire Canal Society helped to develop a new organisation, the Birmingham Canal Navigations Society (B.C.N.S.), to protect and restore the Birmingham Canals.

One of the first canals under review was the Titford Canal within the Warley Borough boundary. The combination of Warley Council interest in the redevelopment of the canal area, plus the active encouragement of the I.W.A., B.C.N.S., and the Staffordshire and Worcestershire Canal Society, supplied the impetus for another restoration scheme. The Oldbury Locks and Titford Pools were re-opened officially in 1974.

The growth in pleasure craft using the Staffordshire and Worcestershire Canal, and the increased demand for mooring and water space was the driving force behind two other restoration schemes in the area. The need for new moorings forced Stafford Boat Club members to attempt to restore the abandoned Hazelstrine Arm, near Stafford, and the desire to extend the cruising area led a Staffordshire and Worcestershire Canal Society member to propose the restoration of the former Stafford Branch of the canal. Further investigations however, revealed that the latter scheme could not be undertaken.

The momentum generated by the successful restoration of the Stourbridge, Dudley and Titford Canals led local I.W.A. members to consider other restoration schemes. One of these, the Hatherton Branch of the Staffordshire and Worcester-shire Canal, gained local support, but the considerable reconstruction work involved deterred the formulation of firm plans. Another scheme for the Wyrley and Essington Canal between Ogley and Huddlesford Junction was also considered by I.W.A. members. Due to the destruction of the canal line in many places, these restoration schemes were ultimately not considered viable.

On a more successful note, however, the potential loss of Hawne Basin at the head of navigation of the Dudley No. 2 Line persuaded some enthusiasts, who were I.W.A. members, to consider its future use. In 1977 they formed the Coombeswood Canal Company, to restore the basin as a mooring and to provide a boat club base. The scheme gained local council support, and, with the satis-factory conclusion of some rather protracted compulsory purchase negotiations in mid-1979, Dudley Metropolitan Council agreed to lease the former canal and railway interchange basin and wharf area to the company, re-named the Coombeswood Canal Trust as a clearer indication of its charitable status.

The Trust was fortunate that in 1974 Warley Council had already dredged the Dudley No. 2 canal from Windmill End to Gosty Hill Tunnel, so that after the purchase of the basin the West Midlands County Council could justify dredging the remaining section from Gosty Hill Tunnel to Hawne Basin. Thus the Trust members only had to concern themselves with the restoration of the Basin area and the development of its amenities. In September 1979 the Trust appealed for financial support, either through donations or interest-free loans. The Trust also promoted a Rally of Boats, over Easter 1980, at which they demonstrated progress on re-development work.

Local authority support was similarly given towards the development of the Black Country Museum at the Tipton end of the Dudley Tunnel. The museum site incorporated an old canal arm, re-excavated and re-watered, and now includes a reconstruction of a typical canal boatyard, and examples of various B.C.N. Day Boats, many of which have also been restored. The project is being phased over a period of years, but from the date of its public opening, it gained interest in the history and preservation of the Birmingham Canals.

To acknowledge growing council support and to emphasise the great part which Black Country canals might play in urban re-development, and in continuing environmental improvement centred on a revitalised waterway system, the I.W.A. planned to hold its 1978 National Rally at the Windmill End of Netherton Tunnel. However, when inspection of the Tunnel revealed the need for vital repairs costing some £350,000, it was decided to hold it on the nearby Titford Pools, on the Titford Canal at Oldbury. They had been restored in 1974 by the Warley Council, with the B.W.B. and members of the B.C.N.S., who had undertaken the clearance of rubbish from the Oldbury Locks. The Rally proved a huge success and raised over £5,000 towards the I.W.A.'s Restoration and Development Fund, quite apart from the substantial publicity and goodwill which was generated.

In many ways the choice of the Rally site identified the amenity value of the various Basins on the Birmingham Canals, since the whole area surrounding the waterspace could become a focal point for the local community. This theme is perhaps best identified in the re-development of Hockley Port, just off the Soho Loop at Winson Green. This was another old railway and canal interchange basis, which had ceased commercial use in the 1960s. The site was taken over in 1976 to provide facilities for the local youth and unemployed. The revival was organised by Cut Boat Folk, Ltd., who have since developed the two canal arms as residential moorings, with a slipway and dry dock, whilst the old two-storey stable block is slowly being converted into community and sporting areas, and an indoor riding school for the disabled. The whole development was further enhanced in 1979, when West Midlands County Council agreed to spend £200,000 on a project, involving dredging the Soho Loop, clearing the adjacent towpath, and landscaping the embankments to improve the environment of the Inner City area. Completion of the first stage of this work was celebrated by a Rally of Boats at Hockley Port in May 1980.

Before this Rally, on 3 March 1980, the West Midland County Council launched their *Canal Strategy for the 1980s*. This was essentially an advisory document of the County and associated District Councils, and linked with the B.W.B.'s own *Central Midland Canal Plan*, which reviewed the future of the 150 miles of 'remainder' waterways in the region. The County Council's Canal Strategy provided a tremendous boost for the enthusiasts because it identified nearly all the features that they had been campaigning to achieve; the recreational, environmental and commercial potential of the waterways.

The concept of the linear park, with canals providing links between open spaces, was a major theme, and the place of voluntary societies in the development of the canals was acknowledged. The aim of the strategy, over a 10-year span, was to get certain 'remainder' waterways re-classified as 'cruiseways', including the Titford Canal, the Stourbridge Arm, the Dudley Tunnel Branch, and the Dudley No. 2 Canal.

The document paid particular attention to the way in which the projects might be achieved, noting that nearly one-third of all derelict land and wasteland in the conurbation was beside the canals, in an area short of water facilities for recreation. It identified six sources of finance: (1) Inner Urban Area Grants; (2) Sports Council Grants; (3) Countryside Commission Grants; (4) Derelict Land Grants; (5) Nature Conservancy Council Grants; and (6) Local Authority Amenity Development Funds. For each local proposal it identified how it might be implemented, and when it could best be developed in relation to the overall strategy aims.

This long-term commitment to reviving the canals encouraged the I.W.A. to hold its 1982 National Rally on the Titford Pools again, in recognition of the amount local authorities in the West Midlands had already spent on their canals. It was also aimed at emphasising the urgent need for a solution to the prolonged closure of Netherton Tunnel and the Rushall and Wyrley and Essington Canals at Aldridge. It was hoped that additional finance could be found for these links to be re-opened. This issue became even more pertinent when the restored Dudley Tunnel was closed in November 1981, due to deterioration in the brickwork at the narrowest part of the tunnel.

The closure of Dudley Tunnel was crucial for the Dudley Canal Trust, who relied on tunnel trips in their two electrically-powered boats for a large slice of their income. Fortunately, the B.W.B. were able to allow them tunnel access as far as Cathedral Arch for short trips. Even so, closure of Netherton Tunnel and also the Stourbridge 16 Locks, where major repair works were scheduled, meant that over the winter of 1981 all the craft moored at restored Hawne Basin were trapped within their home length of the canal.

Fortunately, the closure of Dudley Tunnel did not have too adverse an effect on the popularity of the Dudley Canal Trust's trip boats operating from the Black Country Museum, and, to cope with the 1983 season, the fleet had to be increased. This was achieved by cutting their double-ended trip boat *George* into two, and by converting the halves into two new craft. At that stage, even though the whole tunnel had not been re-opened, because funds had been given first to work at Netherton, the Trust were planning future restoration, and had submitted proposals to Dudley Metropolitan Borough Council for a £10,000 Urban Aid Grant to enable them to evaluate the feasibility of a new £130,000 underground circular route, so that their trip boats could go through a series of re-opened underground canals, into the spectacular Singer Cavern, and return along a new 300-ft. link to 'the Well' area. This re-opening, it was hoped, would also permit the retrieval of a Dudley Mine Boat—a sort of Black Country version of the Worsley starvationer—for exhibition at the Black Country Museum.

Increasing interest in canal artifacts of the area provided the basis for a further unusual partial restoration scheme. In the mid-1970s the Delph Locks and their surrounds on the Dudley Canal were made a conservation area by Dudley Metropolitan Borough Council. Subsequently, a joint working party of B.W.B. and the Borough was created to consider the site's preservation and improvement, and to encourage visitors. In April 1982, work started on excavating the old flight, curving to the east, with a view partially to restoring the locks, which were filled in 120 years ago, to a 'ruin' condition; highlighting weirs, culverts and paddle holes; and placing old railway sleepers where bottom gates would have been. The project also involved the complete renovation of the new straight line of the present lock flight, and the conversion of the Old Stable Block, at the top of the flight, to an Interpretation Centre and an outpost of the Black Country Museum. Initial work was undertaken by members of the various local societies, but the major restoration work was allotted to the West Midlands Task Force, sponsored by the Metropolitan Borough of Dudley, with Manpower Service Commission support. The whole project, due to be completed in summer 1983, will provide a good example of how an eyesore in the heart of the Black Country can be transformed into a visual amenity.

The development at Delph spurred on the Staffordshire and Worcestershire Canal Society to re-develop the terminus of the Stourbridge Arm, so that the waterway did not again fall into decay. In early 1982 they published a booklet

The Stourbridge Canal—Securing the Future, which noted that, after the completion, at the end of 1981, of a West Midlands County Council sponsored (£68,000) dredging programme, the Canal Arm would again be fully navigable. The study proposed that the old bonded warehouse at the terminus should be renovated as a workshop, canoe club, and boat hire base. The study also proposed that safe moorings, a dry dock and a canal trip operation could be developed in the terminus area. To operate this new complex, it was suggested that a Management Trust be formed of local authority, county council, industry, B.W.B., and canal society interests.

Staffordshire and Worcestershire Society members started to repair the warehouse in late 1982, to make it weatherproof, before the contractors moved in to eradicate the dry rot prior to full renovation.

Progress of national restoration by 1983 could be epitomised by what was happening in the B.C.N. The West Midlands might be regarded as a microcosm within which Council-sponsored projects, Manpower Service Commission funded developments, grant supported schemes, and Task Force Projects were evolving. These extended from major public investments, such as the £120,000 Bumble Hole amenity improvement scheme, to the smaller-scale Park Head Locks' three-year landscape development plan, at a cost of £4,500, or to work of the private developer, Associated Cruisers, who, through self financing, dug out the entrance to the old basin at the top of the Wolverhampton 21 Locks as a new base for their hire boats. The area around the top lock basin was landscaped by Wolverhampton Metropolitan Borough Council as a new parkland in the town centre.

No review of the restoration projects of the Birmingham area can be complete without mention of the work of Birmingham Canal Navigations Society Working Party Group, who have regularly cleared and maintained the various Loops and Arms within the B.C.N. network. Whilst this work, on such canals as the Ridgeacre Arm, does not fall fully into the restoration category, without it the lesser-used waterways of the area would have become rapidly impassable, and a full-scale restoration scheme would be imperative.

The West Midlands region was a major centre in the growth of the national waterways restoration movement, where from the early work of the I.W.A. and the Staffordshire and Worcestershire Canal Society members, various other schemes have developed and multiplied. The significance of the early successes of the Stourbridge Canal and Dudley Tunnel restorations cannot be underestimated in the progress of the national restoration movement, and the recent commitment of the West Midlands County Council and the various District Councils towards revitalising the canals must be a good omen for the long-term future of the region's inland waterways.

* * * * *

14.–AVON AND SEVERN VALLEYS

In the Dark Ages and until Saxon times natural inland navigation was much more extensive than more recently. River channels were unobstructed, and allowed tides to sweep far inland. The river Severn offered perhaps the best example in Britain of this far-reaching tidal influence. Until the early 19th century, barges were able to reach Welshpool, 128 miles upstream of Gloucester. But by 1895 much of this stretch was only navigable by light pleasure craft, due to the change in use of the upper reaches and to the problems created by serious winter floods and the consequent lack of safe moorings.

As the commercial use of the river Severn developed so the demand to make the river Avon navigable grew. The foresight and business acumen of one man, William Sandys, between 1636 and 1639, enabled sizeable craft to reach Evesham and Stratford.

The growth of Birmingham as an industrial centre increased the need to link the mines and works of the Black Country with both the rivers Avon and Severn. The benefits of cheap water transport and easy access to raw materials and markets led to the construction, first of Droitwich Barge Canal, then the Stratford-on-Avon and Worcester and Birmingham Canals, the development of the Droitwich links, and the opening of the enlarged and modernised Grand Union Canal Line.

However, slowly but surely the waterways network became broken as vital links became lost through railway pressure and domination. The motor lorry provided the final blow to canal traffic. Apart from the small amount of regular traffic on the Worcester and Birmingham and Grand Union Canals, which assured their maintenance in fair order, little other revenue-earning traffic remained to finance the repairs needed to keep the waterways open.

The waterway restoration movement in the area went into early action when a lorry damaged and locked a swing bridge over the Stratford-on-Avon Canal near King's Norton in 1946. The founders of the Inland Waterways Association mounted their first successful campaign in removing the obstruction and re-opening the canal. The publicity from this event, and a keen local nucleus of waterways enthusiasts who formed the Midlands Branch of the I.W.A., provided the means for other schemes to develop.

The turning point in the national waterway restoration movement came with the successful union of business acumen, provided by D. Barwell, and I.W.A. ideals, exemplified by R. Aickman, in the development of the Lower Avon restoration scheme by the Lower Avon Navigation Trust, which was founded in 1950. The vision and practical example demonstrated by the Lower Avon restoration offered the waterway restoration movement a measure of success.

This new enthusiasm for the recovery of the waterways led to the formation of the Stratford-on-Avon Canal Society in 1957 to foster local interest in the derelict and decaying Southern Section of the Stratford Canal. Canal Society members managed to navigate sections of the canal by canoe, and it was the toll tickets for these voyages that prevented the canal from being formally abandoned

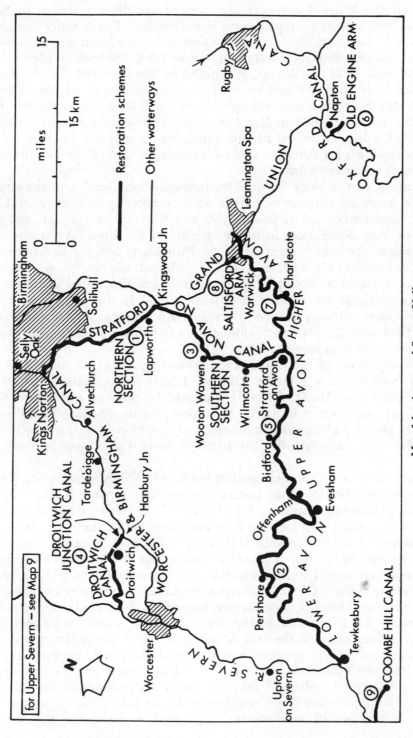

Map 14.—Avon and Severn Valleys

(1) Northern Stratford Canal; (2) Lower Avon; (3) Southern Stratford Canal; (4) Droitwich
Canals; (5) Upper Avon; (6) Old Engine Arm; (7) Higher Avon; (8) Saltisford Arm;
(9) Coombe Hill Canal

in 1959, when the Warwickshire County Council sought permission to block the canal line rather than to repair a canal overbridge. The Stratford-on-Avon Society changed the local climate of opinion and convinced the citizens of Stratford-on-Avon that their local waterway was worth a new lease of life.

The tactical skill of D. Hutchings, a founder of the Coventry Canal Society, combined well with the enthusiasm of J. Smith, chairman of the Finance Committee of the National Trust, who promoted the restoration of the Southern Section of the Stratford-on-Avon Canal in 1960. This scheme for the complete rehabilitation of a heavily-locked narrow canal, was a supreme example of the economic restoration of a derelict canal by volunteers, and of the benefit to be gained from such volunteer work.

The inspiration of the work on the Stratford-on-Avon Canal, and the success of the Lower Avon Trust, both of which were completely re-opened in 1964, provided the momentum for re-joining the two navigations through the long derelict Upper Avon Navigation. In the re-opening of the Upper Avon one must not underestimate the achievement of David Hutchings, and his small team of men, who fund-raised, planned, and built, with remarkable speed, this new waterway. Local expertise in waterway restoration was also useful in promoting the scheme for reviving the derelict Droitwich Canals. In this instance the New Town Development planners helped to evolve the scheme, and it was agreed to form the Droitwich Canals Trust, modelled on the Upper Avon Trust, through which the work could commence.

After the completion of the Upper Avon scheme in 1974, the next challenge for Hutchings was to create a further link, the Higher Avon, between Stratford-on-Avon and the Grand Union Canal at Warwick. To this end the Higher Avon Navigation Trust was formed in 1976. The value of a broad-gauge inland water route, between the rivers Thames and Severn, and of a by-pass to the heavily-used pleasure craft route through the Stratford-on-Avon Canal gave strength to the scheme.

The prospect of reviving another canal in the Severn Valley arose in September 1978, when the Coombe Hill Canal came up for auction. It was purchased by the Severn and Canal Carrying Company for £35,000. They subsequently announced their intention to restore the canal as a 'park-*cum*-museum', and to offer a trip boat service along it from the Coombe Hill wharf to the river Severn.

The rapid increase in the use of pleasure craft in the area provoked two other small restoration schemes. The first was the restoration of the Old Engine Arm, on the picturesque Oxford Canal. This was undertaken as a private development by a local farmer, who saw the need for new moorings. The second, the Saltisford Arm at Warwick, was largely due to the desire of local enthusiasts to retain the amenity of their local canal in the face of an adverse re-development plan. They argued that the additional craft moorings that could be gained by restoring the Arm justified its retention, and its value to local fishermen and the amenity of the towpath substantially enhanced the case against its destruction by a factory development. Local planners, however, believed that jobs were important and allowed part of the factory development to proceed, so restricting the route to the old terminal wharf. Fortunately a bridge, giving navigable headroom, was built over the entrance to the Arm, but the authorities would do nothing to revive the waterway. The campaign to save the whole Arm faltered, and enthusiasts had to wait for a more opportune time to press their case.

Much the same situation applied to the Higher Avon plans, but here the array of objectors caused the delay. This was surprising, because Warwickshire County Council pre-empted the Trust's own announcement of the scheme by publishing a 'synopsis' of their plans late in 1977. At this stage the Higher Avon Navigational Trust were in discussion with the Severn Trent Authority and had only roughly costed the scheme. However, the prospect of an additional 10,000 boat movements a year persuaded Warwickshire councillors to support the scheme, no doubt because of additional trade and jobs that the new waterway would generate!

The Higher Avon Navigational Trust finally published its detailed plans in spring 1978, under the title *The Avon Navigation—Stratford to Warwick*. The fact-filled booklet outlined the plan for nine new locks, including three to raise boats over the 26ft. difference between the Avon and the Grand Union Canal in Warwick. The estimated cost was some £500,000, mainly for new locks and weirs, as the river needed little additional dredging once the water levels were correctly aligned. The aim of the scheme was to complete a chain of broad gauge waterways across the country, from the Severn to the Thames, as well as to form several new circular routes.

The Higher Avon plan received a further boost in 1979 when parliament rejected objections to the form of the proposed Higher Avon Navigation Bill. In doing so, it implied that the 1751 Act, which confirmed the river Avon as a public Right of Way by water, covered the Higher Avon. Thus the Higher Avon Navigational Trust could seek the right to become the Navigation Authority through a smaller private Bill. However, because of local objections, the Trust decided temporarily to withdraw their Bill, in the hope that further discussions with the objectors could result in the Bill passing through parliament without opposition. The main opposers were some riparian landowners and local anglers.

On a smaller scale, the plan to revive the Coombe Hill Canal also ran into difficulties when the new owner, A. Picken, sought planning permission to undertake the work. Gloucester County Council refused this on the grounds that lack of access to the wharf area precluded the opening of the site as a park and museum. When this news broke, waterway enthusiasts were asked to support the restoration scheme, and when the revised plans were submitted to the Council in March 1980, there were over 100 letters advocating the scheme, and requesting the earlier, negative planning decision be over-ruled. The pleas were accepted and permission was granted for work to proceed. However, by then, valuable time had been lost for fund-raising and restoration. Equipment faults added to the delay, so that by 1982 only the first half-mile had been cleared, and the planned trip boat operation had not got underway. Cashflow problems ultimately forced the Severn and Canal Carrying Company into voluntary liquidation in summer 1982. However, it was hoped that a newly-formed Coombe Hill Canal Trust might purchase the canal and continue with the revival plans.

The problem of cashflow has beset all operations at some time, but some have the ability to survive. Such was the case on the Upper Avon, when, in 1980, Welford Weir was likely to be breached through excessive erosion. The U.A.N.T. persuaded local hire-boat firms to donate £3,000 to cover immediate remedial work and prevent its imminent collapse, but the prospect of a bill of between £25,000 and £40,000 to remedy the fault was a major problem, especially when the Severn Trent Water Authority could only make £10,000 available for maintenance work. Hutchings, the Trust's manager, decided that the work must proceed, and accepted a tender of about £40,000 to proceed with the remedial work before the potentially devastating winter floods. His positive attitude was rewarded, and the Countryside Commission very generously agreed to match pound for pound all the funds he could raise elsewhere. With his usual flare, he set out and achieved his goal, and U.A.N.T. were just able to meet the final account.

The Droitwich Canal restoration scheme has similarly been delayed by unexpected problems arising from a shortage of funds as the work proceeded. However, in recent years, they, too, have benefited from a variety of grants and awards to add to their own fund-raising schemes. One such scheme is perhaps unique in the restoration movement. The Trust have sold a limited number of Canal Tokens giving the purchaser free navigation on the waterway, once it is restored—such is their confidence of success!

This confidence has been shared by the local Wychavon District Council who, in 1980, announced their plan to make a grant of about £200,000, spread over two or three years, to the Trust to excavate a new canal route through a previously-infilled section at Vines Park in the centre of Droitwich New Town, and also to build a marina. The first part of this money was paid in 1980 for exploratory work and further allocations were made in 1981 and 1982, as work visibly progressed. In late 1982, the Council allocated to the Trust £140,000, with a grant of £25,000 for the archaeologists to excavate the adjacent Upwich Pit. This will enable the Trust to complete the whole central town section of the canal, and, if all goes to plan, launch their steam-powered trip boat in the re-opened Vines Park area in late summer 1983.

However, before the Droitwich Canals Trust re-opens the whole summit level, there is the task of repairing a major culvert fracture at Salwarpe. Fortunately, the oil company, Shell, were able to make a major Waterways Award of £1,500 towards this work, and the Hereford and Worcester County Council have promised £1,000. Even then the Trust's task will be hardly finished, for they will still have to make the final link into the River Severn, overcoming the road embankment at Hawford which obstructs the original canal route. After that, re-opening the Droitwich Junction Canal will be the next major problem.

Apparently intractable problems have recently beset the Southern Stratford Canal, which was originally restored and re-opened by the Queen Mother in 1964. Since that time the National Trust have run it, but it has proved an ever-increasing drain on their funds, even though some maintenance work has been undertaken by volunteer labour.

By 1978 it was clear to local enthusiasts that the National Trust would be glad to be relieved of their task. In 1980 they stated they could no longer afford to maintain the canal, for which income in 1979 had been £27,500 against outgoings of £52,000, and they wished to hand over the canal to a 'suitable body' by the end of 1981. They approached the Department of the Environment with a view to relinquishing statutory control.

Hutchings, who had been instrumental in the original revival scheme, suggested the creation of a new charitable trust to run the canal. This was one of the options discussed at an informal conference called by the Department of the Environment in June 1981. However, disagreements over the funding of future maintenance presented a stumbling block. At a second meeting, in February 1982, the I.W.A., through an *ad hoc* Stratford Canal Advisory Committee, suggested that a newly-established charitable Stratford Canal Trust could take on the canal on a long lease, provided that funds were available over a three-year period, for the new body to bring the canal to a reasonable state of repair. The parties, however, could not agree on the details of the scheme. In December 1982 the plans appeared to be doomed, especially when the National Trust could not withdraw their objections to the Higher Avon scheme, nor provide land and access for the necessary changes in the river at Charlecote, which were part of the package deal. The Stratford Canal Trust believed that the Higher Avon scheme was essential to the Southern Stratford Canal. It would provide not only an alternative route to the canal when essential works were required, but also would increase the waterway network in the area to the benefit of the public and the local economy. The negotiations collapsed, but the National Trust agreed to keep the Stratford Canal open until a suitable successor could be found, which is where it presently rests. The impasse has meant that the plans for the Higher Avon also have reached a stalemate.

This did not stop other schemes in the region from going ahead. One was a plan evolved by Hutchings for making the Upper Severn navigable again between Stourport and Ironbridge. The idea developed after a Bridgnorth councillor expressed interest. Hutchings conducted a preliminary feasibility study during 1982 and reported that at least 75 per cent of the route was already navigable through to Ironbridge, and that with the construction of 13 new locks and weirs, the remainder could be converted into an attractive tourist waterway. His ideas were revealed in December 1982 at a meeting sponsored by the Town Council of Town, District and County Councillors at Bridgnorth. Bewdley and Telford Councils indicated that they were in favour of the plan, but Shropshire County Council were not so impressed. Subject to the result of further meetings with the Severn Trent Water Authority, it was hoped that a full feasibility study might be undertaken during 1983. However, careful monitoring of local politics and the development of support from the anglers will be vital if the project is to succeed.

Getting the 'timing' right led to the success of the second attempt to restore the Saltisford Arm in 1982. The B.W.B., having fought earlier against plans to construct a road over part of the Arm, were keen by then to see the Arm re-developed. A local enthusiast, D. Amende, suggested that the Arm could be developed in two ways. Firstly, as a site for a local youth water activities centre, with a community project at the town end, and, secondly, to provide new opportunities for the commercial development of boating facilities and moorings at the Junction end of the Arm.

The prospectus found support from the Arthur Rank Centre Leadership Training Unit for Warwickshire, and gained funding from the Manpower Services Commission Community Enterprise Programme. It also met with approval from Warwick District Council and the B.W.B., and permission was granted, and funding quickly arranged, for work on clearing the quarter mile of the remaining length of the Arm to begin in September 1982. Since then Amende and his colleague, R. Hickin, have led local youngsters and the unemployed in transforming the derelict waterway into a new amenity.

The spirit of the waterways movement is exemplified by what has been achieved in the Avon valley. It therefore seems fitting that the living memorial to the late Robert Aickman, who in 1946 launched the national campaign to save the waterways, and for many years led it with fire and faith, should be sited in the valley he loved so much; especially on the Upper Avon Navigation, which he nurtured to new life as chairman of U.A.N.T.

Aickman died on 26 February 1981, when the Upper Avon Navigation Trust were trying to overcome severe silting at Harvington Lock. They decided that a new lock should be built and had purchased the land. The problem was that of finance. The I.W.A decided to launch an Aickman Memorial Fund and this raised £24,000. Two other major grants were received from the Severn-Trent Water Authority and the Countryside Commission, and these paved the way for the new lock. It was designed by Hutchings and constructed by a small team under his direction. The lock chambers were built between 17 January and 29 March 1982, in spite of delays caused by floods! The first boats were able to use the new lock and cut on 2 December 1982. The whole project cost £150,000 —a bargain price.

The Aickman Memorial Lock was officially opened on 21 May 1983, when a bronze portrait plaque set in a small monument on the lockside was unveiled; a fitting tribute to the man who did so much behind the scenes to make the re-opening of the various Avon links possible.

For many, the Avon valley holds the key to the success of the waterways restoration movement. The battles fought by Aickman, Rolt, Barwell, Hutchings, and so many other unnamed enthusiasts, set the pattern for progress elsewhere; and the Royal re-openings of 1964 and 1974 gave the whole movement a sense of purpose it could never otherwise have achieved.

*   *   *   *   *

15.—GRAND UNION CANAL

The Grand Junction Canal, which was later amalgamated with eight other canals to form part of the Grand Union Canal system, was constructed to provide

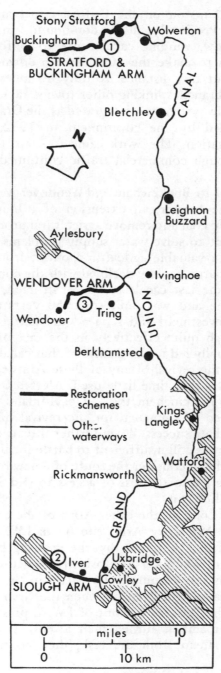

Map 15.—Grand Union Canal
(1) Stratford and Buckingham Arm;
(2) Slough Arm;
(3) Wendover Arm

a short cut between Braunston on the Oxford Canal and Brentford, west of London on the Thames. Previously, all London-bound traffic from the Midlands had to follow the narrow, winding canal route to Oxford, where loads were transhipped into lighters to make the 100-mile trip down-river to London. The Grand Junction Canal cut this distance by fully 60 miles and, with its 14-foot wide locks and various branches linking other towns, rapidly became both busy and profitable. The whole system was integrated as the Grand Union in 1929 and the new company, aided by the government in 1932, launched a massive programme of modernisation. The work came too late to prevent the decline of the main canal, although commercial traffic continued on it until the early 1960s.

The Arms of the canal to Buckingham and Wendover were envisaged as part of the original scheme. The former, an extension of a branch to Old Stratford, was geared both to supply coal and remove agricultural produce from a developing area. The latter was built to solve water supply problems at one of the summit levels, and also offered a valuable agricultural outlet from the Chiltern slopes. The traffic on both these arms rapidly declined with the coming of the railway.

Surprisingly, one of the last canals to be constructed, the Slough Arm, ran parallel to a railway line and was built some 50 years after it. Yet the Arm proved to be a useful investment and serviced the gravel workings at Iver and the town wharf at Slough quite effectively in the face of railway competition. The motor vehicle eventually led to the demise of that canal.

The first stirrings for the revival of any of these Arms came with the threat to the Old Stratford Arm, by that time little used. Alerted by the formal abandonment of the extension to Buckingham, the few local Inland Waterways Association members in the area tried to campaign for the revival of the canal as early as 1961, but with no immediate success. When further threats developed some eleven years later, local support was still insufficient to battle for the canal line. Although a Public Enquiry was held to consider the route of a new road which cut the line, the lack of local activists led to the loss of access to Old Stratford Wharf and of a new future for the derelict spur.

Further south, nearer London, the other Arms of the Grand Union were more actively protected. The Aylesbury Arm, site of an I.W.A. Rally in 1961, was rigorously safeguarded from that time by the growing body of local pleasure craft owners. The adjacent Wendover Arm, which was without the cover of a legal Right of Navigation, was less fortunate. Its decay in the early 1900s left little room for a restoration campaign. Even so, when the Grand Union Canal Society (G.U.C.S.) was formed in 1967 as a result of I.W.A. pressure, this was the first derelict canal to which members turned their attention, and, in spite of many problems that deterred them from the task, they continued to monitor the condition of the Arm.

The G.U.C.S. interest in the Slough Arm, however, proved to be far more successful. From the time the Grand Junction Canal was opened, and even before, various schemes had been promoted to link the west of London by canal to the upper reaches of the Thames at Windsor. This idea was reactivated in 1964 by

I.W.A. member, Viscount St Davids, and discussed by the owners of craft which used the Iver Boat Yard. There was a growing local awareness of the amenity value of the Slough Arm. The threat of closure of the terminal length coincided with the G.U.C.S. interest in the Arm, and the threat of a ring-road led to a very active local anti-road lobby. The combination of the local groups, with I.W.A. pressure, saved the Slough Arm from the road threat.

The 1969 Canal Festival, held at Stoke Wharf, Slough, did more than anything else to prove to the local councillors the value of the canal. Soon after the Festival, the G.U.C.S. formed the Slough Canal Group as a local campaigning body to fight for the Arm. It achieved this through lectures for local organisations, and working parties to clear the waterway and towpath. It also entered into discussions with local authorities and British Waterways Board, to ensure that the interests of all users of the Arms were protected.

One major problem of the Arm was weed growth. To combat this the Group organised a Rally of Boats in 1974, and thereafter offered a plaque and certificate to any boat owner who could prove that he had reached Stoke Wharf. This both persuaded boats to travel the whole length of the Arm, and proved that they still regularly reached the centre of Slough.

The vision of the potential Thames link finally disappeared in 1977, when Slough Council rejected a plea from the Group to retain the land required for the construction of the shortest possible route through the outskirts of Slough to link with the Thames near Eton. Even so, the potential development of the Colne Valley Park, with its link to the Thames, suggested an alternative route from the Slough Arm, giving access to the non-tidal upper reaches of the Thames.

The G.U.C.S. had not forgotten the Wendover Arm, and realised that it, too, had to be used to secure its future. The Society therefore organised the first of its Annual Events on the Arm in September 1978, when seven craft travelled to the head of navigation at Tringford Pumping Station. The trip was reported in *Waterways World,* and would-be navigators were told not to be deterred by the plank across the mouth of the Arm, as this was only there to prevent weed from floating out into the main line of the canal!

Some 25 boats attended the Second Event on the Wendover Arm in August 1979. By then the G.U.C.S. were alarmed at the deteriorating condition of the waterway, rapidly becoming obstructed by reed growth. This prompted them to renew their campaign not only to dredge the first section and to restore the towpath, but for the re-opening of the whole canal, including the restoration of the missing middle section, which had been de-watered in 1904 because of leaks. To encourage use of the navigable section to Tringford, the G.U.C.S. issued certificates to all those who submitted proof that they had managed to reach the Pumping Station by boat.

The scheme proved a success, and at the next Annual Event in September 1980 the waterway was clear enough for a trip boat to run cruises along the Arm. This gained more support, and prompted the G.U.C.S. and the local I.W.A. branch to consider how they could improve the amenity of the Arm still further. In 1981 they started a scheme to clear the towpath along the dry section, and in 1982 and 1983 ran regular working parties. This action bore fruit in various ways. In 1982 the B.W.B. dredged the Arm from its entrance through to Tringford Pumping Station, and also cleared and re-gated the former stoplock. At first the Society thought this was the start of a larger dredging scheme, but it was subsequently learned that the stoplock was to be used to store new lock gates under water, until they were ready to be used. This was confirmed when the section beyond the stoplock was infilled with dredgings removed from elsewhere!

The G.U.C.S. held its Annual Event in September 1982 and some 42 boats attended, well justifying the dredging work. All those boat owners who made the trip were presented with a brass plaque, and it was announced that the Society would offer similar plaques to all future boats navigating the Arm.

Working parties jointly organised by the G.U.C.S. and the I.W.A., Hertfordshire Branch, continued to make progress in clearing the whole dry section of the Arm and by winter 1982 well over a quarter of a mile had been cleared. In February 1983 this progress paid dividends when it was announced that agreement had been reached between the B.W.B. and Aylesbury Vale District Council for a council-sponsored Community Enterprise Project to start work in March 1983 to clear the remainder of the dry section. Although the canal would not be fully restored it might be the first stage in the aim of the I.W.A. and G.U.C.S. to get boats back to Wendover Wharf.

Just as Wendover Arm made progress through the slow but steady pressure of the Group, so events proceeded in a similar way on the Slough Arm. In May 1980 the I.W.A. London Branch organised a spectacular Canal Festival at Slough. Its aims were three-fold: to publicise the amenity of the Arm; to highlight the recreational facilities of the Colne Valley Park; and to raise funds to support and encourage restoration projects on the inland waterways. About 120 boats fought their way through the occasional Sargasso Sea of weeds, and over 10,000 visitors came through the turnstiles to the Rally Site. The event raised some £2,000 and put the Slough Arm on the map. After the Festival, a group of local enthusiasts decided to build on the spirit and enthusiasm that had ensured the success of the Rally. They therefore formed the Slough Canal Society in August 1980, to secure the future of the Arm by upgrading it to 'Cruiseway' status.

The Society quickly gained support from local M.P.s, local councillors, and from the London Anglers' Association, who joined its main committee, and all actively campaigned for the reinstatement of the towpath along the whole canal.

In May 1982 the Slough Canal Society joined with the I.W.A. to celebrate the centenary of the opening of the Slough Arm of the Grand Union Canal in 1882. A Slough Canal Centenary Festival Committee was formed to run the celebrations, which were part of the festivities of Maritime England Year. Once again, the three-day Festival created tremendous local interest, and over 150 craft lined the canal banks. The Festival was timely as the B.W.B. were in the process of presenting a Bill to parliament seeking to upgrade various waterways. The Slough Arm was one of the seven waterways involved, and the local councils had given a commitment of their financial backing to the long-term upkeep of the canal. While the Bill was going through parliament the Slough Canal

Society were given permission by the B.W.B. to clear the towpath and make it 'walkable', a task which was undertaken by various working parties.

In February 1983 the B.W.B. Bill received Royal Assent and the Slough Arm was upgraded to 'Cruiseway' status, thus justifying the long and hard-fought campaign of the G.U.C.S., I.W.A. and Slough Canal Society. It is unfortunate that the revival of the Slough Arm is the only success in an area through which one of the most modern of Britain's old canals passes. It is particularly sad that the battle for the Old Stratford Arm was lost, especially as it could have offered a valuable amenity for the developing new town of Milton Keynes. Even so, the fight for the revival of the Wendover Arm is still underway. Although this presents some major engineering problems, restoration experience has proved that the difficulties of dry sections can now be overcome, if sound financial backing is obtained. Only time will tell if boats will ever return to Wendover Wharf.

*　　*　　*　　*　　*

16.–SOUTH WALES

The waterways of South Wales, which includes Monmouthshire in the area now known as Gwent, were the product of the demand for transport systems following the Industrial Revolution. They climbed the steep river valleys from the ports of Newport, Cardiff, Giant's Grave, and Swansea, to link with the collieries and ironworks of the interior. They were the main means of carrying for 60 years from 1795, and continued, in declining importance, for another 30 years after the advent of railways.

One feature of the South Wales canals, which ultimately had much to do with their demise, was the heavy lockage they incurred. There were numerous flights of locks, such as those at Cwmbran and Rogerstone on the Monmouthshire Canal, while the Glamorganshire Canal had some of the deepest canal locks in the British Isles. In contrast the lines taken by the upper reaches of the canals, high along steep hillsides, provided paths above the industries in the valley floor and offered routes of considerable scenic beauty. It was that beauty that was the inspiration behind a local campaign to retain parts of the canals for pleasure and amenity use.

The beauty of parts of the Welsh canals was well-known. The image of annual Sunday School outings in the former open working boats was very much in the eyes of many older residents, who had benefited from such trips, and the free swimming that the canals offered. The most scenic of the canals was the Brecon and Abergavenny, which traversed the Brecon Beacons. Although pleasure craft were not allowed to use the locks, the owners of canoes and portable craft sometimes used the intervening pounds. With the prospect of the Brecon Beacons National Park, first mooted in the Hobhouse Report of 1947, and envisaged within the 1949 National Parks Act, the amenity of the Brecon Canal came sharply into focus. It was in this light that the Inland Waterways Association started their campaign for the restoration of the canal and its re-opening to

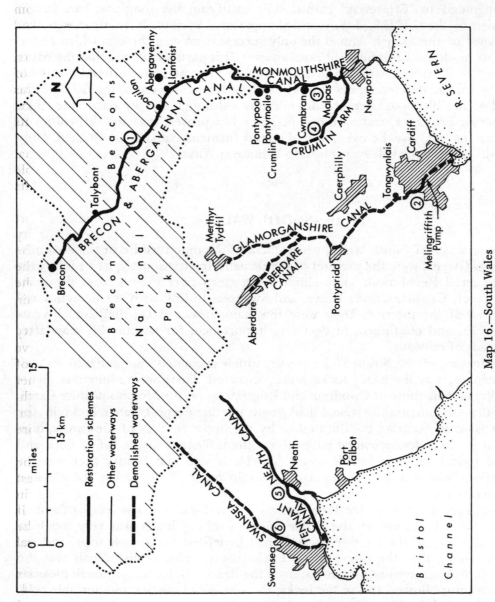

Map 16.—South Wales

(1) Brecon and Abergavenny Canal; (2) Glamorganshire Canal; (3) Monmouthshire Canal;
(4) Crumlin Arm; (5) Neath and Tennant Canals; (6) Swansea Canal

pleasure traffic in 1952. Although the I.W.A. had few local members, their rally at Brecon in August 1952 stirred up local commitment towards the retention of the canal. The final decision to restore the canal fully was taken in October 1968, and the work was undertaken by the B.W.B., financed by a £30,000 grant from Monmouthshire and Breconshire County Councils under the National Parks and Access to the Countryside Act.

As the campaign on the Brecon Canal made progress, so the I.W.A. members, led by W. H. Field, turned their attention to the inter-connected upper reaches of the derelict Monmouthshire Canal, in the Pontypool area. This attention was later focused first on Cwmbran, and then on Newport, as each of the local authorities involved became interested in the future of the canal within its boundaries.

The latter provided the stimulus for the formation of the Newport Canal Preservation Society through which local residents, led by R. Rudd, were able to combine with the waterway enthusiasts, led by Field, to promote its restoration.

The attitude of the Newport Borough Council and the success of the Newport Canal Preservation Society stimulated local anglers and waterway amenity enthusiasts, who lived near the Crumlin Arm of the Monmouthshire Canal in the Risca, Magor and St Mellons area, to form a canal society to promote the restoration of that part of the Crumlin Arm within their area. Although the Arm was not restored for through navigation, parts of it became available again for water-based activities.

The distinctive flight of 14 locks at Rogerstone provided the opportunity for the development of an Open Air Museum, by the local authority, to preserve one of the most remarkable and valuable features of the industrial heritage of the Welsh canals. Local government reorganisation in 1974 enlarged the former Newport Council to encompass both the lower Crumlin Arm and the Monmouthshire Canal, south of Cwmbran, within the new Newport District Council area. This offered a more secure future for the lower reaches of the Monmouthshire Canal, where one lock was substantially restored.

Stimulated by this progress and by local I.W.A. reorganisation in 1974, the South Wales Branch of the I.W.A. broadened its sphere of interest. To the west it investigated the restoration of the Neath and Tennant Canals; at Cardiff, in conjunction with the Oxford House (Risca) Industrial Archaeologists, it reviewed the possible restoration of the Melingriffith Pump and Feeder on the Glamorgan Canal; and to the east it promoted the Torfaen Canal Society to deal with the upper reaches of the Monmouthshire Canal.

By far the greatest success was achieved in the west where local enthusiasts promoted the Neath and Tennant Canals Preservation Society in September 1974. Help from a Manpower Services Commission Job Creation Scheme has combined with local labour to restore Aberdulais Basin and some other sections of the canals.

A blow to other, longer-term plans came in March 1975 when a serious breach closed the Brecon and Abergavenny Canal at Llanfoist. After extensive investigation B.W.B. announced in early 1976 that the canal would remain closed 'until more favourable economic times'. Fortunately a Job Creation Scheme overcame the financial hurdle, and work commenced on restoring the canal in 1977 with a projected re-opening date of Easter 1979.

The problems involved in repairing the breach at Llanfoist were far greater than had been anticipated and the remedial work was not completed until winter 1980. The canal was officially re-opened to craft just before Easter 1981, after some six years of restriction. To celebrate the event and to re-awaken interest in the waterway, the I.W.A. organised a Spring Cruise from Goytre Marina to Govilon and back to enable boats to cruise beyond 'the breach' and to inspect the canal repairs.

In the late 1970s other finance was being devoted to the renovation of canals, although not for boating use. Some grants were devoted to two small sections of the Glamorganshire Canal, earlier designated as nature reserves. At Pontypridd some 450 yards of canal were dredged and the cleared site was rehabilitated as part of a community scheme promoted in the Jubilee Appeal Year by the Prince of Wales's Committee. Prince Charles visited the site on 14 July 1978 to see how the work had progressed, and to study a small exhibition in a restored toll-house showing what had been achieved. Further along the Glamorganshire canal, at Whitchurch, an £11,000 Job Creation project was also devoted to clearing two lock chambers, at Llwynymallt and Forest Lock, for them to be included in the Glamorganshire Canal Nature Reserve, to the south of which was the restored Melingriffith Pump.

Further east, the Welsh Development Agency was providing most of the funds for extensive repairs to the Crumlin Arm of the Monmouthshire Canal, and some £17,800 was allocated in 1978/79 for re-lining the 14 locks at Rogerstone to allow water to flow down the flight, earlier designated as an Open Air Museum; another £26,000 was spent on remedial works on the canal at Risca. The aim was to create 'fun areas', picnic spots, fishing, and localised boating, as it was not envisaged that the Arm would be re-opened for through navigation.

However, in 1978, plans were made to re-open a further section of the Main Line of the Monmouthshire Canal, north of Newport, and to restore Malpas Lock at an estimated cost of some £16,000, with the hope of a second phase in which the canal would be re-watered as far north as Ty-ffnnon Bridge, just south of Cwmbran. Further north, beyond Cwmbran New Town, the Torfaen Canal Society was also working hard to revive 3½ miles of canal between Five Locks, Cwmbran and Jockey Bridge, Pontypool, which had been excluded from the earlier restoration of the Brecon and Abergavenny Canal because it lay outside the boundary of the National Park. The Society were aided by a floating dredger, *Spirit of Torfaen,* which was placed at their disposal in 1979 for dredging the potentially navigable section from Pontymoile to the *Open Hearth* inn, Sebastopol. Much of this restoration work was financed under a £90,000 series of Job Creation Schemes, and Torfaen Council contributed through a five-year plan a canal-side landscaping. This work also enabled the Canal Society to re-open the canal as a good fishery, which was re-stocked with financial assistance from the Welsh Water Authority. It also added weight to the Canal Society's efforts to rebuild Crown Bridge at Sebastopol to navigable height, providing access for boats to the remaining water-filled section of the canal, through to the derelict and partly infilled Five Locks at Cwmbran.

In much the same way as the Torfaen Canal Society galvanised local support between 1974 and 1980, so the Neath and Tennant Canals Society succeeded in re-opening lost sections of their local canals. After their successful restoration of Aberdulais Basin, which was re-opened in 1976, they subsequently concentrated on the Neath Canal, between Rheola and Resolven, where the Rheola Aqueduct had been repaired and sluice gates fitted to the dam walls of the locks for the section to be re-watered for use by small craft.

They also organised a hard-fought political campaign to protect the canal lines from encroachment by a major by-pass plan, and achieved a great success. Likewise, through gaining the local council's support, the towpath of the Neath Canal between Neath and Glynneath was designated a public Right of Way, which gave further protection to that section of the canal route and a chance for more people to enjoy their local canal.

In an effort to influence future developments the Neath and Tennant Canals Society decided to exploit the long-term tourist attraction of their canals, particularly when fully restored, as a basis for public debate. They submitted a discussion paper, *The Next Five Years,* to the West Glamorgan County Council in October 1979. Copies were also circulated to all other interested parties, seeking their comments on, and support for, the plans. The document clearly set out the many assets of the waterways and indicated how easily each could be developed in an economic way. The report set a clear pattern of what could be achieved in the early 1980s, if all united to implement the Society's ideas.

Taking the lead, the Society developed two projects with tourism in mind. One was the restoration of the Neath Canal Company Workshops at Tonna, where the old 1790's forge, joiners' workshop and covered work areas were slowly rebuilt; there were plans to develop a second phase—restoring the Saw-pit and the Long shed—as finance was received. Fortunately, the Manpower Services Commission funded much of the labour required for the initial scheme, and a Community Canals Officer, funded by Urban Aid Grant, provided the means of mobilising other resources to get further grants in aid. The Society's second project was based on further development of Aberdulais Basin, which had originally re-opened in 1976. Unfortunately, the winter floods in December 1979 brought a lot of silt and gravel back into the Basin, and the Society, therefore, had to rehabilitate the area. This work was undertaken in early 1980, when they removed over 600 cubic yards of silt and regraded and seeded the banks. This action prompted the Tennant Canal Company to repair the adjacent Aberdulais Aqueduct, which had been similarly damaged in the floods.

Unfortunately, those same floods seriously damaged the Ynsbwllog Aqueduct on the upper Neath Canal, where the River Neath had swept away a complete masonry arch and some of the adjoining walls. The plight of the Aqueduct was made worse because the Canal Society's permission to work on the canal had expired and they did not have a licence to undertake further work on the Neath

Canal. This brought new urgency to their delicate negotiations to secure a lease so that they could carry out remedial work. It was not until 1983 that the Society was able to see a way towards re-opening the Neath Canal, when the Welsh Development Association offered to fund a three-phase study of the waterway, to include a survey of restoration practicability, an examination of the hydrological problems, and a detailed engineering survey.

The concept of a study report was also developed for the Monmouthshire and Brecon Canal in 1981, when a discussion document was published. This had been prepared by officers of the Gwent County Council Planning Department, the Brecon Beacons National Park Authority, and the British Waterways Board, and offered various options for the future of the canal. These options included the upgrading of the canal to cruising waterway standard, extension of the cruising area to Five Locks, Cwmbran, and the provision of additional mooring facilities at various sites along the whole waterway. A public meeting was held at Abergavenny in July 1981 and it was hoped that a formal development plan for the whole canal would emerge. The first fruit of this strategy was the formal designation of the Brecon and Abergavenny Canal as a 'Cruiseway' in February 1983, when the British Waterways Board Private Bill received Royal Assent. Prior to that, in autumn 1981, a preliminary report on a future Severn Barrage was published, suggesting that further detailed studies on a dam, from Bream Down, Weston-Super-Mare to Lavernock Point, near Cardiff, were justified and should be made. This development offered the prospect of a safer water link between the English canals and the South Wales waterways, with potential for tourism, provided that the Monmouthshire Canal could be completely restored and a new link built into the River Usk.

This plan received a damaging blow when the Cwmbran Development Corporation announced, in 1981, their plan to obliterate part of the Monmouthshire Canal route in the second phase of their new 'Cwmbran Way' road scheme. When the Development Corporation refused to consider alternative plans, enthusiasts appealed to the Secretary of State for Wales for the whole issue to be considered at a Public Enquiry. Such was the strength of local concern that the Public Enquiry was granted, and it was held in Cwmbran on 26 January 1983. Evidence against the road scheme was presented by the Newport Canal Preservations Society, The Torfaen Canal Society and the I.W.A., South Wales Branch. They each argued that the Development Corporation had not properly consulted the various waterway interests, and had not sufficiently considered the range of possible options. The Inspector's decision will clearly either make or break the revival of the Monmouthshire Canal. Enthusiasts, however, believe that the threat of an irreversible blockage will not be allowed to defeat them!

It was the very threat of road schemes which proved to be the saving grace for parts of one of South Wales's other derelict canals. The prospect of losing most of the remains of the Swansea Canal through road developments prompted the Royal Commission on Ancient Monuments in Wales to organise a four-year field study of it. In 1978 S. Hughes lectured to the Swansea Valley History Society on their progress, and an exhibition of their findings was organised at

Pontardawe. At much the same time a resident and well-known weight-lifter, J. Bryce, was campaigning to have the disused Ystalyfera Aqueduct listed as an Ancient Monument, and so preserved. The outcome—a new surge of local interest—prompted the Swansea Valley History Society to try and save what remained of the waterway. At about this time the local Lliw Valley Borough Council also put forward plans to reconstruct a section of the waterway, between Clydach and Pontardawe, and improve the towpaths elsewhere. It was then discovered that the Ystalyfera Aqueduct was the first aqueduct to be built using hydraulic mortar—even earlier than the one at Chirk on the Llangollen Canal in North Wales. This new evidence immediately changed its status, and it was promptly listed as an Ancient Monument.

Looking for some early results, the Swansea Valley History Society investigated the possibility of raising the derelict remains of an old canal barge. They subsequently located a reasonably intact craft at Clydach, and organised working parties to raise the barge. The substantial publicity helped towards their aim of restoring the 100-year-old craft for exhibition.

In 1981 the Swansea Canal Society was formed by local enthusiasts, who planned to revive parts of the canal. They aimed at landscaping the canal at Clydach, clearing the Ystalyfera Aqueduct and the Ynysmendwy Locks, and restoring a stone-arched bridge at Hafod. In the longer term, they hoped to develop a strategy for protecting and restoring other sectors of the derelict canal. This Society received a strong incentive when they heard that the Council for British Archaeology Committee Annual Forum was to be held in Swansea in October 1983, and that the Swansea Canal study by the Welsh Royal Commission was to be featured at the conference, linked with site visits.

The rapidly growing interest in the historic importance and the heritage value of the South Wales canals clearly will do much to aid their restoration and preservation, especially as new access to public funds is offered. An example is the publication in 1983 of a colourful tourist leaflet, partly funded by the Thompson Organisation and circulated by the Welsh Tourist Board, extolling the virtues of Aberdulais Basin, and highlighting it as the focus for 'attractions that provide a complete day out for the whole family'; the prospect of a trip boat for the disabled on the Neath Canal (scheduled to operate in 1984) presents that waterway in a new light and helps more people to enjoy its facilities. In a similar way the new Interpretation Centre at 14 Locks Rogerstone provides a novel outdoor museum of their local canal.

From a slow start in the early 1950s, through partial success on the Brecon Canal in the 1960s, to the rigorous enthusiasm of, and spread of interest in, the mid-1970s, the waterway restoration movement has now made its mark on the main Welsh canals. For many the outstanding challenge is the full restoration to navigation of the Monmouthshire Canal, through Cwmbran to Malpas Junction at Newport. This is still the goal of the enthusiasts. The combination of problems created by road improvements and severe lack of finance are the major hurdles. For many the second re-opening of the whole of the Brecon and Abergavenny Canal, just before Easter 1981, demonstrated the rapid revival of pleasure traffic on that restored waterway as a means of generating substantially more public support for the complete revival of the Monmouthshire Main Line in the late 1980s. This will offer a new access to the Brecon Beacons National Park, and so bring new life back to the old water route. A far cry from the 1950s, when the whole Welsh canal network was rapidly falling into disrepair through lack of interest and through neglect.

*   *   *   *   *

17.–THAMES AND SEVERN LINKS

Links between the navigable rivers, Severn and Thames, was one of the earliest canal schemes to be promoted, yet one of the latest to mature. The development of the Avon, Kennet and Stroudwater Navigations each offered a means of providing the cross watershed link. The first to be completed was the Thames and Severn Canal, linking Lechlade with Stroud, in 1789. As the Oxford Canal had not been completed by this time, the Thames and Severn Canal offered the first complete inland water route from Birmingham to London, but suffered considerably from the poor state of the upper Thames Navigation because of its shoals and staunches. Although opened some 20 years later, the Kennet and Avon Canal provided a more reliable link between the two great rivers, but it suffered from the hazards of the lower Severn Navigation between Sharpness and Bristol, Avonmouth. The broad gauge of the locks and the vision of the structures that Rennie created, made for the optimum use of the Kennet and Avon Canal, while the strictures imposed by the difference in gauge between the Stroudwater and the Thames and Severn Canal retarded the development of the latter.

Both canals quickly felt the impact of railway development. By the 1880s both were owned by the Great Western Railway Company, who by then had little sympathy for canal traffic at its former high level. The first link to fail was the Thames and Severn Canal. Water leakage from the summit level and low toll revenue made its retention unwarranted, and by 1927 part of the canal was abandoned. Thereafter the canal, and its interlinked Wiltshire and Berkshire Canal, gradually mouldered and became infilled.

The Stroudwater Navigation and the Kennet and Avon Canal both survived the war years 1939 to 1945, but were by then in a poor state of repair. The plight of the Kennet and Avon Canal was the first to interest the waterways enthusiasts who formed the Inland Waterways Association in 1946. One of the I.W.A. founders, L. T. C. Rolt, spent the war years living on board his boat, *Cressy,* at Hungerford. It was from that base that his best-known book, *Narrow Boat,* was written, which pleaded so well for the retention of the canals.

The history of the campaign to restore the Kennet and Avon Canal is one of the most famous accounts of the restoration movement, as is the growth, development and work of the Kennet and Avon Canal Association, which later became the Kennet and Avon Canal Trust. Over nearly three decades the small body of enthusiasts, who saw the last boat pass through the full length of the

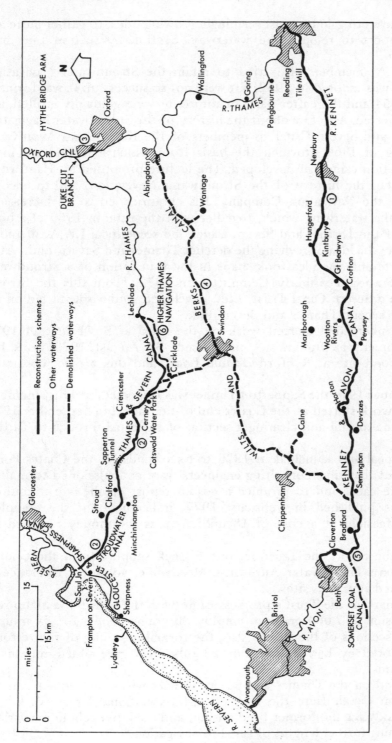

Map 17.—Thames and Severn Links

(1) Kennet and Avon Canal; (2) Thames and Severn Canal; (3) Hythe Bridge Arm; (4) Wilts and Berks Canal; (5) Somerset Coal Canal; (6) Higher Thames Navigation

canal in 1951, have struggled against seemingly growing odds, to gather more and more public support to re-open the waterway. Section by section they have achieved their aim.

The local I.W.A. members also tried to retain the Stroudwater Navigation, when its closure was mooted in 1952, but were not so successful. It was formally abandoned in 1954 and thereafter parts of the route were gradually infilled, and some bridges culverted. A lecture about the history of the Stroudwater Navigation and the Thames and Severn Canal to members of the Kennet and Avon Canal Trust in Reading in 1964 provided the basis from which a second and more successful restoration campaign developed. The lecture prompted M. Hanford to investigate in detail the history of the Stroudwater Navigation, and to become a shareholder in the Navigation Company. His enquiries led to an increase in local interest in the waterway, which, together with the issue in 1969 of a book on the history of the Thames and Severn Canal, led some local I.W.A. members actively to resume the idea of reviving the derelict Thames and Severn Link. After some abortive attempts the idea took shape in the foundation of a Stroudwater Navigation Restoration Feasibility Committee in 1972. From this the Stroudwater, Thames and Severn Canal Trust, Ltd., developed, and work started on the restoration of the second Thames and Severn link.

The Trust members first started work on the canal at Bowbridge in 1973, purchasing equipment as fund-raising progressed. By August 1973 work had started on a second site at Ryeford Double Lock, and this project continued throughout 1974.

During September 1974 the Sapperton Tunnel was inspected by Trust members and, as a result, work started at the Coates end of the tunnel in September 1975, restoring the tunnel portal and clearing a section of the canal through to Tarlton Bridge.

A national appeal was launched in 1976 to raise funds for the Coates Portal restoration. About that time consulting engineers were commissioned to make a full survey of the canal and to produce a costed report on the work required. Their report was published in February 1977, indicating that the complete restoration was feasible at a cost of £8 million, plus the money required for land purchase.

Armed with the report the Trust set out to seek support from the County Council and Severn–Trent Water Authority. Meanwhile, volunteer clearance of the canal continued at various sites.

A major landmark in the Trust's progress came with the award of a Manpower Services Commission £17,000 grant to employ 20 young people for six months to clear further sections of the canal. Also, the formal unveiling of the restored Coates Tunnel portal by Earl Bathurst on 23 July 1977 gave added impetus to their long-term aims.

Work progressed on the Thames and Severn Canal revival, and equally on the Kennet and Avon Canal. Here the Kennet and Avon Canal Trust worked in unison with the B.W.B., the former fund-raising, and the latter rebuilding various locks and re-opening further lengths of canal to navigation.

Perhaps the greatest advance came in 1977 with the facility to rebuild the two-mile Limpley Stoke dry section, financed from a Job Creation Grant. Work on this section was completed in July 1978. Earlier the same year an extension of the Job Creation Scheme to a second site, the Devizes 29 Locks, provided the means to overcome the other major barrier to the complete restoration of the canal. For this project the Trust had to find the £300,000 required for new lock gates. This, with their share of the finance for the earlier Job Creation project, and a forward commitment by B.W.B. to restore other sections of the canal over the next four years, meant that the Trust had to find a further £500,000. To do this a national appeal was launched in April 1978, aiming at the complete re-opening of through navigation from Reading to Bath and Bristol by 1985.

On a lesser scale was a project proposed by the I.W.A. Oxford Branch in 1973 for the restoration of the quarter-mile Hythe Bridge Arm of the Oxford Canal, to provide short-term moorings near the centre of Oxford. The project finally got underway in 1976 with the blessing of Oxford City Council and the B.W.B. Volunteers cleared the banks of the Arm, and a B.W.B. dredger completed the restoration work in October 1977, allowing boats to use the Arm again after a lapse of 17 years.

The only other major derelict waterway linking the Thames also gained some support in 1977 when the Wiltshire and Berkshire Canal Amenity Group was formed. Their aim was to protect the remaining sections of the canal and to revive short stretches of the dormant waterway as a public amenity. The group started work in early 1978 on a short stretch of canal at Kingshill, on the outskirts of Swindon, with the assistance of Thamesdown Council, who owned it. About one-third of a mile of weed-choked canal was to be cleared, and facilities provided for angling and small boats. This project was subsequently helped by a local Manpower Services Commission Work Experience Scheme.

To extend its rôle, the Group made contact with all the parish councils along the route of the canal during 1978. Thus they gained permission to work at a second site, at Shrivenham, in 1979. Here a minor road bridge crossed the canal, and the adjacent canal bed was used as an illicit rubbish dump by 'fly tippers'. The Group held a series of monthly working parties to remove the rubbish, and Oxfordshire County Council provided free skips for material that could not be burned. The Group's reputation grew from this, and some members undertook a survey in January 1979 of the 12 miles of canal between East Challow and Bourton to extend the restoration site. None of the landowners objected to the study and so the Group were able to publish a two-part report in May 1979. The first section contained a full account of the state of the surveyed section of the canal, while the second discussed the range of options. In particular it suggested that a drawbridge could be rebuilt at East Challow. For this, the Group received the support of the local Parish Council and the County Council, who were able to place a temporary footbridge across the canal until the new bridge could be built by the Group.

They aimed to start two new developments during 1980. The first was at Dauntsey, where the owner of the section was sympathetic towards the restoration of about a mile of canal. However, the second, at Wootton Bassett, proved more difficult to get underway. Here nearly a mile of the canal was owned by Wiltshire County Council, who announced that they planned to use it as a rubbish tip. Both the Group and the local Town Council found this proposal unacceptable and the Group decided to press for planning permission to renovate the canal. The issue finally went to an Enquiry, after the County Council had rejected the planning application, but the Group subsequently won their appeal, and in 1981 were given permission to develop the site as an amenity area. However, in spite of winning the appeal, the Group were again temporarily thwarted when the County Council allowed a builder to fill in a short section of the canal and construct a foul sewer across it, right in the middle of the very section which the Enquiry Inspector had given them permission to restore! Fortunately they were more successful on another Wiltshire site at Calne, where they had permission to restore 1,200 yards of the canal Branch. This work included a brick-arched bridge, for which the Group gained a Shell Waterways Award of £275. Here they linked with the Calne Civic Society to develop their plans, and published a joint report, setting out various long-term ideas, including the creation of a museum associated with the canal in the old Wiltshire and Berkshire Canal Company headquarters building in Calne itself.

On a totally different scale were the long-term aims of the Kennet and Avon Canal Trust, whose fund-raising efforts to re-open the Thames and Severn Link dwarf almost every other canal restoration scheme. It is impossible in a short review such as this to identify even part of the restoration work they were able to complete each year, but some impression can be gained when it is appreciated that by 1979 their 5,000-plus members had already financed restoration work at over £407,000, and, during the preceding financial year, they had actually raised £132,679 from subscriptions, donations and other fund-raising schemes, with the prospect of even more in subsequent years as their major Devizes Flight Fund-Raising Appeal reaped its rewards. This fund-raising capacity meant that they could place orders quickly for the new metal top gates at Devizes, with a view to starting on the re-gating of the whole flight of 29 locks in 1980.

Perhaps of even more immediate practical importance to local boaters was the re-opening in August 1981 of part of the canal from Newbury through to the Crofton Pumping Station, after 30 years of closure. This enabled craft in the then landlocked Newbury section to have a greatly extended cruising ground. It also considerably enhanced the amenity value of, and the revenue from visitors to the restored Crofton Pumping Station, which provided a useful fund-raiser for the Trust. At the re-opening ceremony the Chairman of the Trust, Admiral Sir William O'Brien, was able to spell out the Trust's next objectives. Although the Trust accepted that there were three urgent projects to be undertaken, it also realised that lack of funds would mean that priorities had to be drawn. Because of this, they had decided that the continuation of the restoration through the remaining six locks of the Crofton Flight should be postponed for the short term. Instead, the Trust decided to concentrate its resources towards re-opening the canal in Berkshire, where the major problem involved the six turf-sided locks, all of which needed complete rebuilding to meet modern safety standards. They also agreed to press ahead with the installation of back pumping plants, especially for Bath, where the canal had officially been re-opened in 1976 but then closed to boats through lack of a reliable water supply.

In 1981 Berkshire County Council provided the means for another break-through towards the full re-opening of the waterway, when they committed themselves to replacing the defunct Aldermaston Swing Bridge with a new lifting bridge designed to meet the needs of heavy modern road traffic. The whole scheme was undertaken as part of a trunk road improvement programme to eliminate a high risk accident spot. When it was completed in 1982, the new structure was unique in that it could be operated by the boater on demand, simply by using a push-button system to activate the barriers and flashing lights, and automatically to open the bridge. This removed one of the major obstacles to the full re-opening of the eastern section of the canal.

In 1982 the major event for the Kennet and Avon Canal Trust was a Rally of Boats and a cruise from Bathampton to Dundas to celebrate the re-re-opening of that stretch of the canal. This was made possible by a formal maintenance agreement between the Trust and B.W.B., whereby the Trust agreed to pay £15,000 a year over the following five years to keep the canal open at Bath, between Easter and October, along with a new auxiliary water supply pump at Claverton. It was unfortunate that a leak in the Dundas Aqueduct prevented the reconstructed former dry-section at Limpley Stoke from being re-opened officially at the same time.

However, the Dundas Celebration Cruise provided an opportunity to launch yet another small restoration scheme, when several members of local councils and B.W.B. officials were shown the first 400 yards dry length of the old Somerset Coal Canal which two local residents, Timothy and Wendy Wheeldon, planned to restore for use as a mooring and focal point for the re-opened section. Their scheme involved the construction of a new swing bridge across the entrance to the old canal, and clearing out the rubbish and debris from the canal line, part of which was used as a car repair yard and the remainder was simply overgrown scrubland. The scheme envisaged the provision of facilities for boats, including a slipway, fuel, water, and toilet and rubbish disposal, as well as secure moorings for boat owners along the hillside route from Dundas Aqueduct to *The Viaduct Hotel*, on the A36 road.

In summer 1982 the Kennet and Avon Trust produced its long-term plans for the Interpretation of the Canal to the public, as part of its aim to develop fully the range of its waterway amenities. This project was sponsored jointly by the Carnegie United Kingdom Trust and the Countryside Commission. It set out a strategy for enhancing the buildings and areas of historic interest along the canal, so that more people could benefit from the revived canal.

The Canal Trust, Ltd., celebrated its 21st anniversary in 1983. An article by Ken Clew in *Waterways World* (June) detailed its major achievements over the years and showed how rapidly the momentum of restoration had increased in the last decade. By early 1983 the Trust announced that a new, major Manpower Services Commission scheme was to be sponsored by Berkshire County Council, Newbury District Council, and the Trust themselves, who had to find £50,000 towards the cost of materials and equipment. The scheme covered the restoration of the derelict Aldermaston and Widemead Locks, together with exploratory work at Monkey Marsh Lock and the clearance of intervening pounds. In combination with other works already in hand, it meant that by mid-1984 only five miles of canal, five turf-sided locks, and a couple of swing bridges would obstruct the through route, from its link with the Thames at Reading to the Crofton Pumping Station.

Elsewhere, after that, six remaining derelict locks at Crofton and the provision of bottom gates for the Devizes Flight would be the only obstacles. Finance was to be the key. However, when one considers the tremendous fund-raising capacity of the Trust, who in the 19 years to January 1982 had raised £834,648 towards the full restoration of the canal, the final target is at last seen to be coming within their grasp; particularly during the preceding six years the Trust's record for financing restoration work is remarkable in its own right:

Money Spent On Restoration Work over the Five-Year Period 1977–1981 Inclusive

Year			£	Year			£
1977	..	..	78,278	1981	..	..	95,694
1978	..	..	73,977				
1979	..	..	32,623	Total spent	..	£417,596	
1980	..	..	137,024				

A date for the full re-opening of the waterway was clearly in the Trust's mind when, in March 1983, they announced publicly that they had resolved, after the canal was completely restored, to continue to support the maintenance costs of waterway for which they and their predecessors had fought for over thirty years.

This sort of time span was also in the minds of the Stroudwater, Thames and Severn Trust when they celebrated the Bi-centenary of the Stroudwater Navigation on 21 July 1979. At that time, they were busy clearing a section of the waterway between Eastington and Ryeford, having gained approval in principle from the proprietors of the Navigation completely to restore the Stroudwater Canal from the Gloucester and Berkeley Canal at Saul to the junction with the Thames and Severn Canal at Wallbridge.

On the Thames and Severn Canal itself, in 1979, working parties were putting the finishing touches to the restored eastern Sapperton Tunnel Portal at Coates and clearing the canal and the lock at Cerney Wick. There were also negotiations to gain access to further work-sites up and down the canal route. It came as a complete shock, therefore, when Gloucester County Council announced their plan to replace a minor road bridge at Daneway, near the western end of the tunnel, with a culvert and embankment. Fortunately the Trust were able to have the bridge listed as a structure of Architectural and Historic Interest, and the County Council subsequently agreed to strengthen the bridge, rather than continue with their earlier plans for its destruction.

In 1980, the Stroudwater, Thames and Severn Canal Trust re-structured its operations to improve its work on either side of the Sapperton Tunnel. A new Thames End Branch was formed, initially to concentrate on a new site near Cricklade, which was over 3½ miles long with four locks. As most of this project fell within the new Cotswold Water Park, an area of flooded gravel pits, the scheme increased the prospect of an alternative link with the Thames and with the Water Park itself.

This idea coincided with the plan of the I.W.A., Oxford and South Bucks. Branch, who had made a submission to Shell, under a second Inland Waterways Restoration Awards Scheme, in July 1979, for finance to undertake a Feasibility Study to improve the Higher Thames upstream from Lechlade to Cricklade, thus extending the cruising area by some ten miles. Fortunately, Shell felt able to make a £300 award for the project and, following a successful appeal for further funds, the consulting engineers, Sir Alexander Gibb and Partners, were instructed in 1980 to carry out the study and to prepare a preliminary report. The I.W.A. formed a Higher Thames Steering Committee to co-ordinate the scheme. They produced a Companion Report for wider distribution, which briefly outlined the consultants' findings. It also fell to this Steering Committee to present to the public the longer-term plans.

The consultants concluded that from an engineering point of view the scheme was entirely feasible and could best be achieved by the construction of three new locks and associated weirs. Although three main roads crossed the river, no major bridge re-construction would be required, other than the dredging and protection of existing foundations. The cost of the scheme was estimated, in October 1980, at £1.6 million.

The Higher Thames Improvement Project was launched officially at a Public Meeting at Cricklade on 11 May 1981, and received a favourable response. By the time the meeting closed, the Steering Committee had already laid its future plans. These not only included the development of the Thames through to Cricklade as a cruising route for motor cruisers, but more importantly embraced the idea of creating a connection with the line of the Thames and Severn Canal, in the vicinity of Cricklade, by use of the River Churn, thereby extending further westward the new cruising route, as sections of the canal were restored.

To promote public interest in these aims, Rallies of Boats were held between Lechlade and Cricklade in both June 1982 and June 1983. These brought the attention of local authorities to increased job opportunities and leisure amenities if the scheme went ahead.

The prospect of developing public support led the Stroudwater, Thames and Severn Canal Trust, Western Branch, to concentrate their efforts in 1980 on the section of the Stroudwater Navigation, between Stonehouse railway bridge and Ryeford Double Lock, in order to clear and dredge the intervening pond and introduce a trip boat on it to increase their funds. The Trust's dredger was floated in October 1980 to speed up the clearance work. Work also started on the clearance of the Thames and Severn Canal bed at Daneway, from the *Daneway Inn* to within sight of the Western Sapperton Tunnel Portal. Discussions also took place with the local landowners to obtain a restoration licence for the revival of this length of canal.

In January 1981 the Trust obtained two mud boats to help with the dredging, and these were moved to the Stroudwater Navigation at Ryeford in the hope that full-scale dredging could soon get under way. In the interim, clearance of the towpath and canal banks proceeded apace so that full restoration could be undertaken as soon as all the equipment and funds were available.

All did not proceed as planned, and by the close of 1981 the Trust faced a major problem when Gloucester County Council announced plans to infill a quarter-mile section of the canal in Stroud as a route for a proposed by-pass road. Fortunately, the Trust were able to show that the canal line could be preserved at little extra cost, by the use of an alternative route, and after a rigorous public campaign their views were accepted.

In February 1982 Stroud District Council passed a resolution that there should be no further obstruction, whether by road or building development, which would involve infilling or blocking of the canal line, which would be prejudicial to eventual complete restoration. This was followed, in July 1982, with acceptance by Gloucester County Council that the proposed Stroud by-pass route should not encroach on the canal line. These moves were a tremendous boost to the Trust as they showed, at last, that local government was thinking in more constructive terms towards the full restoration of the canal.

Summer 1982 saw further progress at the Daneway end of the Sapperton Tunnel, where most of the collapsed masonry had been lifted from the canal, giving an indication of the extent of the amount of stone required to repair the tunnel portal. Likewise, a week-long Work Camp, organised by the British Trust for Conservation Volunteers, started rebuilding the off-bank approach wall of the canal near the tunnel mouth. Tentative thoughts were then turning to rebuilding the portal of the tunnel as a major project for summer 1983, provided that finance was available.

The Trust therefore appointed a professional fund-raiser (a member who offered the service for a nominal fee) in 1982, and set out to raise some £250,000 to get the restoration fully underway. About that time a formal application was made to the Manpower Services Commission for a team of six men to work on the Stroudwater dredging project. It was also hoped that the support of Cotswold, Cricklade and Latton Councils for restoring the canal to full navigation and linking it to the Water Park and the Thames, would lead to the provision of funds for similar work at the eastern end.

A remarkable breakthrough for the Trust's fund-raising efforts came in October 1982 when B.B.C. T.V. broadcast a 'Good Cause Appeal' on behalf of of their work. This raised over £7,700, and brought in some offers of physical assistance, materials and equipment.

The launching of the Trust's refurbished tug boat at Ryeford completed their equipment for dredging, which proceeded on the Stroudwater in advance of the M.S.C. Community Enterprise scheme, due to start in May 1983. Plans were also well advanced to replace Ryeford Pedestrian Bridge with a new swing bridge, the cost of which was to be met by the Company of Proprietors.

Elsewhere on the Thames and Severn Canal a bridge across a gap in the towpath had been rebuilt by Trust members near Cerney Wick, and work was proceeding in the restoration of Cerney Wick Lock. The towpath between Latton Junction and South Cerney had also been cleared completely and provided an ideal walkway to study that stretch of the canal.

In spring 1983 it was decided to employ a part-time manager to enable the Trust to build on the political work that had already been undertaken and to convert the 'behind the scenes' efforts into tangible results. It was hoped that this would provide the means to capitalise on the various other Job Creation Schemes and Grants funded by central government, which offered the most direct means to revive more sections of the waterway at a far faster pace.

Clearly, the waterway restoration movement in the region is rapidly gaining momentum. The first scheme in the area, the Kennet and Avon revival, is nearing its final goal. The rebuilding of the remaining turf-sided locks should be the last major problem to be overcome. Thereafter all else will depend on the Kennet and Avon Canals Trusts' ability to raise the necessary finance. They seem sure that they can do this within the next four years.

When the Kennet and Avon Canal is re-opened in the mid-1980s, the more active local enthusiasts may well turn their attention to the second Thames and Severn Link, where the groundwork undertaken so far by the Stroudwater, Thames and Severn Trust should provide a reasonable basis for opening that waterway by the turn of the century. If the Higher Thames scheme comes to early fruition, then that could well advance the Thames and Severn restoration timescale quite dramatically. Elsewhere, the plans for the Wiltshire and Berkshire Canal now seem to be making steady progress. However, the only completed scheme so far is that of the revival of the Hythe Bridge Arm. This is now regularly used by boats as a safe mooring, near to the centre of Oxford.

Looking ahead, the heavy and ever-growing pleasure traffic on both the Thames and Southern Oxford Canal perhaps provides the best omen for the longer-term future of the waterways in this region. When both Thames and Severn Links are re-opened, these will provide some of Southern England's most sought-after water recreation.

*   *   *   *   *

18.—SOUTHERN ENGLAND

The majority of inland waterways of Southern England derived from the activity of the dockyards at Portsmouth and Southampton and the development of commerce in Surrey, Sussex, and Hampshire in the 17th and 18th centuries. London was by then the major market for the agricultural produce of the area, while the need for a link with the dockyards at Portsmouth and Southampton ensured a regular return of cargo from the metropolis.

In Hampshire the need to import coal and export agricultural produce prompted an Act to make the Itchen navigable in 1663. In that same a Bill reached a second reading in the Lords, which was to make various rivers navigable to London from towns, including Farnham and Petersfield, and also from Southampton to Winchester and Alresford.

The growing importance of Guildford as an agricultural and manufacturing centre by 1651 had led to the canalisation of the river Wey from the Thames at Weybridge as far as Guildford. The opening of the extension of the navigation to Godalming in 1763 boosted the coal and timber trade. This was increased by the carriage of government stores and munitions, destined for Portsmouth during the American War of Independence.

As the value of water transport to agriculture became increasingly evident, and the state of the roads grew worse, with increasing use by coaches and heavy wagons, so various schemes for developing links from the Thames across Surrey, Sussex and Hampshire to the docks materialised. The Wey and Arun and the Portsmouth and Arundel Canals linked the Thames with Portsmouth, while Basingstoke and Winchester both gained water routes for their trade.

Just as the pressure for reliable and faster links gave rise to the inland waterways, so the same pressure later led to early railway links through the area. The London and Southampton Railway was opened in 1839 and a railway line reached Portsmouth in 1841. As more railways spread across the region and the road network rapidly improved, so the value of the waterways declined. The Portsmouth and Arundel Canal was the first to close, and with the loss of this link to Portsmouth the Wey and Arun Canal was abandoned in 1871. The last commercial craft reached Winchester in 1869, and Basingstoke Wharf saw its last in 1914, although little regular traffic had used the upper reaches since the 1860s. With the loss of commercial traffic, so the navigations mouldered and decayed, except for the lower reaches of the Basingstoke Canal and the Wey Navigation, both of which were used by commercial craft until the late 1940s. After this only H. Stevens's barges between London Docks and Coxes Lock grain mill on the Wey Navigation continued until 1969. This traffic was revived for a short time in the early 1980s.

Long before then the strange lure of the Basingstoke Canal, which had previously been the centre of several revivals, had attracted the attention of the waterway restorers. The news of the sale of the Basingstoke Canal in 1948 presented the young Inland Waterways Association with an almost impossible decision: to purchase or to lose the canal. A local enthusiast, L. A. Edwards, fought hard to keep the canal. As had happened so often before, the canal's future became the centre of intrigue. Early plans for its full restoration slowly receded, but a cruiser was able to reach the upper level and get to North Warnborough in 1957. This was the last craft to do so, and thereafter the waterway fell into further decay.

By the early 1960s the I.W.A. was recognised as a body concerned about the revival of waterways. Thus they were able to assist in the campaign for the restoration of Ports Creek in 1963. It was not until 1966 that a similar success could be claimed for the Basingstoke Canal. In that year a local enthusiast, E. Woolgar, gathered support for a revival of the Basingstoke restoration

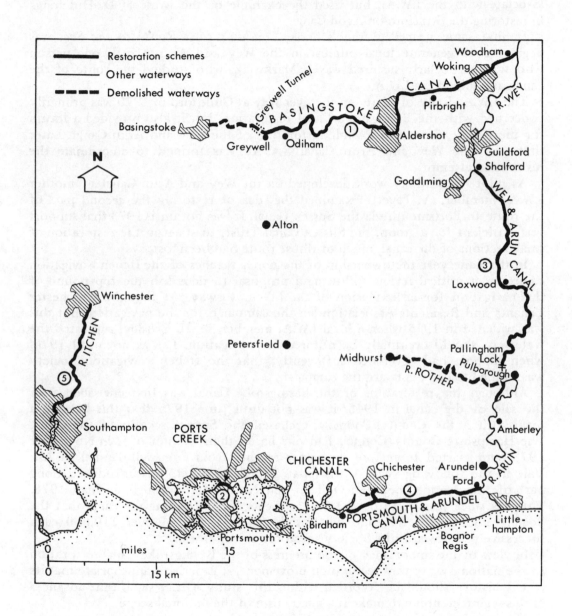

Map 18.—Southern England
(1) Basingstoke Canal; (2) Ports Creek; (3) Wey and Arun Canal; (4) Portsmouth and
Arundel Canal; (5) Itchen Nàvigation

campaign. Because of the conflict between the I.W.A. and the owners of the canal, the New Basingstoke Canal Company, the new group did not openly associate with the I.W.A., but used the example of the work of D. Hutchings in restoring the Stratford-on-Avon Canal.

In that same year Paul Vine's book, *London's Lost Route to the Sea,* was beginning to generate local interest in the Wey and Arun Canal; one person who was particularly inspired was J. Markwick, who studied the route of the canal, and joined the I.W.A.

The I.W.A. Rally of Boats on the river Wey at Guildford in 1970 was primarily concerned with the Basingstoke Canal restoration, but it also provided a forum for the debate about the possible restoration of the Wey and Arun Canal. Later that year the Wey and Arun Canal Society was formed to co-ordinate the restoration attempt.

As pilot restoration work developed on the Wey and Arun Canal so another I.W.A. member, A. Pagett, examined the idea of restoring the second part of the route to Portsmouth via the Sussex Canal. It was not until 1973 that support was sufficient for a group, the Sussex Canal Trust, to start on the restoration of small sections of the canal, much of whose route had been lost.

In the same year the ownership of the upper reaches of the Itchen Navigation came under critical review following a proposal to demolish the top pound of the navigation for an extension of the M3 motorway. At first the Winchester Tenants and Residents Association led the campaign for the navigation, but this was widened in 1975 when a local I.W.A. member, G. H. Crosley, suggested the waterway should eventually be restored for navigation. It was not until 1976, when support had developed sufficiently, that the Itchen Navigation Society was formed to carry forward the campaign.

Although the restoration of the Basingstoke Canal was first envisaged after the sale of the canal in 1948, it was not until June 1975 that this became a reality when the County Council purchased the Surrey section of the canal. The Hampshire County Council had purchased their section of it in November 1973, and started to restore the upper reaches from Greywell Tunnel to Ash Vale in the following year. A trip boat, *John Pinkerton,* was introduced along part of this section, between Odiham and North Warnborough, in May 1978. This has since proved to be the best advocate for re-opening the canal that the Society could wish for, and has raised a clear profit of over £10,000 each successive year towards the Society's restoration expenses.

In view of the importance of the progress of the Basingstoke Canal restoration to the national waterway restoration movement, it is perhaps appropriate that its recent history should be recorded within this study. Other significant advances in this region combine to make it a microcosm of the national scene.

For many enthusiasts the turning point in the battle to restore the Basingstoke Canal was one very wet week-end in October 1977, when some 600 volunteers turned out to work on the canal. The Waterway Recovery Group's 'Big Dig' made a remarkable impact on nine locks of the Deepcut Flight and on two locks at Brookwood, by clearing silt and excavating new by-pass weirs. Afterwards it was estimated that it would have taken normal working parties over a year to do the same amount of work. However, above all else it proved to the Surrey County Council that the volunteers, and the Surrey and Hampshire Canal Society, would keep their side of the bargain to restore the canal completely.

This same commitment had already been demonstrated to the Hampshire County Council when the Canal Society brought a 70-ton steam-powered floating dredger, *Perseverance,* which, after a complete overhaul, was launched at Colt Hill, Odiham, in July 1974. The floating dredger was the ideal tool. Its boilers could be fired from the wood cleared from the towpath and it could work its own way along the silt- and weed-choked canal, so avoiding the problems of bankside dredging. By the close of 1977 the dredger had cleared over three miles of canal eastwards from North Warnborough. To improve this operation the Society purchased, through a donation of £1,000 from Johnson Wax of Frimley, a couple of tugs and some old gravel barges. These, combined with a dragline crane at the canalside tipping site, enabled up to 800 tons of silt and weed to be cleared by volunteers each week-end. Elsewhere, dredging had also been undertaken by various means, the most interesting of which was at Fleet, in 1977, where the Society recovered the cost of the hire of a Hymac excavator, used to clear several hundred yards of canal, by selling the silt to the local council to cover a rubbish tip. For its part the Hampshire County Council employed four full-time canal wardens on general maintenance work, and by 1977 had rebuilt the Whitewater Aqueduct and reinstated a cutting at North Warnborough— both major engineering schemes.

Work in the heavily-locked Surrey section progressed in a very different way. A group of Society members, who were railway enthusiasts, laid a mile-long narrow-gauge line alongside the canal at Deepcut to overcome the problems of lack of road access. By using a small diesel locomotive and skip wagons, the line proved the ideal method of transporting supplies for rebuilding to the various lock sites. By the end of 1977 five lock chambers had been restored, three of them by a team of workers employed by the Society under two grants of £52,000 from the Manpower Services Commission for a 10-month scheme under the Job Creation Programme.

In early 1978 the Manpower Services Commission made the Society a further grant of £129,000, plus £9,000 for operating costs, to employ up to 45 people for a second year on lock restoration work. For its part, Surrey County Council provided £45,000 for building materials and equipment, as well as the professional and technical support needed to ensure that standards were maintained. The Council also organised the dredging of over five miles of canal between Brookwood and Mytchett Lake and in Woking.

Fortunately, the Manpower Services Commission made a third grant to the Society in 1979, making over £250,000 in all, so that by the end of the year 10 of the 14 locks on the Deepcut Flight were complete, apart from gates and lock gear. Even on that front, a special workshop at the top of the flight, financed under the scheme, was producing the gates. Thus the first Deepcut Lock, No. 28, was restored to full working order in September 1979. At the re-opening ceremony the chairman of the Society, R. Higgs, warned that the pace of future restoration could be affected by cutbacks in government aid. In consequence, to ensure that the nucleus of skilled supervisors was not disbanded, the Society decided to raise £30,000 to employ the four supervisors at least until the middle of 1980. The Chairman of Surrey County Council reiterated their policy to see the restoration completed, even if it took a little longer than the five years envisaged in 1977. Fortunately, the Society were able to get an extension grant for three months from the M.S.C., followed by another 12-month Job Creation Grant, to cover the remainder of 1980 and the beginning of 1981. By then it was hoped that the whole of the 14 locks would be rebuilt and the flight re-watered.

Perhaps the other major achievement of 1979 in the Hampshire section was the sealing of the Breach in the Ash Embankment, which had divided the canal in two halves since it occurred in 1968. This work was undertaken by the Hampshire County Council using the spoil from a nearby disused railway embankment. They also started to restore the adjacent Ash Lock, so that the two lengths of canal could be re-united. The Society volunteers were given the task of re-puddling the embankment with clay to prevent a recurrence of the breach. The delivery of the clay along the whole length of the ¾-mile embankment presented a problem which the Society overcame by removing their narrow gauge railway from Deepcut and re-laying it along the embankment towpath from a depot at the southern end. Surrey County Council supplied the clay from the depot, and Society volunteers moved over 9,000 tons along the railway and spread it over the bottom and sides of the whole channel between July 1980 and July 1981.

By the end of 1980 two events ensured the restoration of the canal, which was well over halfway towards completion. These were: the re-opening of a new route for the Society's trip boat, *John Pinkerton*, eastwards from Odiham to Dogsmersfield, made possible by achievements of the steam dredger, and, secondly, the start of work on the St John's Flight of locks, after some local Society members won a £5,000 prize in the Spar Groceries 'Improve your Local Environment' competition. Further advances were made with the help of the Construction Industries Training Board, whose apprentices assisted in rebuilding lock walls as part of their training for a large-scale bricklaying project. All this was indicative of the Society's good speed towards their projected re-opening in 1985 of the whole canal up to Greywell Tunnel. It was, therefore, not unexpected when the County Councils set up a Joint Management Committee to plan the future running of the canal. Out of the 18 places on this Committee, six each went to the County Councils, who entirely owned the canal, and six were allocated to user-representatives, of which two were given to the Society in acknowledgement of their leading rôle in the restoration.

Thus the Surrey and Hampshire Canal Society entered 1981 with a more optimistic air. The prospect of regular income from their trip boat *John Pinkerton* enabled them to employ two full-time workers on the canal, which greatly facilitated the development of further Job Creation Schemes. Hampshire County

Council made a grant to employ six jobless school-leavers and a supervisor for 12 months to complete the remaining work on the Ash Embankment, whilst Surrey Council planned to promote a Work Experience Scheme using local unemployed labour. This materialised in the form of a further Manpower Services Commission grant to the Society, for 1981/82, of £103,000 to employ 32 young people and eight supervisors/trainers on the restoration work. Apart from the rebuilding of the lock at Deepcut, the group were also able to rebuild Cowshot Bridge as a replica of the former brick-arched bridge. To speed up the completion of lock-gating work, Surrey County Council agreed to supply wood to a local contractor, who could manufacture top gates in bulk and deliver then in kit form to the Surrey and Hampshire Canal Society workshops. Volunteers could assemble the gates and reduce the cost to about £350 per pair. The Society's own carpenters continued to build the bottom gates. Even so, it meant that the locks were being re-gated at a much faster rate than before. By the end of 1981 the top gates for the whole Deepcut Flight were in place, but a lot more bottom gates were required.

The main body of the Job Creation team concentrated on the repairs needed before the section between Ash Lock and the top of the Deepcut Flight could be re-watered. Major tasks here included the rebuilding of a large run-off weir at Ash Vale, together with a new weir on the embankment itself to protect that stretch of the canal.

By 1982 repair work on the Ash Embankment was nearly complete, and the re-watering was able to proceed. Re-watering also took place down the Deepcut Flight, where the majority of the locks had been re-gated. This evidence of progress enabled the Society to apply for a further Manpower Services Commission grant and gained an award of £68,000 to employ 25 full-time workers during 1982/83.

Unfortunately all work did not proceed as planned during 1982. A considerable bank slip in the Dogmersfield cutting delayed dredging there for most of the year, and a bank breach above Deepcut Lock, No. 26, caused additional delay at the end of the year. However, much was achieved during the year: all the remainder of the Deepcut Lock Flight only required the finishing touches. As a result, the Manpower Services Commission team could start on a new dry dock at the top of the Deepcut Flight, and, further down the line, Lock 5, at Woodham, and Locks 9, 10 and 11 on the St Johns Flight were making rapid recovery to full working state. More important, stop plank grooves were also installed at four bridges in the Ash to Deepcut section, to ensure that the water in this long pound could be more effectively controlled in the event of future bank or aqueduct problems.

It had been hoped to hold an official ceremony during the last week-end in April 1983, to mark the restoration of Ash Embankment and the completion of the Deepcut Locks, but this had to be put back to September 1983. The highlight of the spring event was to have been a cruise by the Society's trip boat *John Pinkerton* from Odiham to Deepcut, showing exactly how far the restoration work on the upper reaches of the canal had progressed. The venture had to be postponed because the trip boat might not have been able to clear the undredged section at Dogmersfield, where subsidence had delayed work on clearance for much of 1982.

Fortunately plans to stabilise the canal banking were completed by the close of 1982, and the work on it commenced in April 1983. The four-month project was undertaken by the Hampshire Canal Wardens and a group of young people funded by the Manpower Services Commission. Materials were supplied by Hampshire County Council out of the £73,000 they had allocated during 1982/83 for capital expenditure on their section of the canal.

The publicity value of smaller craft regularly completing the 14-mile restored section encouraged the Society, in conjunction with the local I.W.A. Branch, to organise a series of small boat cruises between April and October 1983. All boats completing the 14-mile voyage from Ash Lock to Warnborough Lift Bridge were to be presented with a certificate to commemorate their efforts.

The Surrey and Hampshire Canal Society and the two forward-looking County Councils have come a long way in the last 10 years, especially when it is remembered that Hampshire County Council only applied for its original compulsory purchase order on 6 December 1972. The pace of events will certainly quicken over the next two years, and 1985 is still being tentatively mentioned as the date for the 'Grand Re-Opening'. However, it will not be through the lack of effort by Surrey and Hampshire Canal Society members if that target is not achieved.

While there is every chance of the Basingstoke Canal being re-opened fairly quickly, the Wey and Arun Canal Trust have a far longer-term scheme on their hands. Even in 1977, as the Basingstoke Canal was slowly coming back to life, the Wey and Arun Canal Trust were fighting the 'doubters' of their plans. They neither had County Council backing, nor was the whole of the canal line intact. The Trust essentially had three major hurdles to overcome before they could convince local people that the canal could be fully restored. Firstly, they had to persuade the owners of the sections of land through which the canal line passed to allow them to restore the canal. Secondly, they had to raise the money to get the work underway. Thirdly, they had to devise a strategy enabling them to gain credit for their achievements so that they could build on their earlier successes and prove to others that they would be able completely to revive the canal in the long term. It is with this in mind that the Trust's progress over the last decade must be viewed.

When the Wey and Arun Canal Society was formed in 1970, it had to show that it could revive such sections of the waterway as were readily accessible. Early clearance projects were centred on Newbridge, Loxwood, Rowley, Run Common, and Birtley. Thus the Society began to prove its credibility, especially at Birtley where over 1,200 tons of clay, donated by the local brick company and conveyed by local contractors at favourable rates, was used to plug a major breach. Subsequently, the canal was re-watered and re-stocked with fish by the local angling club, to prove what a valuable asset the restored waterway could be.

In 1973 the Society became the Wey and Arun Canal Trust, a limited company and a registered charity. This enabled it to enter into agreements with landowners, and more especially to raise funds. At this time the Trust undertook and published a comprehensive survey of the canal. This examined the problems of regenerating the canal, and offered solutions to the barriers which had arisen in the 100 years since the canal was officially abandoned.

Initially, works were started at two sites in Surrey and three stretches in Sussex, but subsequently the Trust's concentration focused on two sites in Sussex. One was at Pallingham where a bridge over the canal, on a much used bridleway, was close to collapse. Here the Trust had to work under the aegis of the Pulborough Society because of difficult local politics. The local Council and landowner both offered financial aid, and the Trust provided the engineering skills. In just under two years the old bridge and its foundations were virtually dismantled and the whole structure rebuilt to withstand another century of wear. The project later won a Civic Trust commendation and, as the local landowner was so impressed by the restored bridge, the Trust were able to claim full credit for their effort. Their second project was between Newbridge and Malham, where two locks and four bridges, together with culverts and weirs, offered a major engineering challenge, yet when completed they could provide a usable two-mile section of restored canal.

Rowner Lock was the first task to be tackled on the Newbridge to Malham length, mainly because the local landowner was sympathetic to the Trust's aims. During the mid-1970s the lock chamber was cleared and repaired, and the bridge over the lock was rebuilt with reinforced decking and new parapets. A local school project provided the means of obtaining new top gates and subsequently the Trust procured a pair of Grand Union lock gates, which were later adapted in their own workshops.

North of Rowner Lock a second bridge carried a bridle path over the canal. Here the Trust was able to stabilise the unsafe brick arch of Loves Bridge, and the bridge was later strengthened with a new reinforced concrete decking. New parapets also were built to replace the old ones which had crumbled. The Trust subsequently dredged the section of the canal south of this bridge with a J.C.B., free of charge, as a demonstration to local businessmen of their digging machines.

To the north of the restored bridge, one of the Trust's most ambitious engineering works was undertaken. A major culvert under the canal was broken and had fractured the canal bed. The trust's volunteers excavated the old culvert and replaced it with over 80 feet of twin 21-inch concrete piping, which a local contractor had donated. This project was monitored by the Southern Water Authority, who were well satisfied with the result.

In 1977 the Trust started on the renovation of Malham Lock. Before work could proceed the lock chambers had to be cleared of scrap metal that had accumulated over the years. The sale of this scrap produced a useful contribution to ailing funds. Once the chamber was cleared, trees growing in the lock had to be removed before rebuilding could commence. This involved the complete reconstruction of the upper lock walls, and the provision of a new lock bridge.

This was completed during 1980. Once the local farmer had access over the rebuilt lock bridge, the causeway above the lock was removed. A small broken culvert just north of Malham Lock was also mended, and the canal bed re-puddled ready for re-watering, when the new Malham lock gates could be procured.

One of the Wey and Arun Canal Trust's major fund-raising events is its annual sponsored walk. In 1979 over 400 walkers raised more than £4,500. This enabled the Trust to tackle the remaining obstacle to navigation on their restored two-mile length of canal. This was a low-level farm access bridge, which obstructed the canal at Northlands. As there was no room for a conventional bridge, the Trust's design engineer, O. Jones, drew up plans for a lifting bridge. This was made by an outside contractor and the whole structure erected on 24 May 1980, after Trust volunteers had prepared the foundations. Trust members later laid the decking beams and painted the bridge.

During 1980 the Trust also began to restore the derelict hump-backed canal bridge called Cooks Bridge. Here the bricks from the parapets were re-used, and the whole structure rebuilt. This was the sixth bridge restored by the Trust, and it gained them a £550 Award under the Shell Inland Waterways Awards scheme.

In 1981 the Trust saved a further section of the canal at Elmbridge, near Cranleigh in Surrey, where a site adjacent to the canal was being re-developed for retirement homes. Here the Trust paid for contractors to clear and shape the canal bed ready for re-watering at a later stage. During that year the Trust also installed the bottom gates at Rowner Lock, and after these gates had been fully adjusted, the Trust hoped to re-flood that section of canal to bring the lock back into use. This was delayed through lack of water supply, but, after the canal was filled by heavy rains, the first boat to use the lock for over 100 years passed through on 10 October 1982. This was the Trust's own working boat, *Aeneas*. Once the Trust has secured a reliable water supply for this section, it is hoped to use the lock regularly, perhaps as a run for their first trip boat.

On the northern section, work proceeded during 1981 and 1982 with the rebuilding of Lock 17 at Rowley. The work centred firstly on rebuilding a stream culvert under an access track to the lock, to enable machinery and materials to be taken to the site. After that, plans were made to rebuild a bridge over the lock, as well as to restore the lock itself. For this work the Trust received from Surrey County Council a long-awaited consignment of a group of youngsters, employed under a Manpower Service Commission scheme, to rebuild the lock bridge. Work started on this in October 1982. At the same time, Sussex County Council also sponsored a similar M.S.C. grant-aided project to repair a lock bridge, which carried a public footpath over the canal. In this instance the local parish council took the initiative, as the landowner did not wish the location to become known.

Elsewhere along the canal line, 1982 saw the general clearance of a six-acre site at Gosden. This involved re-defining the public footpaths and providing rustic seats for local residents to enjoy the canal area. For 1983, the Trust had reached agreement for the clearance of a mile of the summit level, next to Dunsfold aerodrome. Secondly, they hoped to complete the full restoration of

Lock 17 at Rowley and, thirdly, they planned to re-gate Malham Lock. The prospect of the revival of the Wey and Arun Canal must be brighter now than ever in the past. The Trust has gained credibility, particularly with landowners and local authorities. One can only hope that, once the Basingstoke Canal is re-opened, more resources will be devoted to the Wey and Arun towards its full revival.

The other man-made section of the London to Portsmouth waterway route, in addition to the Wey and Arun, was the Portsmouth and Arundel Canal. This has been, and still is, the subject of a restoration scheme. After the impressive start in the early 1970s the first local canal society, the Sussex Canal Trust, faltered and soon fell; with it seemed to go any prospect of ever getting the canal revived. However, a local enthusiast, R. S. W. Pollard, was unwilling to let the matter rest, and he and a small group of former Sussex Canal Trust members called a public meeting in Chichester in May 1979. Representatives of West Sussex County Council and Chichester District Council, together with those of the Chichester Anglers Association, who have fishing rights on the Chichester Arm, and of the newly-formed Solent Branch of the I.W.A. attended the meeting. All present offered co-operation and support for rejuvenation of the canal. As a result a new Portsmouth and Arundel Canal Society was formed to replace the Sussex Canal Trust, which had been dissolved. The new Society quickly gained charitable status and set to work on its longer-term plans. Initially it was decided to concentrate on the Arm of the canal, which was owned by West Sussex County Council, linking Chichester to the sea.

A local management committee was formed, including the Anglers, the Council and the Society, and it was hoped that this Committee could ultimately assume responsibility for running the canal, having directed its revival as an amenity for the area. In the interim, the Society itself took a protective rôle over the old canal line, and began to fight infill proposals that came before the local planning committee. Members also started to clear the towing path of the Chichester to Birdham section for canal walkers. Trusty prisoners from the local Ford Open Prison were allowed to assist with some of the work. To show local residents what had been achieved, the Society organised a Guided Walk along the Arm in July 1981, which increased local support.

By 1982 the Canal Society had drawn up a Five Year Plan for developing the Chichester Arm of the canal. This envisaged repairs to the towpath and banks, dredging the Hunston to Birdham section, and replacing the fixed Poyntz bridge at Hunston with one offering full navigational clearance. The latter scheme received active support from Chichester City Council, who arranged for the work to be undertaken by a joint West Sussex County Council and Manpower Services Commission job creation scheme. This involved the removal for renovation of the old Poyntz Bridge and its ultimate re-siting near Chichester Basin at Southgate. A second Community Enterprise Project, also funded by the M.S.C., enabled Chichester Basin walls to be re-pointed and the banks along the Arm to be improved. It was subsequently hoped this team would carry out some dredging along the line, using equipment hired by the Canal Management Committee.

Interest in the future of the Old Canal between Ford and Birdham increased substantially in 1982, Maritime England Year, when the West Sussex County Council produced a *Walkers' Guide* to the line. This provided a detailed description of the canal's remains, and listed the points of access, especially where these were Public Rights of Way.

The Society plans initially to restore the Chichester Arm, to which there are three obstacles. The first is the restoration of Manhood Lock, which is in good condition, though it has no gates. The other two are more major tasks. These are the culverted Donnington Road and Birdham Road bridges, the latter being on the main road to West Wittering. Given adequate finance, both these barriers could be overcome. For the longer term, the route through to Ford offers many trickier problems. Even so, if the Wey and Arun can be re-opened, then this, too, is possible. It will depend on local support and public will.

It was just such support that inspired the region's other main waterway campaign to restore the old Itchen Navigation. It also led to the formation of the Itchen Navigation Society in November 1976.

As mentioned earlier in this section, the first of these battles was a campaign to protect the navigation route in Winchester, in the face of the threatened plan to build an extension of the M3 across the water meadows, so obliterating a section of the waterway. In an erudite constitutional move to prevent the building of the road, various objectors tried to summon the first meeting for 150 years of the Commissioners of the Itchen Navigation. The seven Acts, dating from 1665, originally creating the Navigation were still legally valid, since they had never been repealed. Under these Acts, the Commissioners must receive complaints about any interference to the navigation. The objectors to the road scheme argued that a stopping or blocking of the navigation, which was illegal, should be dealt with by the Commissioners, who included the Mayors of Winchester and Southampton, as well as the Fellows of Winchester College, among others. Fortunately, the issue never reached that point as, in the face of mounting public concern, the Motorway Enquiry was adjourned. The Inspector recommended that the road should not be built on the proposed line, and directed that the Department of Transport should propose an alternative route. This plan was subsequently published in 1983. It both avoided the water meadows and offered a bridge of navigable height over the line of the Navigation, much to the relief of the Itchen Navigation Society, who had worked so hard in the original campaign.

Part of the early campaign to revive public interest in the Itchen Navigation was organised by the Southampton Canal Society, whose members carried out a survey of the waterway in 1975 and revised it in 1976. It was published as a report in March 1977, and outlined the work required to re-open the navigation. It also made a case for the waterway to be revived in the longer term.

The Itchen Navigation Society used this report for their subsequent campaigns. Initial work organised by the Society was based on developing the well-used towpath as a safe rural walk. Early working parties in 1979 and 1980 tackled bank erosion between Bambridge and Albrook and this work was subsequently extended as far as the site of Withymead Lock. Further working parties, in 1981 and 1982, undertook similar towpath renovation on the section between Eastleigh and Mansbridge.

It was north of Mansbridge that the projected M27 motorway route was due to cross the navigation, and when the plans were published in 1979 it appeared that the motorway would cross the line of the waterway on a very low bridge. It was not possible at this site for a high-level crossing due to the proximity of Eastleigh Airport runway. The knowledge and experience gained from the earlier M3 Enquiry enabled the Society to present a very solid case at the Public Enquiry to review the M27 plans late in 1979. The main points made by the Society were accepted by the Inspector, who agreed that a route for the navigation had to be preserved. The Department of Transport subsequently revised the route and included a half-mile diversion for the navigation. It was, however, agreed that the new channel need not be cut until such time as the remainder of the waterway was fully restored, when it was accepted that the diversion would be at the expense of the Department of Transport. Elsewhere, the Society has continued to protect the route against further obstructions, such as when a railway bridge needed to be replaced over the navigation channel; the route remained unspoiled through the action of the Society.

In the longer term, the Society would like to see the navigation completely restored, but the tangle of legal and 'squatters'' rights has to be sorted out. In the short term, the aim is to keep the towpath clear, and to foster public support for a section-by-section revival, when the climate is right.

The only other restoration scheme, if it can be described as such, in this area, is the renovation of a 1½-mile section of the former Andover Canal, north of Romsey, where the route used a backwater of the River Test. Here the Romsey and District Society, through their Waterway Sub-Committee, cleared this section of the old line for use by canoes. They have no plans to develop other parts of the line, which for the most part has been obscured.

Waterway restoration in Southern England covers the whole spectrum of restoration schemes. The first success was the re-opening of Ports Creek in 1970. Next in line is the revival of the Basingstoke Canal, with a 'Grand Re-Opening' now set for 1985. Thereafter, of the three major long-term schemes, the Wey and Arun seem to be making the most rapid progress but after a false start, the Chichester Arm of the Portsmouth and Arundel Canal could well be the next re-opening. This depends mainly on the County Council allowing new road bridges to be built over the line—which, in the tight economic scene of the 1980s, looks some long way ahead.

*   *   *   *   *

19.—SOUTH-EASTERN ENGLAND

The history of the waterways of South-East England relates far more to the navigability of the rivers in the area than to the few artificial waterways

constructed later to fill gaps in the system. In the south the Eastern Rother
from very early times was navigable to Bodiam, Udiam, and beyond. The
Romans used it up to Bodiam, and in Saxon, Norman and later times it was
navigable for small boats at least to Etchingham. Records exist of the carriage
by water of stone for the building of Bodiam Castle in the late 14th century.
Similarly from the earliest times boats had been able to work on the tidal part of
the river Medway to Maidstone and beyond. In the north the river Thames, with
its tidal creeks, provided an early trade route.

As the demands for navigational improvements grew, so thoughts turned to
making the river Medway navigable between Maidstone, Tonbridge and Penshurst.
A 1627 scheme suggested the value of such a navigation to transport timber and
iron from the Weald of Kent to Chatham Dockyard. It was not until an Act of
1739 that the Medway Navigation through to Tonbridge became a reality. Locks
were built to take 40-ton barges, and wharves were built at Branbridges and
Tonbridge for the new trade. Traffic consisted mainly of timber and iron
downstream, and coal was the return cargo. As trade developed, plans were
proposed for a Thames and Medway Canal, to shorten the route from London
to Maidstone and Tonbridge. The Act authorising the link was passed in 1800,
and further plans were made for the extension of Wealden waterways. In
September 1800 a plan for a canal to link the Thames and Medway with the
Eastern Rother, making a through waterway from London to Rye harbour,
was promoted by A. Sutherland, and found some favour, but was finally
abandoned in 1815 through lack of finance and support.

As work proceeded on the Thames and Medway Canal, the threat of an
invasion from France gave rise to the scheme for the Royal Military Canal from
Hythe to the Rother as a means of defending the vulnerable Romney Marsh.
The scheme began in 1804 and was completed under the authority of an Act
of 1807.

Although the waterways gained some trade, only the Medway and Thames
Navigations substantially prospered. With the arrival of railways in the area in
the 1840s and 1850s, the small local value of the Thames and Medway Canal
and the Royal Military Canal was soon undermined. The Thames and Medway
was the first to fall, once Strood tunnel was converted for railway use in 1849.
Traffic lingered on the Royal Military Canal until 1909 when that also ceased,
leaving only the lower Rother, the Medway and the Thames to carry what
remained of water-borne trade.

Traffic on the Medway Navigation gradually declined as the railways took over
its trade. Although some locks were rebuilt in 1915 commercial traffic never
returned, and for many years thereafter the navigation slumbered, hardly used
by commerce or for pleasure. In 1957 the Inland Waterways Association created
the River Medway Sub-Committee to work for improved conditions on the
Upper Medway. As shortage of money did not allow all locks to be manned
by lock-keepers the I.W.A. Committee sought permission for boat-owners
themselves to work the locks. In 1968, after 10 years' work and experience gained
from a pilot scheme, the Kent River Authority opened the river for use by all

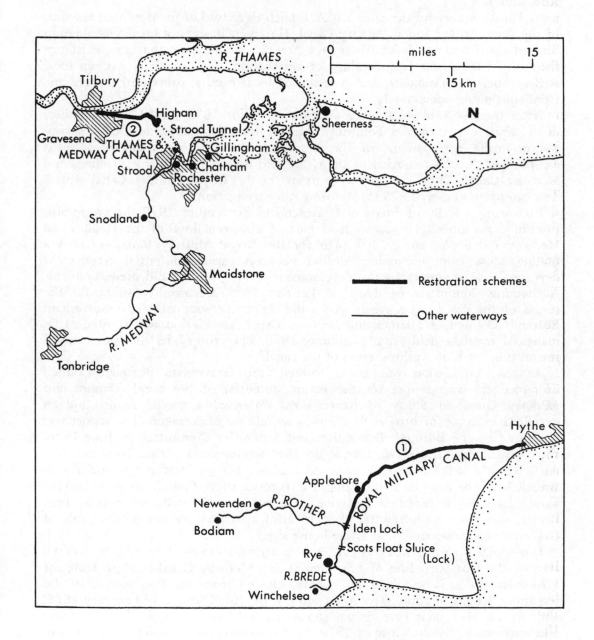

Map 19.—South-Eastern England
(1) Royal Military Canal; (2) Thames and Medway Canal

who paid the appropriate dues. Since that time the members of the London and South East Branch of the I.W.A. have developed the navigation and also produced a booklet on it.

In 1969 members of the same I.W.A. branch were told of the potential amenity of the then disused Royal Military Canal. However, it was not until a local group formed the Romney Marsh Waterways Amenity Committee that any assistance from the I.W.A. was forthcoming for restoration. The conflict between local anglers and restorationists, and pressure of local events, prevented the scheme from continuing immediately.

After the I.W.A. national reorganisation in autumn 1974, local I.W.A. members in the south-east formed a Tonbridge Branch. Branch members decided to survey the potential development of the waterways in their area, and as a result campaigned for the retention of the Gravesend Basin of the former Thames and Medway Canal. They also revived interest in the Royal Military Canal with a new campaign in early 1975 for restoring it for navigation.

Following a Rally of Boats at Gravesend in September 1975 the group also examined the possible restoration of part of what remained of the Thames and Medway Canal. As the group's plan for the Royal Military Canal suffered a further blow from increasing conflict between various potential users, so it devoted more resources to the development of its Thames and Medway plans. A Steering Committee produced in January 1976 a feasibility study for the re-use of the canal. As a result, and with the active support of the Gravesham Borough Council, a Thames and Medway Canal Association was formed at an inaugural meeting held on 26 February 1976. The group later that year started restoration work on a pilot section of the canal.

As the Association was being formed, the Gravesham Borough Council produced its own report on the future potential of the canal—*Thames and Medway Canal: A Study of Recreational Potential*—a model report and an excellent example of how such a review should be undertaken. The report was presented to the Borough Recreation and Amenities Committee in June 1976, who instructed officers to follow up the development plans. They and the Association's officers therefore worked together for an interim agreement with British Rail, the owners of the canal, for its restoration, though adequate fencing would have to be installed between the canal and the adjacent railway line. British Rail later withdrew its plans to infill a further section of the canal at Gravesend for development as a warehouse site.

During 1977 regular working parties were organised to modify the new terminal area of the truncated line of the Thames and Medway Canal at Mark Lane for a boat-launching ramp. Rubbish was also cleared from the first section of the remaining length of canal. The Association's first 'Big Dig' was in February 1978, and on 14 May their first annual sponsored walk raised some £200 for more clearance work. By the close of 1978 the Association had transformed a rubbish-filled ditch at Gravesend into a respectable stretch of water. November 1978 saw the Association's first major working party at the Higham end of the canal. Some 40 people cleared undergrowth from a large area around the Old Higham

Wharf—which attracted more local interest and support. By that time the membership of the Association had risen to over 70, and regular parties worked to clear the Gravesend section of the canal.

In 1980 the Association received a Shell Award of £150 to undertake major dredging work at Higham to improve the water supply of the whole canal line. Clearance proceeded during the year but came to an abrupt halt after problems were encountered in part of the line that had been infilled with industrial waste. After this the Association had to concentrate its working parties at Gravesend, until the difficulties could be resolved.

During 1980 interest in the Royal Military Canal also seemed to revive when Fay Godwin's new book *Romney Marsh and the Royal Military Canal* was published, extolling the unique features of the waterway. Local enthusiasts hoped this would stimulate greater public interest in its future as a recreational amenity and, to build on this publicity, the local I.W.A. Branch organised sponsored walks between Appledore and Hythe on 28 June 1981, and between Appledore and Rye on 13 June 1982. Unfortunately, neither walk was strongly supported, and any prospect of provoking local support for full restoration to navigation seemed very slim. The only boats now regularly using the canal are at Hythe, particularly at the time of the biennial Venetian Fête.

Fortunately, this was not so with the Thames and Medway Canal. Association members were told at the 1981 A.G.M. that the legal difficulties presented by the Higham tip were near resolution. It was also learned that British Rail were sympathetic to the idea that the local council should purchase the canal. The Association, therefore, planned with renewed vigour for the restoration of the only remaining swing bridge on the canal line.

During 1981 Gravesham Council completed its Thames Flood Prevention works. Part of this scheme included the installation of new barrier gates on the old Terminal Basin of the canal, which was also substantially improved. The only eyesore left was the remains of the old canal entrance lock, which was improved in 1982.

By October 1981 the Association's journal was able to report that the problems at the Higham tip had been resolved. This news renewed enthusiasm for developing the canal: the Association held its first Boat Rally on the canal on 6 June 1982 as its contribution to the Maritime England Year. Sailing boats, canoes and rafts raced along the re-opened section of the line, between Mark Lane and the Swing Bridge, for the first time for some forty years.

On the 4 July 1982 the Thames and Medway Canal Association resumed work at the Higham end of the canal. A hired Hymac excavator cleared a 300-yard section to improve the old Wharf area. In October 1982 British Rail detailed its proposals for the sale of the canal to Gravesham Borough Council, and opened negotiations for the takeover of the remains for long-term amenity use. The Council subsequently agreed to purchase the sections of the canal on offer, subject to satisfactory surveys and normal legal reviews.

The success of the restorationists in the South East is very much related to the scarcity of waterways in the area. It now seems that more of the Thames and

Medway Canal will be restored to provide a useful amenity for the Gravesend area. The Royal Military Canal is not likely to be re-developed for navigation, but the Rother and the Medway are both able to meet the recreational needs of the region, in this respect, for the foreseeable future.

* * * * *

20.—SOUTH-WESTERN ENGLAND

The waterways of West Somerset, Devon and Cornwall, 150 miles long at their greatest extent, were of little economic importance compared with those of the Midlands and North. A variety of schemes and projects for canals in the area occupied men's minds for the century between 1769 and 1870 to improve transport links in the South West, particularly from the Bristol Channel to the English Channel. Some materialised as useful local waterways, such as the Parratt Navigation and the Tavistock Canal; others, such as the Bridgwater Bay to Exmouth Ship Canal, remained 'pipe dreams'. Of them all, only the Exeter Canal remains a commercial navigation to the present time.

Apart from plans to restore the inclined plane of the Tavistock Canal at Morwellham as part of a study centre for local industrial archaeology, and the Tamar Manure Navigation Lock, the waterway restoration movement in the South West has been centred mainly on links to the Parratt Navigation.

The first waterway promoted in this area was the River Tone Navigation, from Bridgwater and the Parratt, principally to carry coal to Taunton. From this link grew a small group of navigations, all based on the minor port of Bridgwater. The Parratt Navigation ran through Langport to Westport, with a branch to Thorney; subsequently, the Bridgwater and Taunton Canal replaced the Tone for most traffic to Taunton, though the river remained in some use, both being joined at Taunton to the Grand Western Canal through to Tiverton; a branch from the Bridgwater and Taunton Canal at Creech St Michael ran through tunnels and over inclined planes to Chard. The two latter canals suffered the disadvantages of inclined planes and lifts which were difficult to maintain, and which in part led to their demise. It was, however, the passing of the 1836 Act for the Bristol and Exeter Railway that signalled the end of the Somerset and East Devon group of waterways. The main railway line was opened in 1844, the Tiverton branch in 1848, and that to Yeovil in 1853. By 1868 the Bridgwater and Taunton, Tone, Grand Western, Chard and Glastonbury canals were in railway hands; all expected closure, and some sections had already closed. Fortunately, other sections of the navigations remained, and it is these that have interested waterway enthusiasts in the South West.

The prime navigation was the Bridgwater and Taunton Canal, which first attracted the attention of the Inland Waterways Association. During the Second World War various swing bridges over the canal became fixed and obstructed through navigation. The I.W.A., after its success on the Northern Section of the Stratford-on-Avon Canal, tried to use the same ploy on the Bridgwater and

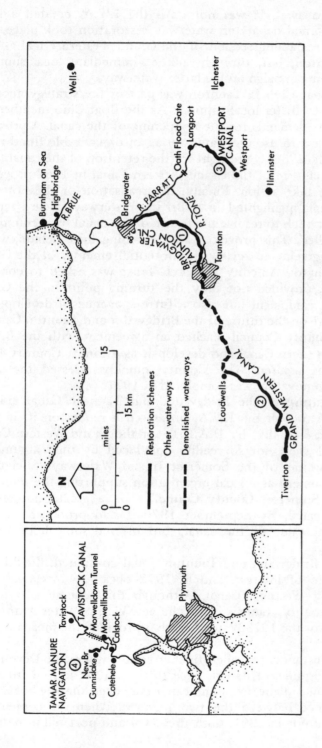

Map 20.—South-West England

(1) Bridgwater and Taunton Canal; (2) Grand Western Canal; (3) Westport Canal;
(4) Tamar Manure Navigation

Taunton Canal, but to no avail. It was not until the I.W.A. created a local committee in 1954 that formal debate on waterway restoration took place. The committee examined the remaining section of the Grand Western Canal as well the Bridgwater and Taunton, but, through lack of immediate local support, decided to concentrate their campaign on the latter waterway.

The foundation of a Boat Club in Taunton was part of the strategy adopted by the I.W.A. Committee to foster local support. As the Boat Club membership grew, the I.W.A. pressed its demands for the re-opening of the canal. A proposal by the Somerset River Board to use the waterway as an unnavigable flood relief channel served to sharpen local resolve to fight for the retention of the canal.

Likewise, the threat of closure of the Grand Western Canal in 1962 provoked the people of Tiverton to take action. Finally, the realisation of the potential cost of retaining the canal, highlighted in a British Waterways Board report, persuaded local planners to seek to resolve the future of the canal by recommending that it should be infilled. This provoked a far-reaching local debate, which ended with the Council agreeing to review the potential amenity of the Grand Western Canal. The Dartington Amenity Research Trust was asked to conduct this review. Their report provided not only the turning point in the Grand Western Canal restoration campaign, but also a further avenue of development for the growing local debate on the future of the Bridgwater and Taunton Canal.

In 1970 the Devon County Council reached an agreement with the B.W.B. to take over the Grand Western Canal and develop it as a Linear Country Park. Thereafter its future was assured. The County quickly assessed the work required and much of the renovation was completed in 1971.

The debate over the future of the Bridgwater and Taunton Canal did not develop so fortunately. Although the I.W.A. presented a report on it, in May 1969, making a similar case to that by D.A.R.T. for the Grand Western Canal, Somerset County Council were not so readily convinced by their arguments. However, after the formation of the Somerset Inland Waterways Society in 1970 and its rapid development as a local organisation supporting the retention of the local waterways, Somerset County Council took a greater interest in the development of the canal. By September 1970 it had produced its own report on the recreational value of the canal, and offered some hope for its future development.

As the debate over the Bridgwater and Taunton Canal continued, the S.I.W.S. broadened its own sphere of interest, and in 1972 began to investigate the restoration of the nearby Westport Canal. Although this scheme also found support in the local and county councils it was the new Wessex Water Authority, created under the powers of the 1973 Water Act, that provided the means for the restoration plans.

Slightly different circumstances prevailed further south, where the Devonshire port of Morwellham owed much of its existence to the traffic derived from the Tavistock Canal. An inclined plane from the canal conveyed the tug-boats over the 237ft. height difference between the two features. When the copper and arsenic mines were worked out in 1901, both the canal and port fell into decay.

1. The Packet House, Worsley, on the Bridgewater Canal.

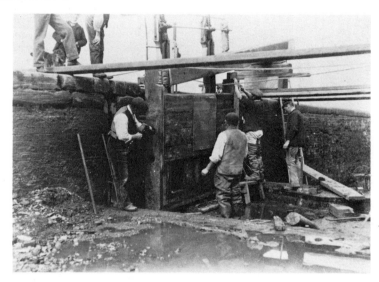

2. This view of lock repairs using traditional methods is most probably taken in the Stoke Bruerne flight in the early years of this century.

3. A christening at Buckby Locks, *c.*1910.

4. Convoy of boats in ice, 1957, between Nuneaton and Bedworth on the Coventry Canal. Nearest the camera are boats owned by Samuel Barlow.

5. (*left*) Surrey & Hampshire Canal Society members at work on one of the St John's Locks, Basingstoke Canal.

6. (*above*) Canal clearance at the Welshpool Lock, October 1969.

7. (*below*) Repairs to a major breach in Howsham Weir, Yorkshire, on the River Derwent.

8. Clearance nearing completion at Castlefields Lock, Rochdale Canal.

9. The Stratford Canal at Wilmcote.

10. A typical signal cabin and swing-bridge layout on the Forth & Clyde Canal, 1950.

11. Clearance of Maryhill Top Lock on the Forth & Clyde Canal, Glasgow by the New Glasgow Society and Peak Forest Canal Society.

12. Ex-Govan ferry being craned into the Forth & Clyde Canal near Kirkintilloch in April 1982.

13. Eastern portal, Hincaster Tunnel, on the Lancaster Canal before restoration by Army Engineers and Trust members, 1980.

14. The Eastern portal of Hincaster Tunnel after restoration, 1981.

15. Lancaster Canal Trust anti-motorway rally, Lancaster Canal, 1968.

16. The derelict flight of locks at Tewitfield, Lancaster Canal.

17. Job Creation on the Rochdale Canal, Rochdale.

18. The junction of the Ashton and the Rochdale Canals.

19. The final lock clearance on the Marple Flight, Lower Peak Forest Canal, 1973. The photo shows the great depth of these locks.

20. Pleasure craft on the restored
Peak Forest Canal at Marple, Cheshire.

21. Dungebooth Lock on the Huddersfield Narrow Canal.

22. Restoration problems on the Huddersfield Narrow Canal at
Stalybridge.

23. A sand barge passes through Linton Lock on the upper River Ouse, Yorkshire.

24. Brigham Landing, Driffield Navigation.

25. Bethell's Bridge on the Driffield Navigation, after restoration.

26. Members of the Pocklington Canal Amenity Society at work restoring Baldwin's Bridge, Pocklington Canal.

27. Osberton Lock, Lower Chesterfield Canal.

28. Morse Lock, Chesterfield Canal, 1975.

29. The upper reaches of the Chesterfield Canal, east of Norwood Tunnel.

30. Bottom Lock, Sleaford Navigation, looking downstream.

31. Members of the Sleaford Navigation Society plan the restoration of Kyme Eau Lock, near South Kyme.

32. (*left*) The new boathouse and Yacht Station on Brayford Mere, Lincoln.

33. (*centre*) Cowbridge Lock, Witham Navigable Drains.

34. (*bottom*) I.W.A. members campaign to keep open the Derby Canal, 1961.

35. Jubilee Dry Dock, Great Northern Basin, Langley Mill, 1978.

36. Cromford Canal Wharf drained for restoration by the Cromford Canal Society.

37. Cromford Canal Wharf with the Cromford Canal Society Trip Boat, *John Gray*.

38. Froghall Basin and Warehouse, Caldon Canal.

40. (*opposite*) The Caldon Canal. Walkers on the towing path near Hazlehurst Aqueduct.

39. Hazlehurst Locks on the Caldon Canal, after restoration.

HAZLEHURST
AQUEDUCT
1841

41. Breach at Trevor on the Llangollen Canal, March 1982.

42. The British Waterways Board constructing a winding hole north of Pool Quay Lock on the Montgomery Canal.

43. The Hay Inclined Plane at Blists Hill, Ironbridge.

44. Preparatory work under way at the Welsh Frankton Locks, Montgomery Canal, 1977.

45. The first boats to reach the new Castle Mills Lock, Great Ouse, in May 1978.

46. Icklingham Lock on the River Lark. Isolated but workable. Photographed 1968.

47. Well Creek at Upwell.

48. *(left)* Mr. L. A. Edwards, Hon. Sec. of the I.W.A. in 1958 takes a message of goodwill from the Mayor of Beccles to the Town Reeve of Bungay as part of the campaign to get the locks to Bungay reopened. They are still closed in spite of the long campaign for Ellingham Lock.

49. *(below)* Lord Greenwood of Rossendale reopens Flatford Lock on the River Stour, Easter 1975.

50. Sudbury Granary before restoration.

51. Sudbury Granary after restoration, and now occupied by the Trust. The Gasworks Arm can be seen to the right. The RST Lighter is under repair in the centre distance.

52. The Wyken Arm mooring of the Coventry Canal Society.

53. Restored wharf buildings on the Welford Arm, 1975.

54. A British Waterways Board hire craft passes through Foxton Locks.

56. (*above*) Old bonded warehouse, Stourbridge Arm.

55. (*left*) Delph Lock Flight, built in 1858, with restored stables (left).

57. (*below*) Restoration work at the Black Country Museum, Dudley Canal.

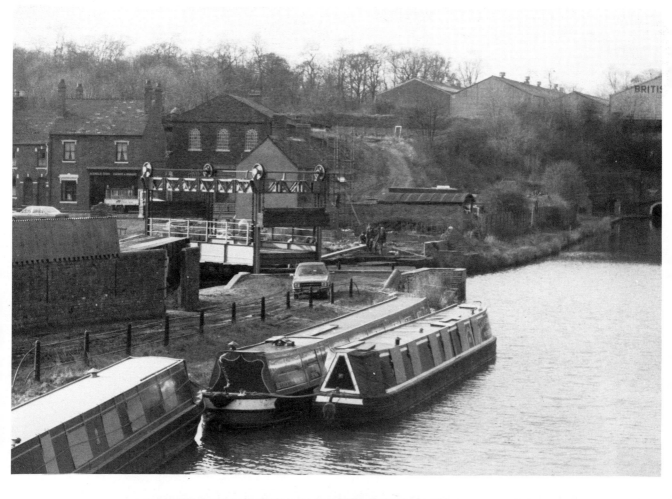

58. Droitwich Gas Works Basin and bridge, 1980.

59. The restored Canal Wharf area at Droitwich, 1983.

60. The opening of the new Robert Aickman Lock at Harvington on 21 May 1983.

61. Rebuilding by-washes on the Southern Stratford Canal during 'Stratford Blitz' in 1978.

62. Her Majesty The Queen Mother arrives at Stratford-on-Avon to reopen the Upper Avon Navigation, 1 June 1974.

63. Canal clearance of the dry section on the Wendover Arm by I.W.A. and G.U.C.S. members.

64. Wendover Weekend, 1982, organised by the G.U.C.S.

65. Slough Arm Terminus at Stoke Wharf, Slough, 1980.

66. Reconstructing the Brecon & Abergavenny Canal after the breach at Llanfoist.

67. Repairing the Aberdulais Aqueduct on the Tennant Canal, October 1974.

68. (*left*) Sidney Gardens, Kennet & Avon Canal, Bath.

69. (*above*) Devizes Flight of Locks on the Kennet & Avon Canal.

70. (*below*) Roundhouse by the culverted Thames & Severn Canal at Chalford.

1. Brickwork repairs, Kings
each, Thames & Severn Canal at
oates.

2. Working party at the Kings-
ill skew-arched bridge, Swindon,
n the Wilts. & Berks. Canal.

73. Members of the Itchen Navigation Society restoring the tow path of the Navigation.

74. Northlands Bridge, Wey & Arun Canal.

75. Restoration of Lock 1, Basingstoke Canal.

6. (*above*) Iden Lock on the Royal Military Canal. It is now used as a drainage sluice.

7. (*above right*) The Thames & Medway Canal Society hold an Open Day on a restored length of the canal near Gravesend, 1982.

8. (*right*) B.W.B. engineers restore Standards Lock on the Bridgwater & Taunton Canal.

9. (*below*) A horse-drawn boat plies the restored Grand Western Canal.

80. Fradley Junction, Trent & Mersey Canal.

81. A hire craft awaits its turn to pass through the reopened Harecastle Tunnel, Trent & Mersey Canal.

82. Chirk Aqueduct on the Llangollen Canal.

83. The late Robert Aickman, founder of the I.W.A.

84. The sign that greeted boats before the Ashton Canal was restored.

85. David Hutchings, M.B.E., Manager of the Upper Avon Navigation.

86. Waterway Recovery Group members restoring the Welsh Frankton Locks on the Montgomery Canal.

87. The restoration of the Rochdale Canal under a Job Creation Scheme.

In 1933 the canal took on a new lease of life, when its bed was dredged and a new cut was made high on the valley side at Morwellham to divert the water into a new storage reservoir. This enabled the canal water to drive an English Electricity Board hydro-electric power plant, sited on one of the old copper mine quays on the banks of the Tamar.

The port of Morwellham itself was saved in 1970, when the Trustees of Dartington Amenity Research Trust leased the site from the Earl of Bradford. They formed the Morwellham Recreation Company Limited to re-create the port and its surrounding area, as a Visitor Centre, in a working display. Although this did not involve the full restoration of the inclined plane, it covered the clearance of much of the site together with the laying out of guided walks.

The development of the Morwellham port area revived interest in former waterway traffic in the area, and led to a display by the National Maritime Museum about the Tamar and its craft, in an old storehouse at Cotehele Quay, a National Trust property further downstream. This exhibition now includes a restored Tamar barge, the ketch-rigged *Shamrock*. It also prompted the I.W.A., West Country Branch, to consider modern usage of the river. In 1977 a preliminary survey suggested that the restoration of the upper section of the river, together with the re-opening of the Tamar Manure Navigation above Weir Head, would encourage craft to make use of the whole river. In early 1978 a Tamar Sub-Committee was established to lead the local campaign, aiming at the creation of a new Society to co-ordinate the planned restoration work. Both the County and local councils expressed interest in the scheme, and the Sub-Committee started to evaluate what had to be done.

One major problem appeared to be the hazy legal background to the demise of the navigation. Whilst this was being investigated, the Sub-Committee members turned to the River Tamar itself, the navigation of which had been severely hindered by extensive flooding on 27 December 1979. Working parties were held both above and below Morwellham to clear numerous large trees which had been washed into the river and obstructed the passage of craft. Perhaps the most important work undertaken involved the clearance of a major landslip, which threatened to prevent craft from reaching Weir Head, Gunnislake.

Unfortunately, when examined in detail, the legal problems surrounding the restoration of the lock at Gunnislake proved more difficult to resolve than had been anticipated, and in 1981 the Sub-Committee decided that the legal costs were far beyond their means. With regret they abandoned their plans, and the Sub-Committee was wound up.

The problems of the Bridgwater and Taunton Canal were fortunately not so intractable; though public pressure was required to overcome them. The main problem concerned the lowered bridges, which had blocked the water-way since the War. In the early 1970s Somerset County Council had raised a number of the fixed swing bridges to allow about four feet headroom. This, however, was insufficient for anything other than canoes. Much of this work had been completed by the time the I.W.A., West Country Branch, was formed in 1975.

On the brighter side the County Council had also financed a programme of other canal works in the 1970s, with the result that Upper and Lower Maunsell and Kings Lock were restored by B.W.B. staff by the close of 1978. Unfortunately, by then the unique double bascule bridge, spanning the divide between the Inner and Outer Basins at Bridgwater Dock, had become unsafe, and a temporary fixed bridge had to be inserted. This blocked access at the River Parratt end of the canal. Even before that the major entrance, through the tide lock and stop lock of the Basin, had been barred by two large concrete dams inserted by British Rail when they formally closed the Dock to shipping in 1971.

These major setbacks did not deter the local I.W.A. members, who started working parties in December 1976 to clear Newtown Lock, which linked the canal to the Bridgwater Dock Basin. They were also instrumental in getting a Job Creation Scheme underway, in 1977, to clear some of the deep cutting above Newtown Lock, which could not be dredged by normal land-based means. Thus, when the Inland Waterway Amenity Advisory Committee (I.W.A.A.C.) toured the canal in September 1978, they were well impressed by the waterway's potential and indicated that they would advocate the revival of the canal to full cruiseway standards in their report.

The I.W.A. members sampled the delights of the first three restored locks when a flotilla of craft journeyed along the canal from North Newton to Bathpool in May 1979, en route for a Rally of Boats. The cruise heightened their wish to restore the canal fully for larger craft, and the Branch decided to organise similar cruises as an annual event. The I.W.A. Committee also reviewed the prospect of creating a viable waterways network for cruising boats in Somerset, following the construction of the planned River Parratt Barrage.

The I.W.A. Committee's report in January 1980 suggested that a network of 111 miles of navigation could be created in a carefully evaluated three-stage scheme. The first phase of this plan envisaged a 50-mile cruising area, which included the full restoration of the Bridgwater and Taunton Canal, the revival of the former Parratt, Yeo and Isle Navigations, and the upgrading of the Westport Canal. The second stage envisaged the upgrading of the River Tone through to Taunton, to complete a cruising ring involving the Bridgwater and Taunton Canal. The third stage looked at a wider area and suggested the upgrading of the River Brue, and, among other projects, the reconstruction of the Glastonbury Canal. Though the whole scheme was dependent on the construction of the Parratt Barrage and a sympathetic Water Authority, it identified the tremendous longer-term potential of the Somerset waterways and showed them in a completely new light. This was exemplified by a re-opening Rally held on the partially-restored Westport Canal in April 1980, organised by the S.I.W.S. Some 30 craft took part, even though the waterway was still land-locked by the lowered Westmoor Bridge, and the terminal basin at Langport had not been dredged.

To encourage local support for the waterways, some I.W.A. members floated the idea in February 1981 of forming a separate Bridgwater and Taunton Canal Society—to complement the existing S.I.W.S. and I.W.A. Branch by organising events and publicity directly related to the Bridgwater Canal. After much debate and a great deal of heart searching, it was decided that the existing groups, with proven support, were better geared to fight future battles. This proved wise, for in summer 1981 the British Waterways Board published an interim report, *The Bridgwater and Taunton: A Canal and its Future*, on the potential rôle of the canal. This was based on the work of a joint group of officers from the Board and the riparian Local Authorities. It noted that Somerset County Council had already provided financial support to restore five of the six locks on the canal and that the County Council were also planning to revive Bridgwater Dock, which it had purchased in 1974, as a recreational amenity and focal point for the town. The report suggested that there were three potential options, namely:

(1) Optimum Development—with the canal being brought up to 'cruiseway' standard.
(2) Interim Development—providing facilities for recreation, but not for larger craft.
(3) No further development.

The report highlighted the major hindrance to full revival as the poor condition of a number of bridges over the canal, 15 of which would need to be replaced or converted into swing bridges, at a cost of £533,000. It called for the views of all interested parties, and encouragingly suggested that 'nothing further should be done to the canal which would preclude its full restoration in the longer term'.

The local I.W.A. Branch immediately committed its full support behind Option One, and campaigned strongly for others to follow suit. It was therefore pleased to learn that Somerset County Council was generally sympathetic to the full restoration plan, and that the repair of Firepool Lock at Taunton, the only one not operational, was to proceed in 1982, with new top gates to be fitted under the B.W.B. normal maintenance programme and the prospect of complete restoration when new lower gates were fitted in 1983.

In early 1982 all three councils, Sedgemore District Council, Taunton Dean Borough Council, and Somerset County Council agreed to support Option One, and all planned to proceed towards the full restoration of the canal, provided that this could be phased to take account of the availability of funds. This news came a few months after Newtown Lock, at Bridgwater, had been restored in late 1981, after the fitting of new paddle gear and the removal of the concrete dam. Thereafter, dredging the adjoining section and the replacement of a low-level fixed pedestrian bridge over the lock chamber were all that prevented craft using the first section of the canal. Fortunately, the Manpower Services Commission, in conjunction with Sedgemoor District Council, financed a £40,000 S.T.E.P. scheme to dredge the channel and repair the Albert Street cutting, and the I.W.A. donated £1,000 towards the cost. After that work was completed in August 1982, it only required Somerset County Council to raise the level of Ham Weir by nine inches to the correct navigable depth for craft to use that section of the canal. This work was scheduled for spring 1983.

During 1983, the main work towards the restoration of Bridgwater Dock was to proceed; the Barge Lock gates are due to be installed in May 1983, and the derelict Bascule Bridge is scheduled for repair and re-opening during the summer, after which craft would have access again from the River Parratt, through the docks to the canal entrance. Thereafter the speed at which the canal can be re-opened fully will rest on the ability of the three councils to finance the renovation and to rebuild the 15 low bridges along the canal line. For this, it was hoped that the Final Report of the Joint Working Group to be published in Spring 1983, would set out a programme for full and speedy restoration.

With the re-opening of the Bridgwater and Taunton Canal firmly in sight, the I.W.A., West Country Branch, turned to ways of developing the recreational use of the waterway. The 14-mile towpath was already popular with walkers, and this prompted them to provide a number of seats at intervals along the canal. The first was installed at Maunsel Higher Lock in 1982, and others are planned as quickly as additional sponsors could be found. Thereafter, the Branch planned to organise regular cruises along the canal, for more people to enjoy the waterway as it came back to life.

The year 1983 was the 10th anniversary of the inauguration of the Grand Western Canal horseboat trips. These immediately proved so popular that the Company quickly introduced a second craft. When the canal was re-opened, it was decided that the eastern end, beyond Fossend Bridge, would be kept as a nature reserve, but because no difference to the habitat of the two sections of the canal could be found, it was agreed that from 1983 the whole canal should be available to unpowered craft. This offered a further 1½ miles of navigation for the horse-drawn trip boats, extending through the tiny Waytown Tunnel to the old lock at Lowdwells, where the old lock chamber was re-excavated by Devon County Council in 1982. When finance becomes available, they plan to make the lock site into a feature of industrial archaeology, adding to the extensive range of items of interest along the route.

The South West of England provides examples of both re-opened canals and battles still to be fought. The restoration of the Grand Western Canal, by the Devon County Council, offers an example of the considerable amenity offered by a canal used as the basis for Linear County Park. The partial revival of the Westport Canal by the Water Authority is an example of the way in which waterways can be improved within the terms of the 1973 Water Act. The recent positive attitude of local councils towards the full restoration of the Bridgwater and Taunton Canal is similarly a step in the right direction towards the re-opening of the canal for larger craft. However, this will still require the full attention of S.I.W.S. and I.W.A. members over the next few years to ensure that it is achieved within a realistic time scale.

In the longer term there is the prospect of spreading the restoration net still wider. This will rest mainly on a commitment to go ahead with the long-planned River Parratt Barrage. Should this develop there will then be a tremendous upsurge of interest in the considerable recreational facilities of the waterways of West Somerset. The former river navigations could well be brought back to life, with the bustle of sailing and other craft there for all to see. In the interim, careful monitoring will be required to ensure that unnecessary barriers are not created to potential routes for larger craft. Such a case is the Telescopic Bridge over the River Parratt in Bridgwater. The British Rail Act of 1981 removed the requirement for the Board to maintain any portion of the structure as a movable bridge. Should this bridge become fixed, however, it will preclude larger craft from moving under it at high tide.

The waterways of the South West have seen a new and positive attitude adopted towards them in the last decade; let us hope that this spirit will continue in the decade ahead.

Chapter Four

THE BOAT HIRE INDUSTRY

THE GROWTH OF INTEREST in boat hire in Britain is of considerable relevance
to the development of the waterway restoration movement since it has supplied
much of the impetus for the provision of additional water space. P. Toyne in
Recreation and Environment (1974) suggested:

> Disused canals have a similar potential in the context of the increasing
> demand for boating . . . One way of solving the congestion which could
> develop if the rate of increase were continued over ten years would be to
> open up the 700km. of rivers and canals which have fallen into decay through
> disuse.

The subject has also been the centre of a major research project, conducted
by the Reading University Amenity Waterways Study Group during 1974-5,
and has been developed by other research organisations, including the Dartington
Amenity Research Trust and the Research Department of British Waterways
Board, who have produced a steady stream of information about the value of
canals as a prime resource for leisure. For this reason there is no need for a
chapter in this book on the amenity value of waterways, but an analysis of the
main features of development of the boat hire industry is included, in the light
of its importance to the restoration movement.

The remarkable growth in the number of hire craft, particularly over the
last decade, has been prompted solely by the spectacular increase in public
demand for water-orientated holidays. This is a significant achievement,
especially when one considers the derelict state of the canals some 30 years ago;
mostly unwanted and certainly under used, and the popular cry was 'fill them in'.
The hire boat industry has helped to introduce many people to the canals since
the early 1950s and has been a major influence in changing attitudes towards
the inland waterways. The majority of hire boaters have returned for second,
third, and subsequent holidays to continue their exploration of the waterway
network. To understand the rapid growth of the hire boat industry it is necessary
to look back and examine the various factors that provided the firm base for this
recent phenomenal increase.

'Messing about in boats' has long been an English disease. It is impossible to
say when people first started to use boats for pleasure, but the fact that many
of the earliest canal Acts enabled canals to be used by pleasure craft points to
the extent of pleasure boating at that time. The Trent and Mersey, and Staffordshire and Worcestershire, Acts of 1766 both contain clauses allowing owners or

occupiers of lands adjacent to the canals to use pleasure craft on them. The Coventry Canal Act of 1768 allowed pleasure craft free of charge, subject to a limit of two miles cruising! The Oxford Canal Act of 1769 had a similar restriction, while the Leeds and Liverpool Act of 1770, and the Ellesmere Canal Act of 1793 permitted free passage of pleasure craft, except through locks.

The earliest craft to introduce most people to canals were the Packet Boats that offered regular passenger services between major towns. The first of these was introduced by the Duke of Bridgewater on his own canal in 1772, and for 70 years, until the railways arrived, boats carried up to 120 passengers a trip between Warrington and Manchester. In the 1800s the *Paddington Packet* offered a comfortable ride between the village of Uxbridge and the developing suburb of Paddington. In the 1830s Swift boats, capable of surging along at 12 m.p.h., were introduced by William Houston on the Scottish canals. On the Lancaster Canal in 1833 a boat regularly covered the 57 miles from Preston to Kendal in seven hours, including the eight locks en route. The last regular Packet boats, which ceased to trade in 1935, were on the twice-daily summer schedule operated by the Gloucester and Berkeley Steam Packet Co. Thus ended an era in which people from all walks of life were introduced to the pleasures of smooth water travel.

Even before most Packet boat services began to decline, various individuals started to hire craft for long pleasure cruises on the canals. One of the first of these to be fully recorded was the voyage of *Crochett's Castle* made by the Peacock family and entourage in 1831. Their fleet consisted of four horse-drawn craft; one for the men, one for the ladies, one for servants and cooks, and one boat that acted as a dining-room and also carried a band!

In 1888 the *Pall Mall* magazine carried a short article, 'On Tour', by Robert Blunt. This described how he and his brother hired a narrow boat and temporarily converted it for a pleasure cruise on the Kennet and Avon, and Wiltshire and Berkshire Canals. This article, no doubt, caused others to follow suit. Perhaps one of them was E. Temple Thurston, who, in 1911, hired a narrow boat, the *Flower of Gloster,* at Oxford, together with its skipper, Harry Eynsham. It cost him the princely sum of £1.50 per week, plus food for the boatman and his horse. The story of his subsequent trip through the now closed Thames and Severn Canal and various other little-used canals gave his many readers a clear insight into the secret world of the inland waterways.

Many Victorians, even before the Temple Thurston trip, were beginning to use the hire fleets of the Norfolk Broads. These started from 1887 when the Press Brothers of North Walsham advertised their five wherry yachts for hire, each with a crew of two to sail them. An added luxury was a piano for an extra 75p. per week. The first boating agent on the Broads is recognised to be Mr. Brown of St Olave's. His brochure for 1890 offered a yacht and crew as a holiday for six people for £8.50 per week. At that time the boating season was only eight weeks long, so the crew looked for rather large tips!

The Blakes hire fleet, so well known today, entered the market with an advert in the *Daily Mail* in 1907. Its first catalogue in 1908 offered some 43 craft for hire during a season from mid-July to the end of August. This was the first boat-owner's co-operative, and has since provided many with the means to have a boating holiday. It also generated the boom period for the Broads in the inter-war years. During this time Harry Blake and Jack Robinson, among others, formed a trade association with a code of practice that set the high standards which today make the boat hire industry so reliable. The second major national hire boat agency, Hoseasons, was not founded until 1945, but has since become a major competitor to Blakes.

The Broads rapidly became the holiday venue for the upper and middle classes; however, school children and some lucky adults from industrial areas were not omitted. A well-known feature of Victorian life was the annual outing on the canal. Rough benches were fitted into the swept-out holds of Humber keels, narrow boats, fen lighters and barges, and between 100 and 200 children were packed into the craft to be taken on a horse-drawn trip from Birmingham, Stoke, Manchester, or one of the other major industrial towns, to the countryside beyond. These trips and Sunday School outings continued well into the 20th century in the Welsh valleys, and many older residents of Neath still recall the Neath Sunday School treat down the Neath and Tennant Canals to Jersey Marine.

The river Thames, in a different way, attracted others to the delights of the waterways. Henley Regatta gained Royal Patronage in 1851 and by 1888 Salters' steamers were offering a daily passenger service downstream from Oxford. Salters started to build their own boats in 1898, and soon their camping boats and punts were offering cheap waterway holidays at prices most could afford.

The 1930s, '40s, and '50s saw the development of today's organised hire fleets on both the Broads and the Thames. In these years, too, the embryo canal hire fleets came into being. The first was the Inland Cruising Association, of Chester, run by Mr. Wain and formed in 1935. This subsequently became Inland Hire Cruisers, Ltd., of Christleton, and in 1939 had a fleet of 13 boats. A second fleet, Canal Cruising Co., Ltd., of Stone, was formed by R. H. Whyatt in 1948 and in 1950 Canal Pleasurecraft (Stourport), Ltd., was founded.

The first canal hotel boat company, Holidays Afloat, was inaugurated by T. Whitley in 1952, and in 1953 Michael Streat started the Inland Waterways Cruising Co., which introduced so many people to canals. In 1954 Lionel Munk, through his boat hire firm, Maidline, started to promote the use of canals by Thames-based hire craft, and by 1960 had generated sufficient interest to justify opening a base in the heart of the canal system at Brinklow. Sir Reginald Kerr, the General Manager of British Transport Waterways, inaugurated a hire fleet at Chester in 1956. This was the forerunner of the current B.W.B. fleets, which now operate from Nantwich and Hillmorton. Since those early days, many others have followed, and now there are hire bases throughout the canal system, including the Caledonian Canal.

No review of the development of the hire boat industry can overlook John James and the *Jason* trip, introduced on the Regent's Canal in 1951, who has provided so many with their first experience of the enjoyment of a canal trip. Mention must also be made of the annual *Canals Books,* first published in 1966,

and of the additional publicity gained from the Boat Afloat Shows at Little
Venice, first held in 1962. All these factors combined to ensure there were
over 600 hire craft on the canals by the close of the 1960s—a far cry from the
first fleet of under 50 hire craft in 1950.

The 1970s have seen an even more rapid increase in the canal hire fleet. The
following statistics demonstrate progress:

Year				All Classes of B.W.B. Hire Licences	Potential Number of New Craft for Hire
1971 ..	..	..	..	728	N/A
1972 ..	..	..	..	N/A	N/A
1973 ..	..	..	..	912	184
1974 ..	..	..	..	1,251	339
1975 ..	..	..	..	1,511	260
1976 ..	..	..	..	1,626	115
1977 ..	..	..	..	1,734	108
1978 ..	..	..	..	1,842	108
1979 ..	..	..	..	1,872	30
1980 ..	..	..	..	1,983	111
1981 ..	..	..	..	2,062	79
1982 ..	..	..	..	1,870*	—

*Whilst Annual B.W.B. Hire Licences increased in 1982 by some 24,
   short-term and river registrations fell sharply, from 456 in 1981
   to 240 in 1982.

In addition, there are now some 20 boats especially fitted for canal trips for
the disabled. This venture has been supported strongly by the Prince of Wales,
who through the Prince of Wales's Committee has been instrumental in restoring
and re-opening a length of the Montgomery Canal as a cruising route for one of
these craft.

The increase in the number of boats and the extension in the 1970s of the
hire season to between 25 to 30 weeks, has meant an equal increase in the
number of individual canal holidays available, and some 130 firms offer facilities
on the canal system. Since the 1960s there has been an average of 10 per cent
annual increase in bookings, although the drought in 1976 and recent problems
of high unemployment have stunted progress. The latest statistics for the canal
system are as follows:

Year				Estimated Number of Individual Canal Holidays
1974 ..	..	..	..	155,000 people
1975 ..	..	..	..	197,000 people
1976 ..	..	..	..	200,000 people
1977 ..	..	..	..	225,000 people
1978 ..	..	..	..	240,000 people
1979 ..	..	..	..	242,000 people
1980 ..	..	..	..	250,000 people
1981 ..	..	..	..	220,000 people
1982 ..	..	..	..	200,000 people

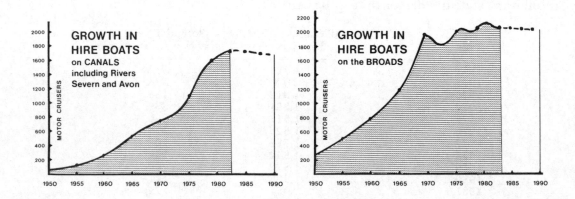

Courtesy: Hoseasons

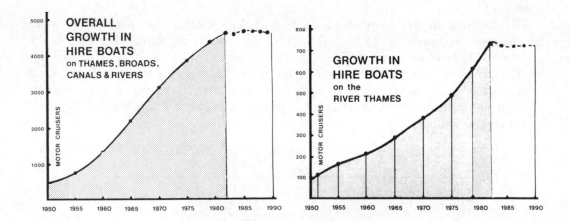

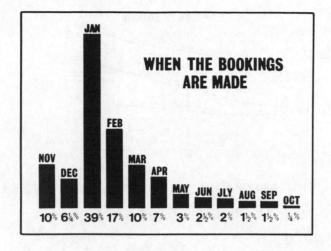

Courtesy: Hoseasons

ONE	40%
TWO	35%
THREE	11%
FOUR OR MORE	14%

Number of wage earners in your hire boat crews

AVERAGE BERTHS PER BOAT

BROADS	4·6 Persons
CANALS	5·45 Persons
THAMES	4·8 Persons
FENS	4·0 Persons

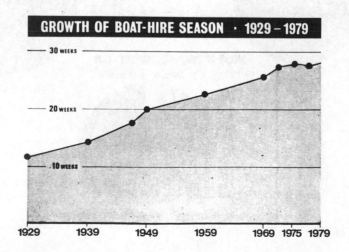

GROWTH OF BOAT-HIRE SEASON · 1929 – 1979

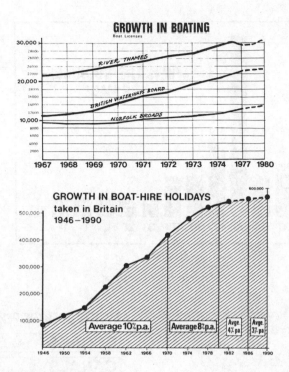

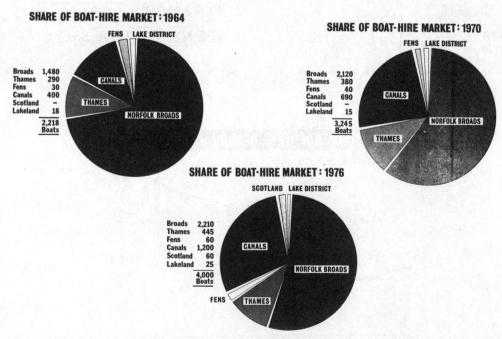

Courtesy: Hoseasons

Although the figures for the 1970s showed a steady upward trend, the drought of 1976 caused many companies to reorganise their fleets, and many holiday-makers found their cruising grounds severely restricted.

Fortunately, summer 1977 led to an improvement in hire boat usage and, in that year alone, it is estimated that the industry on the canals earned £5 million, with an additional £2 million being spent in canalside towns. That same year Blakes fleets had 220,000 bookings, which produced a gross revenue of £4.72 million, and 15 per cent of this trade came from foreign visitors. In 1978, Hoseasons, the hire boat market leaders, had 380,000 customers; and, on the canals alone, they had made over 80,000 bookings by the time the summer season had reached its peak.

Early in 1978 the British Waterways Board announced its decision to limit the number of canal hire craft licences for the period 1 March 1978 to 28 February 1979 to the same number issued for 1977/78. This seemed to many to be killing the goose that laid the golden eggs, since it prevented the introduction of about 100 new hire boats, and lost the additional revenue which was much needed to finance canal repair work. The embargo was to enable the Board to conduct studies into the development of boating on the waterways under its control, and, in particular, into the rôle of hire boating. The restriction ironically came in the year in which the Association of Pleasure Craft Operators (A.P.C.O.), the trade organisation for the inland waterways boating industry, celebrated its Silver Jubilee. The British Waterways Board were particularly concerned that some canals were deteriorating very rapidly through extensive use by powercraft—often traffic levels were even higher than when the waterways were at the peak of their working life! They believed there was a need to examine how future development could more readily spread the load, perhaps by developing lesser-used routes. After detailed research, they agreed a strategy for the development of further bases and started to accept new applications for hire craft licences.

In mid-1979, the English Tourist Board produced a report entitled *Holidays on England's Rivers and Canals.* This concluded that, although waterway holidays constituted a relatively small part of the English holiday industry, they utilised an outstandingly attractive asset and should therefore be encouraged. In particular, it was noted that most hirers tended to come from the younger age group, 18–35 years, with up to 40 per cent being one-family units. Some 21 per cent were two-family hirers, 13 per cent. were families plus friends, and 23 per cent groups of friends. About 50 per cent of the people were first-time hirers, and there was a 1 in 9 chance that they might ultimately purchase a boat. The report noted that hiring of boats by visitors from overseas, though a relatively small part of the total market, was increasing steadily. This was especially due to the efforts of the four national booking agencies—Blakes, Boat Enquiries, Central Booking Agency, and Hoseasons—who marketed almost two-thirds of Britain's hire craft. It also pointed to the fact that, of the 129 businesses hiring boats, 30 per cent had been established for over ten years; a further 27 per cent had been operating for between five and ten years; whilst

43 per cent had only recently come into the market. The number of firms had trebled in the previous decade, but none of the individual companies was large. The report suggested that 75 per cent of the firms had 12 boats or less, and of these 29 per cent had five boats or less. Two-thirds of the boats on offer were between four- and six-berth. Some of the larger firms operated boats from several bases, and although in recent years there had been a marked increase in the average size of hire fleets, no individual firm was of a size to handle international marketing.

The overseas marketing of canal holidays had already received some attention from both Blakes and Hoseasons. Both companies appreciated that boating holidays were priced at the top of the self-catering holiday range. Partly to balance this, they had started to try to attract a growing number of foreign holiday-makers. The first direct flights from Switzerland to Norwich, for Broads holidays, started in 1971, and in 1978 additional charter flights were organised from Denmark to enhance this trade. Between 1971 and 1978 Blakes' business from foreigners had grown from less than one per cent. of their total bookings to nearly 15 per cent. Hoseasons also were able to sell between one-tenth and one-third of their peak season hire allocation to visitors from overseas. This was particularly evident when the extremely favourable exchange rate of the pound, in the late 1970s and early 1980s, induced a disproportionate number of visitors to come to Britain.

The British Waterways Board also saw the chance of compensating for the downturn in the British economy at this time by seeking additional overseas trade. Their Research Officer, Sally Ash, was granted aid by the British Travel Education Trust to investigate the United States market for holidays on British waterways. Her report, published in May 1981, suggested that the decline in domestic bookings in the early 1980s could be offset, to a degree, by increasing the level of overseas marketing. In particular, the U.S. market might bear somewhat higher prices for canal boat hire; the U.S. travel market was more resilient to economic recession. For these reasons, the report suggested that hire boat companies should make greater overseas marketing investments, in particular in the U.S.A.

As a result, a consortium of boat hire companies was set up in early 1982 by the British Waterways Board and the Association of Pleasure Craft Operators. U.K. Waterway Holidays, Ltd., was particularly aimed at selling holidays on the inland waterways to the major European, North American and English-speaking markets. The key words were: *Waterways cruising in Britain is different, afford-able, and fun, and a great way to get acquainted with the local people.* The consortium got off to a very good start, and in 1983 was able to expand their range to include 'economy charter boats', catering for larger parties and youth groups. In addition, these were offered for holidays combined with tuition in English, to give double benefit from the holiday break!

The concept of hire boats as the saviour of the canals can be taken too far, but one argument in its favour, made by the B.W.B. in research reports, is that the funds from government needed for proper waterway maintenance are more likely to be forthcoming if the canals can show their success as income earners. This can also be applied to the regions through which the canals pass. A survey carried out in 1979 into the *Economic Benefits of Cruising Waterways* studied boaters' expenditure on the Stratford-upon-Avon Canal (North). This showed that shops, pubs and boatyards close to the canal received something in the order of £50,000 in net income from pleasure-boat traffic, much of which was hire craft (an average of £5,000 per mile of canal). At a time of recession this cannot be ignored.

The British boat hire industry on the Broads, rivers, fens, and canals by 1982 had some 4,700 craft available for hire, 80 per cent of which had been built in the last eight to 10 years. Most of these craft were in use for up to 30 weeks in a season, offering at least four berths each, thus providing waterway holidays for some 564,000 people each year. Estimates suggest that the boat hire industry generates a turnover in excess of £22 million, after all factors are taken into consideration. On the canals alone, 100 new hire craft cost over £1 million, and the normal fleet replacements a further £500,000, thus providing jobs to the value of £1.8 million, after allowance is made for the ancillary trades.

The hire craft industry has thus come a long way in the last 100 years. The public usage it has stimulated has brought the inland waterways to life again. Their future development very much depends on the economic climate and governmental attitude to their value as an amenity. This, in turn, will influence the entrepreneurs' attitudes to the increase of the hire fleets. However, because of scarcity of land and the need to develop resources for optimum use, it is realistic to expect that disused and derelict canals will have an important future.

During the 1970s the number of people using the canals for hire boating, pleasure cruising, angling, walking, and other forms of recreation has increased each year. It has caused some congestion at better-known places. If there is a move towards a shorter working week in the 1980s, this pressure is likely to increase. One way to solve the problem would be to open the 700km. of rivers and canals which have fallen into decay. The restorationists' concern is that during this period of recession nothing will be done to hinder or negate the longer-term development of new cruising routes. Once the economic outlook improves, they hope that there will be a real commitment by all in authority for many derelict waterways to be re-opened, providing a greater variety of holiday opportunities and more leisure space. Thus, a greater opportunity will be available for people to sample the delights of the water highways, which many have used already, thanks to the existing hire fleets.

Chapter Five

THE WATERWAYS RESTORATION MOVEMENT IN PERSPECTIVE

A SERIES of full-page advertisements, many in colour, and sponsored by Shell U.K., Ltd., appeared throughout the national press during 1981 under the bold heading: 'Fancy helping weed a river?' They showed an old converted narrow boat cruising along an idyllic rural canal. The text included the following statement:

> How about helping . . . restore life and beauty to a dry canal?
> Of Britain's thousands of miles of inland waterways, long stretches are in desperate need of some kind of restoration, and each week-end, all over Britain, groups of dedicated enthusiasts hack, weed, burn and dig, taking the task upon themselves . . . the problem is vast, but luckily it's a problem that's fun to solve . . . Next week-end you could be weeding riverbeds instead of flower beds.

This advertisement, perhaps, marked the turning point in the efforts of waterway restoration enthusiasts, over a period of some 30 years, to obtain a wider public understanding of what they were about.

More official recognition of the value of their work came in a series of national advertisements, placed by the Manpower Services Commission, in early 1983, to develop support for their Community Enterprise Programme. Among the schemes that were actually recommended by the M.S.C. to help those who had been out of work for some time and to help local communities, were projects for clearing canals and derelict areas to improve the environment. Truly official blessing, indeed! But what is it all about?

Waterway restoration means different things to different people; to the canal enthusiast it means full recovery to navigation; to those interested in amenity development it means revitalising dead stretches of water; to others interested in industrial archaeology it means an opportunity to reconstruct a past era. For the great majority, however, waterway restoration means a chance to revive part of the national heritage which was created by man for the advancement of the nation. This is perhaps best shown by the considerable growth of interest in waterway museums, restored boats, and reconstructed water routes, now available for all to use.

One feature links each different idea about waterway restoration: this is that the inland waterways are still today of a scale that the individual can comprehend.

When the canals were constructed, they were made by men using their hands. Equally, when they are reconstructed, individuals can still use their hands and and achieve personal satisfaction in re-creating a former working environment.

Why has waterway restoration gained so much of a hold over the past few years, and what does it involve? Perhaps understanding of the present position can be gained best by looking back to the past. In 1800 there was a system of inter-connected inland waterways offering some 4,250 miles of navigation. By 1960 this had been reduced to a disjointed system of only 2,250 miles available for navigational use. The loss of 2,000 miles of navigable inland waterways, and the demise of the attendant way of life, provoked the desire to re-create the former system. Other factors also came into play. Firstly, there was the growing realisation of the shortage of leisure space. Secondly, the waterways offered opportunities for multiple use. Thirdly, society felt a need to cling to past practices, to indulge in nostalgia. All of these combined to create the growth of the waterway restoration movement.

What the movement actually involves is rather more difficult to define. In essence waterway restoration can be epitomised in the Waterway Recovery Group motto, 'We dig canals', but, like the proverbial iceberg, there is far more in it than just digging. Essentially, waterway restoration is a political process. Firstly, there is the battle to awaken interest, to make the case and gain public support, and the ultimate aim to commit those in authority to take action. Secondly, there is the demand by the public to have adequate leisure facilities. The working week has been drastically reduced over the last 30 years and people now have more time to enjoy themselves—water space provides an opportunity for this. Thirdly, there is simply the demand by members of society to be able to do something constructive in their spare time. There is nothing more satisfying than seeing the result of one's labours, and canals provide an immediate indicator of effort expended—a towpath cleared, a section dredged, a lock restored, are all such jobs that can quickly show benefits and only involve simple engineering techniques and hand labour.

Undoubtedly, the waterway restoration movement that has developed during the last 30 years has its roots in the early 1900s, when single schemes, such as the proposal to revive the Avon Navigation were the order of the day. It was not until the Second World War, when the waterways had become under-used, silted and nearly forgotten, and lack of labour had allowed the system to fall into disrepair, that sufficient public concern was provoked to demand action. This revival of interest in the waterways and resulting activity towards restoration developed a three-pronged form. Firstly, Tom Rolt produced his book, *Narrowboat,* which for the first time invited many into a new and forgotten world. Secondly, Ealing Studios produced a film, *Painted Boats,* which highlighted and recorded the silent water roads of England and their way of life. Thirdly, there was in the air an attitude of post-war enthusiasm for reconstructing and re-creating a new and better life.

The new and better life was epitomised by the formation of the Inland Waterways Association in May 1946 to campaign for the retention and revival of the inland waterways. The I.W.A., during its early life 1946–1949, developed a dual strategy. Initially, it tried to reactivate public interest in canals and thus to prove that enough people cared about their future; and, subsequently, it tried to use the law to force those in control of the waterways to repair, refurbish, and re-open those canals that had fallen into disrepair.

The greatest achievement of this early campaign was, perhaps, the restoration of a lifting bridge on the Northern Stratford Canal, and with it the re-opening of the alternative route from London to Birmingham, which had become unusable. The period also provided a test for early waterway restorationists when the Basingstoke Canal came up for sale in March 1949. The I.W.A. was neither constituted to take on the responsibility for the canal, nor did it have the capital to purchase it outright. Although it appeared at first that the Basingstoke Canal had been saved for the nation, the inability of the I.W.A. to raise the necessary finance meant that the canal fell into other hands. However, the I.W.A. was more successful with other restoration campaigns that were forming in 1949.

The first waterway restoration to be completed was at Linton Lock, on the River Ouse in Yorkshire, which was re-opened in 1950 after I.W.A. members had both raised the cash and made a physical contribution towards the restoration work. At much the same time the lessons learnt from Linton Lock and from the abortive Basingstoke campaign were put to good use when the restoration of the Lower Avon Navigation was projected. Thus 1950 saw the first evidence of progress in the waterway restoration campaign with the formation of the Lower Avon Navigational Trust. The growth of public interest was consolidated at a waterways rally held at Market Harborough. In 1950 also the unified toll structure for pleasure craft in the inland waterways was introduced, and a new range of books about inland waterways became readily available.

The foundations for the modern waterway restoration movement were thus laid during the late 1940s and during the following decade public support was strengthened. The greatest single feature of the era, significant in gaining public interest, was perhaps the introduction of the 'Jason' waterway trip along the Regent's Canal. This introduced many people for the first time to the delights of inland waterways. The considerable progress in restoring the Lower Avon also proved to others what even a small band of volunteers could do in restoring a waterway to active use. The example of the Lower Avon encouraged a similar development on the river Ouse in Bedfordshire, but at first lack of effective authority stifled early progress on this scheme.

Thus, people in other parts of the country slowly began to interest themselves in their local waterways. Furthermore, the British Transport Commission, custodians of the nationalised waterways, decided to undertake a far-reaching survey to evaluate the value of the remaining waterways. As a result, a Board of Survey report in 1955 concluded that some 336 miles of waterways should be improved, a further 994 miles of waterways should be retained, but that some 771 miles of waterways should be disposed of. In respect of the last item, the report suggested the need for a further review.

At about this time industrial archaeology was just beginning to bloom, and a new body of people emerged who saw value in retaining monuments to the past industrial era. In the following three years, 1956–1958, various local conflicts arose between those willing to see their local canal disappear and those prepared to fight for its retention. For example, two opposing groups were fighting over the Town Arm of the Coventry Canal, one seeking its conversion to a road, and the other for its revival as a water route to the centre of the town. From this campaign emerged a practical leader of restorationists who has since done much to reactivate the waterways. That man was David Hutchings, who, in 1958, started to restore the derelict Wyken Arm of the Oxford Canal as the first stage in his long career as waterway restoration. His career soon blossomed with a pilot scheme, inaugurated in 1960, for the restoration of the Southern Stratford Canal by the combined forces of the National Trust, the Stratford-upon-Avon Canal Society, and the I.W.A. The successful restoration of the 13-mile rural Southern Stratford Canal gave waterway restorationists their first opportunity to participate in a short-term restoration scheme and thus prove publicly the viability of their ideals.

At this time the embyro Navvies Movement was also clearing a section of the Basingstoke Canal with a working party for a boat rally at Woking at Easter 1962. In that year a boat rally at Stourbridge highlighted the conflict between official attitude and public will, and resulted in David Hutchings clearing a section of the Stourbridge Arm in the face of official protests. By this time, official attitudes were just beginning to mellow, and, under the 1962 Transport Bill, the British Waterways Board was formed in January 1963 to develop the inland waterways.

The Board brought with them a new official attitude to restoration, which permitted such pilot schemes as the restoration of the Stourbridge '16' Locks, and developments leading to the re-opening of the Dudley Tunnel. Later, official willingness to allow volunteers to reactivate canals spread to other parts of the country.

The next significant development came in 1964 with the re-opening of the Lower Avon and the Southern Stratford Canal. This gave waterway enthusiasts the chance to re-open a new waterway ring by restoring the derelict Upper Avon Navigation, linking Stratford with Evesham. The Upper Avon Navigation Trust was soon active and became a spearhead for the waterway restoration movement during the latter part of the 1960s. Similarly, the possible loss of a section of a circular route in the North-West, later named the Cheshire Ring, provoked others to work to restore the waterways of that area.

In 1965 a report, *The Facts about the Waterways*, indicated to all that, whatever happened to the waterways, the government had to meet a bill of £600,000, and yet for only 50 per cent extra a pleasure network could be retained for future generations. It so happened that this information fell on fruitful ground, for the period from 1965 to 1970 was when the seeds of the leisure revolution were being sown. It was a time when people were beginning to realise that the shorter working week offered greater leisure, and that inland waterways offered considerable recreation and amenity. Some also looked for ways to use their leisure hours by taking part in restoration schemes. This willingness to volunteer aided the development of the *Navvies Notebook,* now re-named *Navvies,* which for the first time provided details of various restoration projects and of when work was taking place, so that all could participate. A new approach to accounting for the benefits that restored waterways could offer was being adopted by the Dartington Amenity Research Trust, who produced a report on the Grand Western Canal and convinced the Devon County Council that the waterway should be retained and restored.

The most significant advance of the period came with the 1968 Transport Act, which for the first time enabled local authorities to grant financial support to waterway restoration schemes in their area. The Act provoked local interest still further because it indicated that the future of certain waterways was still in doubt. The very real threat of losing their local canal prompted the formation of many individual waterway groups. Such groups were formed in Slough, Birmingham, Pocklington, in the Erewash Valley, and elsewhere. All had the common aim of reactivating their local waterways.

The 1968 Act stimulated the organisers of the Navvies Movement to exemplify what controlled volunteer labour could achieve, and 'Operation Ashton' was conceived to prove to various authorities that volunteers could be co-ordinated into action to restore a derelict section of canal.

By the late 1960s industrial archaeology movement could also demonstrate progress. Waterway restoration was taking place at the first open-air museum of industrial archaeology at Blists Hill, Ironbridge, where a section of the Shropshire Canal, the Hay Inclined Plane, and the Coalport Canal were designated for revival. In the same area in 1969 a second major waterway restoration dig at Welshpool was planned to support a local campaign to divert a bypass intended to be built on the local canal.

In 1970 the Waterways Recovery Group was formally constituted to promote and co-ordinate waterway restoration on a national scale. It also introduced a new era in waterway restoration, for the period 1971–1975 was a time of success. During these years many local groups experienced a considerable upsurge of public interest, and prompt action by volunteers provided the publicity which led to the turning point of many campaigns. In consequence 1974 provided a year of 'Openings': the re-opening of the Upper Avon, the Caldon Canal, the Ashton and Peak Forest Canal, for example, provided the incentive to work hard on much longer-term schemes, such as the restoration of the long derelict Wey and Arun Canal.

As more waterways re-opened, greater interest developed in their use for hire craft, and a new holiday industry developed offering canal cruises. The growth of boat hire and private boat purchase led to a need for more mooring spaces and marinas. This, too, stimulated the restoration movement and schemes for the Prees Branch of the Shropshire Union Canal and the Old Engine Arm at Napton on the Oxford Canal, among others, added to the list of successful waterways restoration.

The conservation movement in Britain was also growing, and the possibility of defining future development within County Structure Plans became a reality. For an outstanding example of Conservation Area development, the designation of the entire Macclesfield Canal can be quoted. In other places small sections of canals, such as the interchange port at Shardlow, were similarly designated 'conservation areas'.

The Water Act of 1973 meant the creation of new, multi-purpose water authorities. These authorities took an interest in waterway restoration projects, and the re-opening in May 1978 of the Great Ouse to Bedford is a fine achievement in this area. Unfortunately, the benefits of the first part of the 1970s were nullified in 1976 by the drought which brought to light many longer-term problems for the waterways, such as depleted reservoirs. The greatest problem, however, was the lack of cash to take essential action to preserve those sections of canals in need of treatment. Most clouds, however have a silver lining, and later that year the first of various Government Job Creation Schemes, covering the revival of sections of canals, began to materialise, and the Rochdale Canal, the Basingstoke Canal, the Kennet and Avon Canal, the Neath and Tennant Canals, and the Thames and Severn Canal, were all included in the restoration work to be paid for by government grants. Although some 30 years previously the government had been trying to dispose of the canals, it had finally had a change of heart, and began again to promote their restoration as a means of creating jobs as well as of gaining additional leisure space.

Other sources of finance emerged in the late 1970s, especially when Shell U.K., Ltd., linked with the I.W.A. to sponsor a series of three bi-annual Waterway Restoration Awards. These awards not only financed restoration work, but also enabled various development plans to be properly explored. For example, one scheme developed for the Higher Thames, between Lechlade and Cricklade, and not only offered an additional 10 miles of cruising navigation, but also the prospect of a link into the Thames and Severn Canal, near to the Cotswold Water Park, and so possibly surmounted some problems of that canal restoration scheme.

The late 1970s and the early 1980s were also a time of restoration by report. Perhaps this way forward was indicated by the publication of the *Fraenkel Report,* and a resultant government commitment to inject more funds to deal with the maintenance backlog developing on parts of the canal system. This backlog of repair work on the southern section of the Stratford Canal led D. Hutchings to publish a report in 1978, *The Avon Navigation—Stratford to Warwick,* which showed how easy it would be to extend the Avon Navigation through to Warwick, where it could link with the Grand Union Canal. The scheme's merit was that it provided an alternative route to the over-used Southern Stratford Canal, so facilitating its rejuvenation.

Other reports produced about this time dealt with specific canals. Nearly all set out a range of alternatives for future development; with full restoration invariably figuring as a longer-term option. Such reports included the *Forth and Clyde Canal: Draft Written Statement*; *A Plan for the Monmouthshire and Brecon Canal*; *The Bridgwater and Taunton: A Canal and its Future*; *The Stourbridge*

Canal: Securing the Future; (The Sleaford Navigation) *Bottom Lock Restoration Appeal*; *A Proposal for the Restoration of the Huddersfield Narrow Canal from Marsden to Slaithwaite,* and many more. All the reports had a common theme: without restoration the canal will simply deteriorate to the detriment of all. Restored it can bring pleasure to everyone and an asset to the community.

These reports came at the right time for, with rising unemployment, the local authorities and central government were looking for ways in which environmental achievements could be gained and the unemployed found work. The I.W.A.A.C. in August 1980 produced their study, *Inland Waterways—Arteries for Employment and Spending,* which suggested that the financial return from further investment in inland waterways could be greatly enhanced, and further employment created, if the canals were revived.

For each mile of waterway restored to navigation, the local community could benefit, both from extra trade and extra jobs, from additional recreational and tourist activity. This theme was subsequently taken up by individual groups, such as the Huddersfield Canal Society, Ltd., in *A Report on the Job Creation Potential of the Huddersfield Narrow Canal, as a Navigable Waterway,* in which it was estimated that 260 additional permanent jobs would be created when the canal was revived.

It was also realised at this time that Manpower Services Commission, Countryside Commission, and Tourist Authority grants could be used for earlier restoration ideas to be achieved. This led to the revival of some previously discarded schemes, and the prospect of restoring the first section of the Saltisford Arm and the final mile of the Ripon Canal were now more likely to be achieved.

This new enthusiasm in the 1980s also spread to other schemes, such as the restoration of the Foxton Inclined Plane, the reconstruction of the Whitchurch Arm of the Llangollen Canal, and the construction of a new Upper Severn Navigation, from Stourport through to Ironbridge. Each in its own way demonstrates the changing nature of public attitudes towards canals. A report produced in 1980 by West Midlands County Council, *A Canal Strategy for the 1980s,* suggested that the local network of canals offered considerable potential for recreation and for improving the local environment. The study, therefore, listed schemes which pursued this theme, such as reviving the old Delph flight of locks as an industrial archaeology site, or the rejuvenation of the Stourbridge Arm and Hawne Basin, where facilities for boaters were to the fore.

By 1983, the restoration movement was full of hope. Major schemes, such as those for the Kennet and Avon and Basingstoke Canals, at last appeared to be on the home straight, though finance was still a barrier to their success. Even so, the wider range of Manpower Services Commission grants, through the Special Temporary Employment Programmes and Community Enterprise schemes, seemed to be smoothing the path ahead. Local authorities also looked more favourably on longer-term restoration plans, and policies for the preservation of canal lines were to be written into the majority of County Structure Plans. The major development was provided by a B.W.B. Private Bill to reclassify various restored waterways into the 'Cruiseway' category, and this received Royal Assent on 8 February 1983. This proved that nearly all the early efforts of the 1970s had been worthwhile, by giving those waterways the 'permanent' status that their restorers always believed they had deserved.

What of the future for the waterway restoration movement? There are four areas in which developments are likely to take place. Firstly, there is a need for new facilities to cope with the growth of the tourist and leisure industry. The restoration of the Hythe Bridge Arm in Oxford provides a ready example of additional mooring space created on the much-used Oxford Canal; developments such as the renovation of the old Shropshire Union Canal Basin at Ellesmere Port and its conversion into a Museum of Inland Navigation, or the revival of the old flight of Delph Locks as an industrial archaeology and conservation area, show the range of opportunities in the tourist area. Many other derelict canal-side buildings and arms will also be restored for this purpose.

Secondly, there is a demand to re-open Touring Rings. The 'Pennine Ring' is one of the best long-term aims, and the restoration of both the Rochdale and Huddersfield Narrow Canals will provide a northern waterway circuit; in the Avon Valley, D. Hutchings' masterly scheme to open the Higher Avon, between Stratford and Warwick, as the missing link in a broad gauge route across England as well as making a new circuit, deserves success. In the east, the idea of linking the upper Great Ouse to the Grand Union Canal at Cosgrove offers another holiday circuit in the very much longer term.

Thirdly, there will be a quest for new routes to link detached sections of the current system. Perhaps the most enterprising plans are to link the Lancaster Canal to the river Ribble and thence, via the river Douglas and the Rufford Arm of the Leeds and Liverpool Canal, to the main canal system, or that proposed by the Rase-Ancholme Navigation Trust, to unite the Lincolnshire waterways. Without doubt, the greatest long-term prospect will be the re-opening of the Thames and Severn Canal, which will offer a new water-route in the south. Should the scheme for a Severn Barrage also materialise, then the restored Kennet and Avon Canal, the river Avon, and the lower reaches of the Severn could offer yet another cruising ring with the prospect of reaching even the Brecon and Abergavenny Canal through a restored Monmouthshire Canal.

It is reasonable to suggest, then, that more leisure time will encourage people to come forward to restore old canal structures and to re-develop lost canals. Thus all will be able to utilise the fruits of the waterway system created by the Industrial Revolution. In this way, the past will continue to provide the key to future enjoyment for the many who take pleasure from the silent waters of British canals.

Appendix I

CHRONOLOGY OF LEGISLATION

MANY FACTORS that have assisted, or retarded, the progress of the Waterway Restoration Movement over the past 30 years can be directly related to legislation that has been in some way influential on the management of the inland waterways and their associated finance. Mostly, the main items of legislation were preceded by government White Papers or consultative documents. These often provoked particular lines of development or initiated publicity campaigns.

Any diagnostic review of the evolution of the Waterway Restoration Movement must define the chronology of this legislation and its political bias, and must note the chronology of the associated consultative documentation.

The analysis that follows has been prepared for this purpose. It is not completely comprehensive since it omits, among other items, various Annual Bills that were promoted by the British Transport Commission. Such omissions are made both for brevity and, more particularly, to focus attention on the most influential items.

1945	Labour Government elected.
1946	*New Towns Act* (area planning),
1947	1. *Transport Act* (canals nationalised under B.T.C.).
	2. *Town and County Planning Act* (Derelict Land Control).
1949	*National Parks and Access to the Countryside Act* (National Parks created).
1950	Labour Government re-elected.
1951	Conservative Government elected.
1953	1. *Transport Act* (B.T.C. split—Docks and Inland Waterways Executive).
	2. *Historic Buildings and Ancient Monuments Act* (grants to local authorities).
1954	1. (B.T.C. internal Board of Survey led by Rusholme.)
	2. B.T.C. Report—*Canals and Inland Waterways* (three groups of Waterways).
1955	1. Conservative Government re-elected.
	2. B.T.C.—British Transport Waterways.
1956	Committee of Inquiry into Inland Waterways (Bowes).
1957	Conservative Government reformed.
1958	*Report of the Committee of Inquiry into Inland Waterways* (Cmnd. 486). (Canals for purposes other than commerce.)
1959	1. *Government Proposals following the Report of the Committee of Inquiry into Inland Waterways* (Cmnd. 676). (Inland Waterways Redevelopment Advisory Committee.)
	2. Conservative Government reformed.
1962	1. *Transport Act* (British Waterways Board).
	2. *Local Authorities (Historic Buildings) Act* (grants to L.A.s).
1963	*Water Act* (River Boards—Resource Control).

172

1964   1. B.W.B. *The Future of the Waterways* (Interim Report).
        2. Labour Government elected.
1965   B.W.B. *The Facts about the Waterways* (Amenity Development).
1966   1. Labour Government re-elected.
        2. *Transport Policy* (Cmnd. 2928).
        3. *Local Government Act* (Land Reclamation Grants).
        4. *Leisure in the Countryside* (Cmd. 2928).
1967   1. *Civic Amenities Act* (Conservation areas).
        2. *British Waterways: Recreation and Amenity* (Cmnd. 3401) (Amenity Waterways—
            L.A. finance).
1968   1. *Countryside Act* (Countryside Commission—Country Parks).
        2. *Transport Act* (Powers for Amenity development using L.A. Finance—Remainder
            Waterways). (Inland Waterways Amenity Advisory Council.)
1970   Conservative Government elected.
1971   1. *Town and Country Planning Acts* (Development Plans).
        2. D.o.E. *Circular 92/71* (Consultative document proposals new Water Authorities).
1972   *Local Government Act* (New Local Authorities, 1 April 1974).
1973   1. *Water Act* (New Water Authorities, 1 April 1974).
        2. *First* and *Second Report from Select Committee of the House of Lords on Sport
            and Leisure*.
        3. Water Space Amenity Commission.
1974   Labour Government elected (February and October).
1975   1. *Sport and Recreation* (Cmnd. 6200).
        2. (October) Manpower Service Commission, Job Creation Grants.
1976   (February) *Review of the Water Industry in England and Wales: A consultative
            document*. D.o.E.
1977   1. *The Water Industry in England and Wales: the Next Steps* (Cmnd. 6876).
        2. *Development of County Structure Plans* proceeds.
1978   Sheffield and South Yorkshire Navigation (Modernisation). £10 million investment
            approved on 8 September 1978.
1979   1. Conservative Government elected.
        2. Government announces it does NOT plan to abolish B.W.B.
        3. I.W.A.A.C. under threat of abolition.
1980   *Anglian Water Authority: Recreation Byelaws*.
1981   1. D.o.E. agreement for *B.W.B.* to sponsor a *Private Bill* to upgrade certain 'Remain-
            der' canals.
        2. Anglian Water Authority—Byelaws Enquiry.
        3. *Water Bill* to increase B.W.B. borrowing powers.
        4. I.W.A.A.C.—reprieve for two years.
        5. *Transport Bill*—Section 8/36 Grants to assist in the development of water transport.
1982   1. Maritime England Year.
        2. B.W.B. given additional maintenance grants.
        3. *Water Bill*—W.A.S.A.C. to be abolished.
1983   8 February, Royal Assent given to the *B.W.B. Private Bill* to upgrade to 'Cruiseway'
            status the following canals:
                    Ashton Canal.
                    Caldon Canal.
                    Erewash Canal.
                    Grand Union Canal: Slough Arm.
                    Leek Branch: Caldon Canal.
                    Lower Peak Forest Canal.
                    Monmouthshire and Brecon Canal.

WATERWAYS CLUBS AND SOCIETIES

Ancholme Navigation
Rase-Ancholme Navigation Trust,
c/o The Marina,
Brandy Wharf,
Waddingham,
Gainsborough, Lincs.

Ashby Canal
Ashby Canal Association
c/o 22 Grove Park,
Burbage,
Hinckley,
Leics., LE10 2BJ

Basingstoke Canal
Surrey & Hampshire Canal Society,
c/o 'Meadow Vale',
Guildford Road,
Normandy, Surrey

Birmingham Canal Navigations
Birmingham Canal Navigations Society,
c/o 'Brades',
Lower Penkridge Road,
Acton Trussell,
Stafford, ST17 0RG

Coombeswood Canal Trust,
c/o 11 Regis Road,
Rowley Regis,
Warley, West Midlands

Dudley Canal Trust,
c/o 27 Trejon Road,
Cradley Heath,
Warley, West Midlands

Waterways Activities Group,
c/o 36 Camden Street,
Walsall Wood,
Walsall, West Midlands,
WS9 9BQ

Bridgwater & Taunton Canal
Somerset Inland Waterways Society,
c/o 'West View', Westport,
Langport, Somerset

Bridgwater & Taunton Canal—*cont.*
I.W.A., West Country Branch,
c/o 'Hazelbank',
Church Road,
Redhill,
near Bristol, Avon

Calder & Hebble Navigation
Calder Navigation Society,
c/o 26 Coley View,
Northowran,
Halifax, West Yorkshire

Caldon Canal
Caldon Canal Society,
c/o 'Long Barrow',
Butterton,
Newcastle-under-Lyme,
Staffs, ST5 4EB

Chesterfield Canal
Chesterfield Canal Society,
c/o 5 Sunnyside,
Worksop,
Notts, S81 7LN

Chichester Canal
Portsmouth & Arundel Canal Society
c/o 39 Langdale Avenue,
Chichester, West Sussex

Coventry Canal
Coventry Canal Society,
c/o 64 Broad Lane,
Coventry,
West Midlands, CV5 7AF

Cromford Canal
Cromford Canal Society, Ltd.,
c/o Old Wharf,
Mill Lane,
Cromford, Derbyshire

Derwent Navigation (Yorks)
Yorkshire Derwent Trust,
c/o 21 Burgate,
Pickering, Yorkshire

Droitwich Canals
  The Droitwich Canals Trust,
  c/o 1 Hampton Road,
  Droitwich,
  Worcs., WR9 8PB

Driffield Navigation
  Driffield Navigation Amenities Association,
  c/o Swing Bridge Cottage,
  Hempholme,
  Driffield, Yorkshire

Grand Union Canal
  Grand Union Canal Society,
  c/o 65 Whitby Road,
  Ruislip,
  Middx., HA4 9DU

Foxton Inclined Plane Trust
  c/o Bottom Lock,
  Foxton,
  Market Harborough,
  Leics.

  Slough Canal Society,
  c/o The Boatyard,
  Mansion Lane,
  Iver, Bucks.

  Aylesbury Canal Society,
  c/o N. B. Kalamaki,
  Canal Basin,
  Aylesbury, Bucks.

  Saltisford Canal Trust,
  c/o 40 Coventry Road,
  Warwick, CV34 4LJ

  Brent River & Canal Society,
  c/o 7 Manor Court Road,
  Hanwell,
  London, W7

  Old Union Canals Society,
  c/o 5 Dunslade Road,
  Market Harborough,
  Leics., LE16 8AQ

  Erewash Canal Preservation & Development
     Association,
  c/o 31 Derby Road,
  Risley,
  Derby, DE7 3SY

Grantham Canal
  Grantham Canal Restoration Society,
  c/o 3 Barratt Crescent,
  Attenborough,
  Nottingham,
  NG9 6AH

Great Ouse
  The East Anglian Waterways Association,
  c/o Wych House,
  St Ives,
  Cambs., PE17 4BT

Huddersfield Canal
  Huddersfield Canal Society,
  c/o 38 Paris Road,
  Scholes,
  Huddersfield, West Yorkshire

Itchen Navigation
  Itchen Navigation Society,
  c/o 43 Taunton Drive,
  Bitterne,
  Southampton, SO2 5BX

Kennet & Avon Canal
  Kennet & Avon Canal Trust, Ltd.,
  c/o Devizes Wharf,
  Couch Lane,
  Devizes,
  Wilts, SN10 1EB

Lancaster Canal
  Lancaster Canal Trust,
  c/o 74 Margaret Road,
  Penwortham,
  Preston, Lancs.

Macclesfield Canal
  Macclesfield Canal Society,
  c/o 4 Endon Drive,
  Brown Lees,
  Biddulph, Staffs.

Linton Lock
  Linton Lock Supporters' Club,
  c/o 47 Irwin Avenue,
  Heworth Green,
  York, YO3 7TU

River Medway
  Medway Preservation Society,
  c/o Springhill Cottage,
  Yardley Park Road,
  Tonbridge, Kent

Market Weighton Canal
  Market Weighton Canal Society,
  c/o 47 Market Place,
  Market Weighton,
  York, YO4 3AJ

Monmouthshire Canal
  Newport Canal Preservation Society,
  c/o 12 Melfort Road,
  Newport,
  Gwent, NP1

Monmouthshire Canal—*cont.*
  Torfaen Canal Society,
  c/o 'Hadley Cottage',
  33 Wern Road,
  Sebastopol,
  Pontypool, Gwent

Neath & Tennant Canals
  Neath & Tennant Canals Society,
  c/o 16 Gower Road,
  Sketty,
  Swansea, West Glamorgan

Nottingham Canal
  Nottingham Canal Society,
  c/o 164 Charlebury Road,
  Nottingham

Oxford Canal
  Oxford Canal Action Group,
  33 Oxford Road,
  Old Marston, Oxford

Peak Forest Canal
  Peak Forest Canal Society,
  c/o 28 Delamere Street,
  Higher Openshaw,
  Manchester 11

Pocklington Canal
  Pocklington Canal Society,
  c/o 74 Westminster Road,
  York, YO3 6LY

Ripon Canal
  Ripon Canal Restoration Society,
  c/o 46 Whitcliffe Lane,
  Ripon,
  North Yorks, HG4 2JN

Rochdale Canal
  Rochdale Canal Society,
  c/o 24 Passmonds Crescent,
  Rochdale, Lancs.

Shropshire Union Canal
  Shropshire Union Canal Society Ltd.,
  c/o 'Oakhaven',
  Longdon-on-Tern,
  Salop. TF6 6LJ

Slea Navigation
  Sleaford Navigation Society,
  c/o 8 Kirby Close,
  Southwell, Notts.

River Stour (Suffolk)
  River Stour Trust,
  c/o 6 Bulmer Road,
  Sudbury, Suffolk

Staffordshire & Worcestershire Canal
  Staffordshire & Worcestershire Canal Society,
  c/o 26 High Arcle Drive,
  Woodsetton,
  Dudley, West Midlands

Stratford-upon-Avon Canal
  Stratford-upon-Avon Canal Society,
  c/o 91 Geoffrey Road,
  Shirley,
  Solihull, B20 2HN

Swansea Canal
  Swansea Canal Society,
  c/o 47 Waun Penlan,
  Rhyd-y-Fro,
  Pontardawe,
  Swansea, West Glamorgan

Thames & Medway Canal
  Thames & Medway Canal Society,
  c/o 49 Sun Lane,
  Gravesend, Kent

Thames & Severn & Stroudwater Canals
  Thames & Severn Canal Trust,
  c/o 1 Riveredge,
  Framilode, Gloucestershire

Trent & Mersey Canal
  Trent & Mersey Canal Society,
  c/o 26 Chaseview Road,
  Alrewas,
  Burton-on-Trent,
  Staffs, DE13 7EL

**Upper Avon Navigation/Higher Avon
    Navigation**
  Upper Avon Navigation Trust,
  Station House,
  Harvington,
  near Evesham,
  Worcs.

Wey & Arun Canal
  Wey & Arun Canal Trust,
  c/o 24 Griffiths Avenue,
  Lancing, Sussex

Wilts. and Berks. Canal
  Wilts. & Berks. Canal Amenity Group,
  c/o 14 Chestnut Avenue,
  Buckhurst Hill,
  Essex, IG9 6EW

Worcester & Birmingham Canal
  Worcester & Birmingham Canal Society,
  c/o 71 Birmingham Road,
  Alvechurch,
  Birmingham, B48 7TD

SCOTLAND

Scottish Inland Waterways Association,
c/o 25 India Street,
Edinburgh,
EH3 6HE

Forth & Clyde Canal
Forth & Clyde Canal Society,
c/o 20 Crosshill Avenue,
Crosshill,
Glasgow G42 8BY

Strathkelvin Canal Park Group,
c/o 12E Ellisland Road,
Cumbernauld,
G67 2HD

Union Canal
Linlithgow Union Canal Society,
c/o Canal House,
Linlithgow,
West Lothian,
EH49 6AJ

GENERALIST WATERWAY GROUPS & SOCIETIES

East Anglian Waterways Association,
c/o Wych House,
St Ives,
Cambs., PE17 4BT

Inland Waterways Association,
114 Regent's Park Road,
London, NW1 8UQ

Inland Waterways Protection Society,
c/o 18 Wentworth Drive,
Bramshall,
Cheshire, SK11 8QN

Railway & Canal Historical Society,
c/o 83 Sunny Bank Road,
Potters Bar,
Herts., EN6 2NL

Southampton Canal Society,
c/o 4 Somerset Avenue,
Southampton, SO2 5FL

Waterways Recovery Group, Ltd.,
c/o 12B Oakdale,
Harrogate,
North Yorkshire, HG1 2LL

BOAT PRESERVATION SOCIETIES

Humber, Keel & Sloop Society,
c/o 'Glenlea', Main Road,
New Ellerby,
Hull, North Humberside

Narrow Boat Trust,
c/o M. Denny,
Chapel Street,
Thatcham,
Newbury, Berks.

Norfolk Wherry Trust,
c/o 63 Whitehall Road,
Norwich,
Norfolk, NR2 3EN

BIBLIOGRAPHY

(A) BOOKS AND PAPERS

Anon., *Macclesfield Canal Conservation Area* (Macclesfield Borough Council, Macclesfield 1975).

Anon., *The Rochdale: Then and Now* (Rochdale Canal Society, Rochdale 1974).

Barr, J., *Derelict Britain* (Pelican Books, Harmondsworth 1970),

Bracey, H. E., *People and the Countryside* (Routledge and Kegan Paul, London 1970).

Braithwaite, Lewis, *Canals in Towns* (A. and C. Black. Ltd., London 1976).

British Transport Commission, *Canals and Inland Waterways* (Report of the Board of Survey) (B.T.C., London 1955).

B.T.C., *British Transport Commission Report and Accounts for 1948* (London 1949).

British Waterways Board, *Address Book: 2nd Edition* (B.W.B., London 1973).

British Waterways Board, *The Facts about the Waterways* (H.M.S.O., London 1965).

B.W.B., *British Waterways Board Annual Report and Accounts* (H.M.S.O., London 1963–1975).

British Waterways Board, *Waterway Users' Companion* (B.W.B., London 1975, 1976).

Burton, A., *The Canal Builders* (Eyre Methuen, London 1972).

Burton, A., and Pratt, D., *Canal* (David and Charles, Newton Abbot 1976).

Button, K. J., *No. 6: The 1968 Transport Act and After* (University of Loughborough, Dept. of Economics, Loughborough 1974).

Clew, K. R., *The Kennet and Avon Canal* (David and Charles, Newton Abbott, 2nd edn. 1973).

Edwards, L. A., *Inland Waterways of Great Britain* (Imray, Laurie, Norie and Wilson, St Ives, Huntingdon 1972).

Farrington, J. H., *Morphological Studies of English Canals* (University of Hull, Occasional Papers in Geography No. 10, Hull 1972).

Fullerton, B., *The Development of British Transport Networks* (Oxford University Press, Oxford 1975).

Gayford, Eily, *The Amateur Boatwoman* (David and Charles, Newton Abbot 1973).

Gladwin, D. D., *The Canals of Britain* (Batsford, London 1973).

Gladwin, D. D., *The Waterways of Britain: A Social Panorama* (Batsford, London 1976).

Gladwin, D. D., and White, J. M., *English Canals: Part I, A Concise History* (Oakwood Press, Lingfield 1967).

Hadfield, C., *British Canals: An Illustrated History* (David and Charles, Newton Abbot, 5th edn. 1974).

Hadfield, C., *The Canal Age* (David and Charles, Newton Abbot 1968).

Hadfield, C., *Introducing Canals: A Guide to British Waterways Today* (E. Benn, London 1955).

Hadfield, C., *Introducing Inland Waterways* (David and Charles, Newton Abbott 1968).

Hamer, M., *Transport and Society*. Background Notes on Social Studies, No. SS 24. (Workers' Educational Association, London 1975).

Hopkins, W. G., *An outline account of the Glamorganshire Canal: 1790–1974* (Cardiff Naturalists' Society, Cardiff 1974).

Hoskins, W. G., *The Making of the English Landscape* (Pelican Books, Harmondsworth 1970).

Ives, W. L., 'The Problems of our Inland Waterways', *Paper to the Metropolitan Section, Chartered Institute of Transport* (London, 4 February 1959).

178

I.W.A.A.C., *Priorities for Action on the Waterways of British Waterways Board* (Inland Waterways Amenity Advisory Council, London 1975).

Jackson, T., *Uses and Abuses of the Countryside*. Background notes on Social Studies, No. SS 21/22. (Workers' Educational Association, London 1975).

McKnight, Hugh, *The Shell Book of Inland Waterways* (David and Charles, Newton Abbot 1975).

Owen, D. E., *Water Rallies* (Dent, London 1969).

Patmore, J. Allan, *Land and Leisure* (Pelican Books, Harmondsworth 1972).

Pratt, E. A., *British Canals: Is their Resuscitation Practicable?* (John Murray, London 1906).

Raistrick, A., *Industrial Archaeology* (Eyre Methuen, London 1972).

Ransom, P. J. G., *Waterways Restored* (Faber, London 1974).

Rolt, L. T. C., *Landscape with Machines* (Longman, London 1971).

Rolt, L. T. C., *Narrow Boat* (Eyre and Spottiswoode, London 1944).

Rolt, L. T. C., *Navigable Waterways* (Arrow Books, London 1973).

Rolt, L. T. C., *The Inland Waterways of England* (George Allen and Unwin, London 1950).

Russell, R., *Lost Canals of England and Wales* (David and Charles, Newton Abbott 1971).

Salter, H. (ed.), *The Broads Book* (Waterways Series, Link House Publications, Croydon 1973).

Salter, H. (ed.), *The Canals Book* (Waterways Series, 1976 edn., Link House Publications, Croydon 1975).

Savage, C. I., *An Economic History of Transport* (Hutchinson, London, 2nd edn. 1966).

Squires, R. W., *Canals Revived* (Moonraker Press 1979).

Stevenson, D. and others, *Organisations and Youth: 50 Million Volunteers* (H.M.S.O., London 1972).

Thompson, D., *England in the Twentieth Century* (Pelican Books, Harmondsworth 1965).

Toyne, P., *Recreation and Environment* (Macmillan, London 1974).

Vine, P. A. L., *London's Lost Route to Basingstoke* (David and Charles, Newton Abbot 1968).

Vine, P. A. L., *London's Lost Route to the Sea* (David and Charles, Newton Abbot, 3rd edn. 1973).

Wilson, Harold, *The Labour Government 1964-79* (Penguin Books, Harmondsworth 1974).

(B) MAGAZINES, PERIODICALS AND NEWSPAPERS

Canal and River Boat, 1978—monthly (Lockgates Publications, Ltd., Nottingham).

Hansard, 1946–daily (H.M.S.O., London).

Motor Boat and Yachting, 1946–occasional (I.P.C. Transport Press, Ltd., London).

The Spectator, 13 September 1946 (London).

The Times, 1946–daily (Times Newspapers, Ltd., London).

Waterways News, 1971–monthly (Staff Newspaper of British Waterways Board, London).

Waterways World, 1972–monthly (Waterway Publications, Ltd., Burton-on-Trent).

(C) SOCIETY JOURNALS AND NEWSLETTERS

Broadsheet (occasional) (Journal of Staffordshire and Worcestershire Canal Society, Birmingham).

Bulletin (occasional) (Journal of the Inland Waterways Association, London, renamed *I.W.A. Waterways* in 1976).

Institute of Transport Journal (occasional) (Institute of Transport, London).

Mercian, 1969–1978 (occasional) (Journal of the Inland Waterways Association, East Midlands Branch, Nottingham).

Navvies, 1966–1983 (occasional), formerly *The Navvies Notebook* (Journal of the Waterway Recovery Group, Inland Waterways Association, London).

Onward, 1958–1983 (occasional) (Journal of the Inland Waterways Protection Society, Sheffield).

(D) GOVERNMENT PUBLICATIONS

Department of the Environment, *Review of the Water Industry in England and Wales: A Consultative Document* (D.o.E., London 1976).

Department of the Environment, *Sport and Recreation* (Cmnd. 6200) (H.M.S.O., London 1975).

Department of the Environment, *Water Act 1973. Chapter 37* (H.M.S.O., London 1973).

Ministry of Land and Natural Resources, *Leisure in the Countryside, England and Wales* (Cmnd. 2928). (H.M.S.O., London 1966).

House of Lords, *Second Report from the Select Committee of the House of Lords on Sport and Leisure* (H.M.S.O., London 1973).

Ministry of Housing and Local Government, *Circular 44/68, 2 August 1968* (H.M.S.O., London).

Ministry of Transport, *Government Proposals following the Report of the Committee of Enquiry into Inland Waterways* (Cmnd. 676) (H.M.S.O., London 1959).

Ministry of Transport, *Reorganisation of the Nationalised Transport Undertakings* (Cmnd. 1248) (H.M.S.O., London 1960).

Ministry of Transport, *Transport Policy* (Cmnd. 3057) (H.M.S.O., London 1966).

Ministry of Transport, *British Waterways: Recreation and Amenity* (Cmnd. 3401) (H.M.S.O., London 1967).

(E) LEAFLETS AND MANUSCRIPTS

Aickman, R., *The River Runs Uphill* (unpublished MS.).

Boundary Post, Commemorative Edition. Titford Canal Restoration Rally March 1974 (B.C.N.S., Birmingham 1974).

Co-operation '72 (British Waterways Board, London 1972).

News Release (various) (Inland Waterways Amenity Advisory Council, London).

1429320

386.409

SQUIRES, R.W.   The New Navvies.

PR. 10.83   £9.95

-0. JUN. 1984

Please renew/return this item by the last date shown.

So that your telephone call is charged at local rate,
please call the numbers as set out below:

	From Area codes 01923 or 0208:	From the rest of Herts:
Renewals:	01923 471373	01438 737373
Enquiries:	01923 471333	01438 737333
Minicom:	01923 471599	01438 737599

L32b

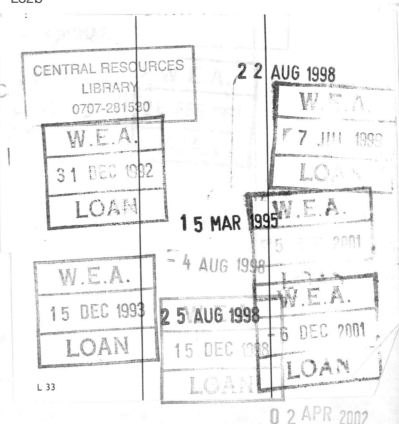